Vietnam Stories

VIETNAM
Stories

A Judge's Memoir

∽

COLONEL JACK CROUCHET
U.S. Army Retired

COPY 1

UNIVERSITY PRESS OF COLORADO

Copyright © 1997 by the University Press of Colorado

Published by the University Press of Colorado
P.O. Box 849
Niwot, Colorado 80544
(303) 530-5337

The University Press of Colorado is a cooperative publishing enterprise supported, in part, by Adams State College, Colorado State University, Fort Lewis College, Mesa State College, Metropolitan State College of Denver, University of Colorado, University of Northern Colorado, University of Southern Colorado, and Western State College of Colorado.

The paper used in this publication meets the minimum requirements of the American National Standard for Information Sciences—Permanence of Paper for Printed Library Materials. ANSI Z39.48-1984.

Library of Congress Cataloging-in-Publication Data

Crouchet, Jack, 1923–
    Vietnam stories: a judge's memoir / Jack Crouchet.
        p.   cm.
    ISBN 0-87081-453-2 (casebound: alk. paper)
    1. Trials (Military offenses) — United States.   2. United
States — Armed Forces — Vietnam.   I. Title.
KF7641.C76   1997
343.73'0143 —dc21   97-15887
                                                         CIP

10 9 8 7 6 5 4 3 2 1

This book is lovingly dedicated to:
My wife Sonja
My son Michael
My daughter Carolyn
and
The memory of my brother George

Contents

Contents

Preface

Poor Horseface! I often think of him when washing my face. He remains seared in my memory as a legacy from Vietnam. No one knew his real name. His fellow countrymen, who were torturing him, and the Americans, who had captured him in an open field, simply called him Horseface, laughing when they did. He was tied to the ground as his captors placed a soaking towel over his face to prevent breathing. He squirmed, kicked, and sometimes broke the ropes that bound him.

"Wave a finger if you decide to tell us where your comrades are!" the interrogators advised. But his fingers never waved, although his whole body shook with terror. When it appeared that he was about to suffocate, they removed the towel, drenched it again in a pail of water, and placed it over his face. Several wet towels and less than a gallon of water drowned the victim. A pathetic ending to one who might have been only a landless peasant! No one protested or shed a tear. No funeral or proper burial for Horseface! Descendants would never pay homage to his remains as they would to other ancestors. His body was rolled into a ditch and dirt was spread over the corpse to keep it out of sight and to prevent the stench from later offending his inquisitors.

Meanwhile, on the spacious roof garden of the Rex Hotel in Saigon, a Filipino band blared away as American men and women danced and dined on steaks inspected by army veterinarians, served by uniformed Vietnamese waiters. Others swam in the adjoining pool or sat in lounge chairs observing the skyline, lit by flares dropped from helicopters, and listened to the distant rumble of bombs and mortar shells. From the top of the Rex, their war was not unpleasant.

Simultaneously, young Americans in cold, wet forests listened for the rustle of Viet Cong or North Vietnamese soldiers. Some were wounded, some were dying, others had just died. All the living were afraid. Across the mountains, deltas, and plains of Vietnam, American soldiers were on patrol, engaged in firefights or sleeping in bunkers or hammocks hoping to remain alive until morning. Nineteen-year-olds were longing for their mothers or sweethearts, praying to live until they could be together again.

I was somewhere between all of those places. My job as a military judge took me to every location where commanders ordered trials by general courts-martial. It was in those proceedings that I learned of the torture of the "Horsefaces" and other offenses committed by soldiers and officers in Vietnam. It is not pleasant to be reminded of those horrors, but they were an inevitable result of the engagements of more than half a million American troops in Vietnam. To think that no crimes would be committed there is as unrealistic as to expect that large cities in the United States would be free of criminal activity.

While living at the Rex Hotel, I enjoyed the amenities available to Americans in Saigon. I also had the opportunity to observe the contrast between United States and Vietnamese citizens, especially the million refugees forced into the city, longing to return to little plots of land where they had worked and their ancestors had died for centuries.

There were three United States Army military judges in Vietnam, all living in Saigon but constantly traveling around the country, when I was stationed there from July 1968 to July 1969. We worked long hours, more often than not into the night. Being a judge wasn't as difficult as assignment to a combat unit, but we were in combat zones four or five days each week. We had our share of sleeping in bunkers, running to shelters during mortar attacks, and flying in helicopters and small planes over hostile territory. But, when we returned to Saigon and our comfortable rooms, we also had the pleasant opportunity to experience the culture of the city as well as meeting reporters, newscasters, movie stars, sports celebrities, and visiting firemen from Washington.

The duties of a military judge are similar to the duties of any judge in a criminal case in the United States with unlimited jurisdiction. He rules on objections, motions, and other matters of law as well as instructs the members of the court on their duties prior to findings and, if necessary, sentence. The court members' duties are similar to those of jurors in civilian criminal cases.

The official title of the prosecutor is trial counsel, but he is frequently referred to as prosecutor. The person being tried is the accused, but frequently is also called the defendant. The staff judge advocate is the legal adviser to the commanding general who orders the general court-martial, but does not participate in the trial itself. During the trial, the members of the court (jury) are frequently addressed, or referred to, as "the court": for example, "the court will disregard the last statement of the witness."

Because of the nature of my assignment in Vietnam, much of what I have written in this memoir naturally concerns crimes and courts-martial. These subjects, however, are only a portion of my experience there. Other matters that I have observed, as well as my opinions of prevailing American attitudes, are also included. All references pertaining to conditions and titles are those that existed during 1968–1969.

All of the trials in which military judges in Vietnam participated were general courts-martial. Special courts-martial and summary courts-martial, with which I was not involved, were used for lesser offenses. Neither of those types of courts had the authority to administer a punitive discharge or impose confinement at hard labor in excess of six months. Additionally, certain commanders had the authority to impose nonjudicial punishment for minor offenses, which never resulted in confinement at hard labor or discharge from the service.

Except for the chapter "Love's Labor Lost," all of the cases described or referred to are based upon cases actually tried in Vietnam during the period of my tour there. Liberties have been taken in a few of the cases by changing the names of persons whose mention might cause embarrassment so many years later. "Love's Labor Lost" is a story based upon many different events that I witnessed or heard about, none of which resulted in a court-martial.

This memoir is not a scholarly report with statistical accuracy, but is written with the purpose of presenting to readers an interesting overview of the cases tried, and sharing with them my own unique experiences. For example, "Silent Night" is compiled from four different cases over which I presided. "Riot at the LBJ," although written as one chapter, is in fact based upon the testimony of about thirty witnesses I heard in six different cases resulting from the same incident. The quotation from the Court of Review at the beginning of "Rape and Murder at the Americal" is verbatim. The testimony of witnesses in that chapter is quoted from several records of trial. The accounts of "I Want a Body Count," as well as the facts reported in other cases, are based upon evidence introduced during those trials. Organizations, when mentioned, are accurately stated.

The war in Vietnam, which lasted longer than any other American military experience and was fought against a determined and indigenous enemy, was so different from all of our subsequent military involvements that comparison with them for military justice purposes is impracticable. In Vietnam, ground troops were officially restricted to fighting within the confines of South Vietnam (except for the brief excursion into Cambodia in 1970), although the enemy retreated into Laos, Cambodia, and North Vietnam at any time. Body count and kill ratio were considered to be measures of success or failure. Most soldiers were draftees as opposed to later military operations with all-volunteer forces.

In 1969, after I returned from Vietnam, important changes in military law were made by both the president and Congress.

The accused, for example, was provided the option of being tried by military judge alone, a choice not available while I was in Vietnam. At the same time, although our duties did not change, the title of law officer, as we were officially designated in Vietnam, was changed to military judge, a term that had been in common usage for many years. For convenience, and because the duties were the same, I have used the term military judge throughout this memoir. We were usually addressed as such.

Other changes to the Uniform Code of Military Justice and the *Manual for Courts-Martial* have been made over the years, including the renaming of what were previously known as the Court of Military Review and the Court of Military Appeals. The terms used in this memoir are those that existed during the time when I was in Vietnam.

The literature of our Vietnam experience is voluminous. There are hundreds of histories, novels, memoirs, and criticisms in existence, in addition to the thousands of short stories and articles that appear in anthologies, magazines, journals, and military publications. In my opinion, the best account describing events that eventually led to a court-martial and the court-martial itself is Daniel Lang's *Casualties of War*, which first appeared in the *New Yorker*. There are several excellent books, in addition to official reports and investigations, describing the My Lai massacre, which occurred in March 1968. Twelve members of the unit responsible for that incident were tried, but only one conviction resulted, that of Lieutenant William L. Calley. Recommended books describing that event are the earlier works of Seymour Hersh and the more recent *Four Hours in My Lai* by Michael Bilton and Kevin Sim.

Twenty years after I left Vietnam, Colonel William S. Fulton Jr., Clerk of Court at the United States Army Judiciary in Falls Church, Virginia, assisted me in obtaining over six thousand pages of material from records in cases over which I presided in Vietnam and almost as many pages of other courts-martial tried during the same period but in which I did not participate. It is the memories recalled from reading and copying those records that form the core of the cases described in this book.

I am especially indebted to retired Colonels Richard Arkow, Darrell Peck, John Webb, and Herbert Green, who reminisced with me about certain cases and circumstances that made the cases tried long ago come to life again for me. I would like also to thank Professor Myrek Land of the University of Nevada–Reno who first encouraged me to write these stories, and to Dr. Stephen Leonard, chairman of the History Department of Metropolitan State College in Denver, for encouraging me to continue writing.

Jack Crouchet

The Parable of the Old Man
and the Young[1]

So Abram rose, and clave the wood, and went,
And took the fire with him, and a knife.
And they sojourned both of them together,
Isaac the first-born spake and said, My Father,
Behold the preparations, fire and iron,
But where the lamb for this burnt-offering?
Then Abram bound the youth with belts and straps,
And builded parapets and trenches there,
And stretched forth the knife to slay his son.
When lo! an angel called him out of heaven,
Saying, Lay not thy hand upon the lad,
Neither do anything to him. Behold,
A ram, caught in a thicket by its horns;
Offer the Ram of Pride instead of him.
But the old man would not so, but slew his son,
And half the seed of Europe, one by one.

Wilfred Owen
Killed in action on November 4, 1918

1. From the collected poems of Wilfred Owen, edited by John Stallworthy.
   Acknowledgment is made to New Directions Publishing Corporation; the
   Executor of the Estate of Harold Owen; and Chatto and Windows, Ltd.

Vietnam Stories

CHAPTER ONE

Departure

I was on a Braniff jet that lumbered down the runway of San Francisco International Airport and climbed into the sky heading for Vietnam on the morning of July 8, 1968. As the plane leveled off, a stewardess told the 160 officers on board to make themselves comfortable, it would be a long trip. What a way to go to a dirty war! I thought to myself, as each of us was given a pair of blue-and-white knitted booties. "It's going to be first class all the way," she said, "so leave your troubles behind!"

I had left my family and friends behind and, as far as I could tell, my troubles lay ahead — first class or not. Yet, strangely enough, there were no evident signs of depression among the passengers. The farewells were finished — we had said our goodbyes.

The chartered civilian plane offered every amenity I would have expected if our destination had been Washington. Hostesses, stereo sets, hot food, and movies. There was scarcely time to test the reclining seats before a stewardess offered free drinks. Nothing lacking in the way of creature comforts. But I was in no mood for roasted peanuts and hot towels, and wanted only to escape by sleeping and keeping to myself.

I don't recall who my seat companions were on that long flight to Saigon. I ate the meals served and briefly got off the plane in Honolulu, but mostly I slept and dreamed about the life I left behind.

I had spent one week in Saigon eight years before. I stopped there on a flight between Korea, where I had just completed a tour of duty, and Switzerland, where my family was waiting. My intention was to meet a friend on a diplomatic mission to Vietnam, but I was informed at the American embassy that he had not yet arrived. To my chagrin, I learned that transportation to Europe would not be available until the following week when an embassy flight would be stopping on its way from California to Spain through the Far East.

Ton Son Nhut Airport in Saigon was relatively quiet in 1960. We were met at planeside by Vietnamese hostesses in colorful *au dais*, the national women's dress consisting of a fitted bodice, loose-fitting pajama-like trousers, covered front and back with rectangular silk pieces, reaching almost to the ground and blowing aimlessly in the wind. They spoke with delicate voices and charming accents, explaining what was expected from us during our stay in Vietnam. Do not use the black market, be careful of the drinking water, watch out for terrorists. At that time, there were about one thousand Americans in the country, mostly acting as advisers to the South Vietnamese army. A few had been killed, mostly in the provinces. In Saigon, President Ngo Dinh Diem, America's surrogate, seemed to be firmly in control.

Among the people who deplaned, a young army dentist from California, Captain Len Steinberg, and I were the only two on unofficial visits. Others were reporting for assignments or returning from duty elsewhere. Len and I were told that we would be provided transportation to a United States billet where we would be allowed to stay for the duration of our visit.

I was fascinated with Saigon from the moment I arrived. Riding to our assigned quarters, I was impressed by being in a city the world was reading about, yet everything seemed normal: farmers in rice paddies, large hotels, painted villas surrounded by walls covered with flowers, French restaurants, modern shops, and an exciting atmosphere. The streets were crowded with virtually all modes of transportation, motorized and otherwise. Citroën taxis and pedicabs, or *cyclo pousses* as they were called in Saigon, were everywhere. It was the people, though, who captured my attention more than the environs. Mode of dress and tools often indicated profession or trade. I especially remember the women carrying bamboo poles across the back of their shoulders with dangling ropes at each end holding pans stacked one on top of the other, filled with a variety of cooked Vietnamese food ready for consumption. I looked forward with great anticipation to exploring the city.

Len and I were taken to the Five Oceans Hotel in Cholon, the Chinese section of the city. It was a typical army transient facility that offered nothing exceptional in the way of physical comforts, but was quite suitable for our needs. From our windows, we observed a nightly ritual that added atmosphere to the environment. About midnight, farmers began arriving in an empty parking lot to set up little stalls, stocking them with vegetables, dry goods, and trinkets that they transported on bicycles or little carts. By 2 a.m., the first customers arrived, and buying continued for a few hours. The noise from the market was not disturbing, but rather soothing. After awakening in the morning about seven o'clock, I would see only the empty parking lot. The farmers had vanished into the villages and the townspeople into their homes.

My friend and I learned quickly that our transportation problems could be solved easily by hiring a pedicab for the entire day and as late into the night as we wished. Chao Tan, the Chinese man who operated the vehicle running his with his bare feet, soon became our friend and waited each morning for us to leave the hotel. He was quite willing to transport us to whatever destination we desired, and some that we did not.

One evening, we allowed Chao Tan to take us to a sophisticated night club in Cholon where we were accosted at the entrance by a dozen or so Vietnamese and Chinese hostesses, in single-line formation, dressed in their finest national costumes. We expressed no interest in attaching ourselves to any of the girls, but our desires had no effect on what was about to happen. A waiter led us, and two hostesses followed, to a table in a room with a band the size of Woody Herman's Thundering Herd. We were not so naive as to believe that the hostesses would sit with us for the pleasure of our company, but after a short discussion, Len and I decided that the experience would be worth the expense. Within minutes, one of the girls stood up and said as she departed: "Please excuse me, I have to see the boss!"

The hostess returned thirty minutes later and the conversation among the four of us resumed. Five minutes later, the second girl stood up and said: "Excuse me please, I have to see the boss!"

"Why do you girls always have to visit the boss?" Len asked.

"Oh, he is very important, and he is very strict!" was the reply, and the remaining hostess began to talk rapidly in an attempt to keep our interest high.

The charade of one girl leaving and the other returning occurred again shortly after the second hostess returned. Len then took a turn at excusing himself and returned a minute later quite beside himself.

"These girls are working two tables!"

"Oh no, no, no, sir, we never do that!" said our lone companion.

"Oh yes!" replied my friend, "I saw the other girl at another table with two Americans."

"Oh, they are only very good friends. She only tells them hello!" was her reply.

"Hello, my ass! She's holding hands with both of them. Let's get out of here!"

I tried to calm Len down but failed to do so before the manager appeared, asking what the problem was. Not wanting to remain in the club or participate in a dispute, I settled hastily with the manager, even though Len refused to share the costs. The girls were in a rage as they returned to the end of the line outside the large room where they would have the longest wait for new customers.

We found Chao Tan asleep in his vehicle. "Take us to Saigon!" I said.

"Aha, Saigon number one! I will show you around! We go to the Rue Catinat!" he replied, and off we went into the balmy night through the streets of Cholon and Saigon. The driver took us by the presidential palace where Diem and his family were ensconced. Len and I talked about the fortuitous circumstances that put us physically so close to people we had read so much about. Chao Tan next took us to the great French cathedral in the center of Saigon and past the Continental Palace and Caravelle hotels down the Rue Catinat. Although Diem's sister-in-law, Madame Nhu, had closed the dance halls and night clubs along the famous street, there was still entertainment to be found. Just sitting in an outdoor cafe drinking beer in the warm evening air, watching the parade of exotic people and beautiful women in flowing au dais was more exciting to us than a night club would have been. This was the street of novels and history. Graham Green would have felt at home!

We sat at an outside table of a restaurant on the Rue Catinat until it closed, and started back to our hotel in the open cab well past midnight. Along the main street that joined the cities, we observed a large tent with people inside. I ordered the driver to stop and walked into the tent past dozens of motorcycles and bicycles. There were hundreds of men, all looking at me, the only Caucasian there. A fiery, patriotic speech in progress came to a halt, but I was not harmed or bothered. My act was more foolish than brave. It contrasted with my action the next day when I merely wanted to cross a small bridge into another part of Cholon, but graciously accepted the advice of a Vietnamese policeman who advised me not to do so.

Colonel Paul Durbin, a judge advocate officer whom I had previously known, was stationed in Vietnam and living in Saigon at the time of my visit there. When I called, he extended an invitation to visit his office and offered to act as a guide to the city.

Len and I went to the United States compound, located between Cholon and Saigon, where Colonel Durbin's office was located. As we casually spent a few minutes observing some Vietnamese concessionaires within the enclosure, Lieutenant General Samuel T. Williams, who commanded all the American forces in Vietnam, walked out of the headquarters building. When his eyes lighted on the two of us, he came to an abrupt halt. It was quite unsettling to be stared down by a three-star general. The Vietnamese had not bothered us as we walked along their streets, but now I was concerned that we might be ordered to leave the country, or at least be restricted to our hotel, by a fellow American. Without changing his focus, the general whispered something to his aide who came quickly to check our identifications. He reported back to the general who then continued his march, not letting us out of his line of sight, until he reached the gate to the compound. I thought he might be suggesting that we had no business in Saigon and should take the next flight out of town.

Colonel Durbin had invited the judge advocate general of the South Vietnamese Army to meet me in his office, for no reason other than the latter was once in the United States and had expressed an interest in meeting American lawyers. By coincidence, I had previously met the general when he was visiting the Pentagon and I had been assigned as his escort while touring the building and viewing a training film. We had a delightful visit that flattered me because his French was superior to mine, and he really seemed to remember me from the Pentagon.

After the visit, Len excused himself and Colonel Durbin took me to the beautiful home where he and his family lived, together with servants, on the Rue Pasteur. On the following day, we had lunch at the Cercle Sportif, which had been the gathering place of the French upper class before World War II and during the first Indo-Chinese war. It was then frequented by Americans, high-ranking Vietnamese officers and politicians, and some of the remaining French civilians who made Saigon their home. At the Cercle Sportif, sitting beside the swimming pool sipping a *citron presse,* I saw a bikini bathing suit for the first time. After lunch, we toured the Saigon golf course, the spacious Phu Tho race track, the temples and gardens surrounding the zoo, a few pagodas, and the beautiful tree-lined boulevards on which the opera house, cathedral, presidential palace, and grand hotels were located.

On the plane from San Francisco eight years later, drifting in and out of sleep, these pleasant memories of my former visit to Vietnam haunted me. I wondered idly how much Saigon and my own life would be changed.

CHAPTER TWO

Arrival in Saigon

A half hour before landing at Ton Son Nhut on July 10, the pilot announced that we were approaching Vietnam. Beneath us were golden beaches on either side merging into lush green mountains and forests that, under other circumstances, might have been a garden spot of the world. How could this beautiful land and sea, which appeared so peaceful from above, contain such misery below? My eyes riveted on the landscape until we landed in Saigon.

What a contrast from 1960! Ton Son Nhut had been transformed into the busiest airport in the world. Military and civilian planes of all descriptions in the air and on the ground; helicopters like birds in the sky; military people everywhere. There was nothing romantic about landing this time. No pretty girls in au dais to meet us. We grabbed our luggage without ceremony and entered the terminal for a brief processing. That done, I felt lost among soldiers from several nations and Vietnamese civilians, some rich with servants and others carrying all their worldly possessions in rags or cardboard boxes.

I found my way to a military phone. I contacted the judge advocate office of the Military Assistance Command Vietnam (MACV), a joint command for all American armed forces, from which military judges received logistical support, including offices. The sergeant major promised to dispatch a vehicle for me immediately.

While waiting for transportation, I witnessed the first of a thousand little scenarios one did not read about, but were endemic to Vietnam. A group of Korean officers, their country's finest, were also waiting for transportation. Surrounding us were beggars, some with babies, all poorly dressed, and some with apparent diseases. I gave a few small coins to one family, but the Korean officers abused them by speaking harshly and pushing them aside. The irony of foreigners acting superior to victims in their native land struck me as particularly cruel. The beggars, however, did not react adversely to the insults, but submitted passively to their apparent fate in life.

Within minutes, I was pleasantly surprised to see a jeep coming toward me driven by an old friend, Lieutenant Colonel Joseph Ammerman. Joe was an army lawyer assigned to MACV, with whom I had previously served in Europe. We greeted each other warmly but could have no serious discussion because of the noise from planes, people, and traffic. In less than ten minutes, however, we were at MACV headquarters, which was on the periphery of Ton Son Nhut.

"My God, Joe, this looks like a little Pentagon!" I said.

"It is," he replied. "Come in."

The one-story air-conditioned building, newly built by the United States government, spread over several acres of land, afforded welcome relief from the heat and noise of the outside world. The personnel in the judge advocate office consisted of approximately twenty United States military personnel and ten Vietnamese civilians. The separate office for the military judges displayed the names of Colonel Paul Tobin and Lieutenant Colonel Richard Snyder. After introductions all around, Joe took me to the judges' office, which was equipped with three large desks and chairs, many books, and several phones, but was devoid of human beings.

"Where are Paul and Dick?" I asked, referring to the other judges in Vietnam.

Joe sat down in one of the leather chairs to make himself comfortable before replying: "They're both out of the country."

"Where?"

"Well, Paul went to Korea, Japan, and Okinawa. This is unusual, because judges ordinarily try cases only in Vietnam and Okinawa. Dick went to Japan on leave and is not scheduled to try any cases after his return since he'll be here only a few days."

"When is Paul coming back?" I asked.

"I don't know. I see he's blocked out on the calendar for about ten days or so. He has no cases scheduled after his return, whenever that might be."

I looked at the three large homemade charts on the wall to which he pointed. They represented the months of June, July, and August, 1968. Each chart contained thirty-five spaces, five rows of seven blocks over which the days of a specific month were entered on an acetate covering. In addition, the names of the judges and places where cases had been tried or were scheduled to be tried were entered with different-colored grease pencils. Paul used black; Dick, yellow. Since Dick was leaving soon, only the word "goodbye" was written in yellow after the date of his scheduled return from Japan. The black line indicated approximately where Paul was at the moment.

"For heaven's sake, who's trying cases in Vietnam now?" I asked Joe.

"That's the problem! All the jurisdictions have been calling for judges and there was no one here. The sergeant major has been recording all messages, though. I thought you'd want to see those!" he said, pointing to a stack of notes on the desk that was assigned to me. " And, by the way, I hate to tell you this, but I've authorized the setting of a case for you in Long Binh tomorrow. The people there are in a panic because half their witnesses are due to return to the United States in a few days. I thought you would understand."

"Great!" I said "Where is Long Binh?"

"No sweat," he replied. "It's about twenty-five miles north of here but we've got transportation all set up. I'll take you to Hotel 3, the helicopter pad at Ton Son Nhut. A helicopter will be waiting, and you'll be met in Long Binh by someone from the judge advocate office in USARV, which is an acronym for United States Army Vietnam, the army element of MACV. Now, why don't you read your messages? We have a couple of hours before leaving for the Rex Hotel, where Paul said you could use his room. Do what you have to and I'll get some of my own work done."

When Joe left the office, I read through the messages, all requests for judges. Before answering any of them, I chose a red grease pencil and added my name to the legend below the chart, indicating that I would henceforth be accounted for with the color red on the acetate. I wrote "Long Binh" and my name in the block over July 11. I took a couple of steps back and looked at the calendar with a touch of pride. I was already scheduled for a case in Vietnam and had not yet sat in the chair I was to occupy for one year.

After that small accomplishment, I began to answer the messages, and before Joe returned at six-thirty, I had notes and a red line running through the rest of July and part of August. I had the dubious pleasure of looking forward to trips to Camp Evans, which was near the Demilitarized Zone; Pleiku; Lai Kai; and three to Long Binh, where several different jurisdictions were located.

The ride from MACV to the Rex Hotel, where Joe and the judges lived, was an experience that made me regret my decision not to retire from the army when I had an opportunity to do so. The uncontrolled traffic had increased exponentially since my first visit to Saigon. Joe drove the office sedan and did not hesitate to claim the right of way, whether he had it or not. Who was to know who had the right of way! I mused, with traffic streaming in all directions. Not unexpectedly, we were jolted by an impact with another vehicle which I heard but did not see.

"You had better stop, Joe. We've been in an accident!"

He looked at me and shrugged his shoulders. "I'd never find the son of a bitch who hit me!"

"But maybe you hit him!" I replied.

"Be reasonable, man, this isn't the United States. The people here don't know how to drive!"

I could only speculate as to who "the people" were, since there were hundreds of vehicles being driven by people of different nationalities.

This was no longer the beautiful Saigon that I had known. The shade trees were poisoned by carbon monoxide; the bougainvillea and hibiscus, which had given color to the city, had disappeared. Wire fencing surrounded the tables of sidewalk cafes to protect patrons against "zappers." Soldiers stood guard in strategic places along the road. But downtown Saigon was familiar to me, both from my previous visit and pictures in current newspapers and magazines.

Within the mass of humanity in the city, I was surprised to see a large number of Caucasians on the streets. I first thought that they were French civilians who had remained behind after the loss of their own war. Joe advised me, however, that the numbers of civilians associated with the armed forces, including Department of Defense personnel, business people, and laborers from many countries, were staggering.

After passing the Continental Palace Hotel, which I recognized immediately, we turned right, off Tu Do Street, which had been the Rue Catinat during my prior visit, on to Le Loi, which was the main artery between Saigon and Cholon. On the left side of the first block was Lan Son Park, once beautifully landscaped with flowers and shrubs, but now the site of a gigantic statue of two Vietnamese soldiers in a crouched position. On the right side of the first block was a conglomeration of five-story buildings contiguous to one another. Within the buildings, which occupied an entire square block, were stores, bars, cafes, shops of many descriptions, and apartments on the upper level, some occupied by American civilians. A maze of alleys ran through the buildings at street level, and elevators located near the entrances provided passage to the upper floors.

On the right side of the second block of Le Loi was another park, across which people walked in all directions. The first building on the right side of the third block was the seven-story Rex Hotel, crowned by a roof garden, clearly visible.

The creaky Rex elevator chugged its way to the fifth floor where the judges' rooms were located. Paul's room was quite large, located on the inside of the building, having no view other than structures within the square block in which the Rex was located. It was furnished with a single bed, a shower, a writing table, several chairs, and a divan, which I considered to be luxurious surroundings. I felt a sense of excitement to be in Vietnam, but perhaps that feeling resulted from the fact that I felt secure in the room that I occupied.

At about eight o'clock, Joe came to pick me up for dinner. We walked to the roof. On the right side of the top of the staircase, there was an officers' open mess, which was more than adequate for wartime conditions. But there were better things than that. "Let's eat in the steakhouse tonight," Joe suggested.

"Whatever," I replied.

We turned left and entered the roof garden with tables in the center, a bandstand in one corner, and a long bar along the inside wall. Joe told me that Joey Bishop, Martha Ray, Georgie Jessel and other "walking through Vietnam" celebrities were frequently seen here. The bar and its surroundings, however, was not the pièce de résistance. Through the wall beyond the bar was a door leading to a room that contained pleasant surprises. In the center was an open grill with burning charcoal next to a table of the finest steaks I had ever seen. Surrounding the grill and steaks were tables with tablecloths where people were eating and drinking. We had to pay to eat here, but that was an expense worth the price. The steakhouse on top of the Rex was the place where war correspondents in Saigon and important official United States visitors came to dinner. Some of the diners in our presence were recognizable from the television news back home. There were many fine restaurants in Saigon, but the top of the Rex was the favorite for those authorized to be there. Here was beef inspected by the United States Army Veterinary Corps, at a very reasonable price.

After dinner, Joe and I walked a few yards to the rooftop swimming pool, which was surrounded by lounge chairs. Waiters attended people enjoying drinks in the evening air, observing flares dropped from helicopters all around and over the center of the city. Near the railing on the roof by the side of the pool, we talked about our past and future lives.

When I looked directly below us, my sense of serenity evaporated. There were people on the street with outstretched hands, begging from every American or foreigner passing by. These people were some of the tens of thousands who overflowed from the tents and tin shanties that surrounded Saigon. They were victims of the war, displaced from their villages, hungry and poor. What we left on our plates would have fed many of them. I regretted having eaten.

"What about those people, Joe? Who is responsible for them?"

"They are just a handful of refugees, many from the Tet Offensive in January and February," he replied. "There are two million people in Saigon, a city not big enough for half that number. I'm not smart enough to say where the responsibility lies. Perhaps you will get used to the sight."

Suddenly, from somewhere in the vicinity, we heard a burst of rifle fire. Military training caused us to drop to the concrete floor. From the floor, between the pillars of the railing, I looked down again at the people below, still begging. They did not seek refuge from the rifle fire. To them, perhaps, danger was a necessary risk to survival.

CHAPTER THREE

Surprises

On the morning following my introduction to the Rex, Joe drove me to Hotel 3. Eight hundred helicopters took off and landed there each day. Even at seven in the morning, they were coming in and departing like flies on a dunghill. But the operation was efficient. I merely announced my presence to the radio operator on duty and proceeded to the VIP lounge, where I waited until the helicopter designated to take me to Long Binh was ready for departure.

My first helicopter flight from Saigon seemed surreal. The crew consisted of a pilot, copilot, and two soldiers manning machine guns mounted near the spaces where the doors had been. From the air, Saigon was still unbelievably beautiful. An astonishing number of architecturally diverse buildings, villas, pagodas, churches, parks, and swimming pools with clear green water were visible. Forests and rice paddies with sporadic evidence of earth and trees torn apart by bombs and artillery fire were never out of sight. All around us were the ubiquitous helicopters and airplanes. I was still in awe when we landed at Long Binh fifteen minutes later. An officer from USARV was waiting and drove me to the courtroom.

USARV headquarters was in a compound consisting of several long buildings, connected in a U-shape, equally as impressive as the ones at MACV. They were made of concrete and glass, two stories high, completely air conditioned. A news magazine had recently reported a story about the construction of a sixty-thousand-dollar flagpole with concrete base to complement the existing structures.

The courtroom in Long Binh was as accommodating as any I had used in the United States and far superior to anything I would see elsewhere in Vietnam. Five feet from the back wall was a long table reaching from one side of the room to the other, behind which were nine leather chairs. This area, for use by the court members, could only be entered from a deliberation room in the rear. The judge's bench and leather chair rested on an elevated platform. Furniture for the prosecutor, defense counsel, accused, and court reporter was new, and there was a railing separating the court area from the spectators.

The prosecutor handed me the necessary docket papers. Happily for me, the case was a simple one and disposed of in a few hours, with time out for lunch. All during the trial, members of the court stared curiously at me. The prosecutor later suggested the probable reason; I was the only person in the courtroom (or possibly in Long Binh) not dressed in combat gear. I had not yet had time to secure the proper clothing.

The case ended at three o'clock in the afternoon, affording time to hustle back to Saigon to unwind from my Trans-Pacific flight. But departing from Long Binh was not as well organized as leaving Saigon. I was brought to the helicopter pad by the prosecutor, who assured me that sooner or later there would be transportation back to Saigon. Indeed, I was there but a moment when I noticed a helicopter with its engines revving up, a sign of hope. Within minutes, a staff car arrived flying a flag with two stars, indicating that a major general was the passenger. I recognized him immediately as the commanding general of a major command. More interesting than that was the fact that I had known him as a brigadier general in Stuttgart, Germany, and had written his will. During the period when we were client and law-yer, he was most cordial, serving coffee and even offering a drink over our legal discussions. Yet, after alighting from his car in Long Binh, he passed me without a glance, and walked quickly to his waiting chopper. Not wanting to appear obviously in need of a ride, I tried to appear nonchalant, as if I were waiting for my own transportation. Immediately after entering the chopper, the general's aide, a prim and proper lieutenant colonel, tapped me on the shoulder and asked courteously: "Are you going to MACV, colonel?"

"Yes, I am," I answered, with a look of hope on my face.

"You may join us in the general's chopper, if you wish."

Of course, I was delighted. "Thank you very much, sir!" I said as I entered, passing in front of the passenger already seated near the door.

The general did not acknowledge my remark, nor my exist-ence, for that matter, but only looked straight ahead with steely blue eyes. Perhaps he grunted but I could not hear because of the engine noise. I fastened my seat belt and we were off on a trip as exciting for me as the one earlier in the day. No words were spo-ken nor glances exchanged. I could not help but ponder the odds of a crash killing both client and lawyer in which the former did not recognize the latter. Surprise at the probate hearing! I thought. When we arrived at MACV, which had its own landing pad, I exited the helicopter with my briefcase and once more thanked the general. Again, no audible response. Perhaps a grunt.

I began my walk to the headquarters building, passing a parked sedan flying a two-star flag, obviously waiting for the main passenger. As I was walking, the general's car stopped beside me. The aide opened the door on his side, courteously offering me a ride in the front seat, which I gladly accepted. I thanked the general again, but received only a grunt in response. We rode the remaining distance to the main entrance of the building in silence. Upon arrival there, I once again thanked my benefactor. Again, he did not respond, but his aide smiled and said, "You are welcome, Colonel. Have a nice day!"

When I returned to my office, there was a note on the desk from Colonel Red Benoit saying that he and I were invited to General William Westmoreland's house that night. Red was an air force officer assigned to the MACV office whom I had met the previous day. I could hardly contain myself with the thought of such an exalted invitation, and rushed over to Red's office. "Don't be too thrilled, Jack. You are not going to meet General Westmoreland. We're going to see Colonel Harvey."

Colonel Hank Harvey was the MACV judge advocate, a personal friend and former classmate of General Westmoreland. He shared the general's house on Tran Quy Cap near the Cercle Sportif. I think that Red was more excited than I, because he was carefully plotting the route through Saigon to insure arrival at the general's house on time. Red was not sure whether we were being invited for a drink or for dinner, but he assumed it was for dinner. We would play it by ear.

The residence in which General Westmoreland and Colonel Harvey lived was surrounded by a large wall. Vietnamese servants and guards lived within the compound. The large white residence reminded me of an antebellum mansion in the old South. On arrival, we were met at the door by Colonel Harvey, who graciously escorted us into a small sitting room with several over-stuffed chairs and a divan.

In addition to the area we occupied, there were living and dining rooms that were air conditioned and separated from the remainder of the downstairs by a large glass partition. A stairway led to a second floor where the occupants lived. At that particular time, General Westmoreland was in the United States awaiting reassignment as chief of staff of the army and would soon be replaced by General Creighton Abrams, who would move into less imposing quarters closer to MACV headquarters.

I surveyed as much of the setting as possible, trying not to be obvious while doing so. This must have been the house of Emperor Bao Dai, I thought, or some other princely official, or perhaps the home of a French governor. I noted that Vietnamese houseboys were fussing around the dining room table set for four:

crystal, china, silver, fresh tablecloth with matching napkins, flowers, the whole bit. I felt uncomfortable in the uniform that I had been working and traveling in all day.

Colonel Harvey mixed drinks as we made small talk, which included a toast to my arrival in Vietnam. The conversation was progressing pleasantly enough when two American men in neatly pressed sport shirts and trousers descended the stairs. After introductions, we knew that one was a colonel in the office of Public Affairs at MACV and the other was a Doctor Somebody, a civilian adviser to General Westmoreland. They poured themselves drinks and joined the conversation. The doctor spoke of his day, but not to Red and me, whom he completely ignored. The colonel joined in the general conversation and, although he did not ignore Red and me, he expressed no real interest in either of us. It did not take long for me to be convinced that our invitation for a visit did not include dinner. I finished my drink quickly.

"Well, Colonel Harvey, this has been delightful, but we must be leaving," I said as I stood up.

"What's your hurry, Jack? There's no need for us to leave now," replied Red, who apparently had not noted the dinner setting for four.

"Of course not. Keep your seats and have another drink!" That was Colonel Harvey speaking, a true gentleman, whose response brought discomfort to his housemates.

While we were passing time with the type of conversation that can be terminated at a moment's notice, there were rumblings in the distance. The glass partition shook quite noticeably. I thought perhaps there was a small earthquake somewhere until the civilian commented, with a smile on his face: "The 52s are out tonight!"

"B–52s?" I asked, rather stupidly.

The civilian stared at me, rattling the ice in his glass, but the others nodded politely. The insipid conversation continued.

Good God in Heaven! I thought. People a few miles from here are being torn to bits as we are sitting in splendor, ignoring the passing of life and destruction of property.

When I stood up a second time, Red joined me as we excused ourselves. No objections were made as we prepared to make our departure. Colonel Harvey was escorting us out when the doorbell rang. All three of the residents walked quickly to the door to welcome their expected guest who proved to be the major general who had favored me with a ride to Saigon in his helicopter a few hours earlier. They happily exchanged greetings and handshakes, but Red and I received only a perfunctory nod and a grunt.

Red and I ate that night in the open mess on top of the Rex without much conversation, watching a bat zooming back and forth between the rafters under the roof. It was little consolation to know that General Westmoreland himself had stayed at the Rex when he first reported for duty in Saigon.

CHAPTER FOUR

Pleiku

My first two cases in Vietnam requiring travel by plane were scheduled for the Fourth Infantry Division at Camp Enari, near Pleiku in the Central Highlands. I took it upon myself to arrange transportation and was directed to report to the military terminal for in-country travel at Ton Son Nhut. I did so at the appointed time, carrying a large briefcase filled with law books and a small suitcase for personal items, wearing a steel helmet, flak jacket, and a .45-caliber pistol with holster, in addition to normal combat gear.

The inside of the military terminal consisted of a long row of wooden desks with various designations crudely written on cardboard attached to the appropriate reporting places. To my chagrin, the line from the desk marked "Pleiku" extended outside the building. There was no place for waiting inside the terminal, nor protection from the sun outside. Servicemen were lying on the grass shielding their eyes from the sun with towels, handkerchiefs, or other suitable items from their duffel bags.

Upon arrival at the Pleiku desk, I was given a slip of paper with numbers and letters printed by hand in ink that constituted my boarding pass. I joined others on the grass outside, used my helmet as a pillow, and tried to shield myself from the sun with arms across my eyes. Paul Tobin had written to his mother that "This is the only place in the world where judicial robes consist of bulletproof vests and steel helmets." I could have added that helmets were also useful to rest one's head.

Shortly before departure, we were each given a box lunch consisting of a peanut butter sandwich, a chocolate bar, and an apple. We were told that there were drinking water and paper cups inside the aircraft.

I had been told at MACV that there were usually two or three spaces in the cockpit where pilots could invite passengers, and I should hope to be so lucky. The first thing that came to my attention upon entering the C–140 was two young women in the cockpit with the pilots. Pretty intelligent young men, I thought to myself, making the same decision I would have made. I think there is something romantic about young pilots flying in a combat zone with beautiful ladies in the cockpit. These women, we were informed over the loudspeaker, were with a USO entertainment group traveling to Pleiku.

The passengers, other than those in the cockpit, were seated on long canvas seats either along the inside body of the aircraft, or in rows set up in conventional seating arrangements. As we leveled off, I carefully surveyed all of the passengers, most of whom were young soldiers newly arrived in Vietnam, identifiable by new clothing and boots, going to uncertain destinations.

During the middle part of 1968, there were over two hundred American soldiers killed in Vietnam each week and more than triple that amount wounded during the same period. Statistically, some of these young men on board, whose average age I presumed to be about nineteen, would be among the casualties of the Fourth Infantry Division, a unit that had already participated in many engagements with the enemy, including the recent Tet Offensive. It was constantly fighting, attempting to rid the highlands of Viet Cong and North Vietnamese regular army forces. As I looked into each of their faces, I pondered whether this one or that one would be later counted among the expected casualties.

There was no horseplay or loud talking among the soldiers, but neither, to my surprise, was there an obvious sense of great apprehension. I was twice the age of most of the passengers and pilots, and felt a sense of relief because I was not expected to go into combat. Perhaps it was better that they could not know the future.

I was happy to arrive in Pleiku where the wet season had not yet ended and the temperature was rather mild. The contrast from Saigon was most welcome. Unlike the soldiers with whom I traveled, who were huddled into formations and marched off to waiting trucks, I was met at planeside by Lieutenant Colonel Darrell Peck, the division staff judge advocate, who was waiting for me in the office jeep. He would take me from the airfield to Camp Enari.

As we drove through Pleiku, I remembered it was here that an incident took place which precipitated the first great escalation of the Vietnam War. On February 7, 1965, Viet Cong forces attacked the airfield on which I had just landed, killing 9 Americans and wounding 128 others. Several helicopters were simultaneously destroyed. In retaliation, President Lyndon Johnson launched Operation Rolling Thunder, which authorized the bombing of North Vietnam and rained destruction on that country until November 1968, almost without interruption. I was curious then, as I am today, about the code name of the operation, apparently taken from a Christian hymn. The term "thunder" was frequently used in scripture to describe God's awesome presence and power.

Montagnard children from the Jarai tribe in the surrounding mountains played and begged for cigarettes or candy along the route through the city. They seemed happy, even with ragged clothes and dirty faces. For hundreds of years, their ancestors had survived invasions and occupations by people foreign to their culture, including their own Vietnamese countrymen. Living with occupiers was a way of life for the Montagnards. They tolerated and worked well with Americans, who in turn employed some of them who were not suited for military duties to perform menial tasks at Camp Enari. Colonel Peck told me affectionately about an elderly mamasan who cleaned the legal office but continued to remove papers and scrub his desk with dirty water in defiance of his repeated protests.

A row of empty little shacks along the route to Camp Enari with names such as Luscious Louise, Tender Touch Massage, Washing Done, Paris Bar, and Trucks Washed provided amusement to me as well as entertainment for the children, who ran in and out as if the buildings had been constructed especially for them as a playground. These shanties, whose names reflected the ingenuity of their previous owners, were shut down for business by order of an American general who had determined that they were detrimental to the morale of his troops.

In the center of Pleiku, we passed a Catholic church where, judging by the number of persons standing about and departing, services had just concluded. The scene, like so many others in Vietnam, seemed incongruous to me. Praying for peace in the midst of war. The church looked quite similar to those in small Louisiana towns where the French had also once exercised their influence. I had forgotten the day was Sunday. One day was like another in Vietnam.

The courtroom in Pleiku was more satisfactory than all the others I used in Vietnam, except for the one in Long Binh. An important factor was the climate, cool enough so that windows could often be kept closed, thus eliminating outside noises. The room was located in the rear of a long wooden building, which also contained the offices of the staff judge advocate, and could be entered through the back door.

I enjoyed going to Pleiku, which I did on three separate occasions, each for several days. At Camp Enari, I was assigned quarters in a three-bedroom trailer equipped with sitting room and bathroom. Two other trailers, for use by the commanding general and other high ranking officials, were nearby. Together, they formed a separate little compound. A guest register in my trailer recorded the names of important persons who had used these quarters before me, including the military historian General

S.L.A. Marshall, several prominent media personalities, and a couple of movie stars.

I was automatically included in the membership of the general's mess at the Fourth Infantry Division. The building, separate from other messes, was partitioned to make facilities for a lounge where members and guests gathered for drinks before and movies after dinner. In the dining area, the commanding general sat at the head of a large round table with his chief of staff, one or two other members of his command, and invited guests. On one occasion, Bernard Weinraub of the *New York Times* and I were both so favored at the same time. The experience of hearing the division's leaders discuss their daily combat activities was exciting. More often than not, I skipped the after-dinner movie and returned to the legal office for visits with personnel assigned there. They were a cheerful group, writing letters, playing games, reading, or just lounging around. A young court reporter was especially adept at making bargains with whomever such bargains were made to obtain the best steaks outside of Saigon. When he was successful, there was a barbecue behind the courtroom, and on those occasions I did not go to the general's mess. Frequently, I played Scrabble with a captain who, without fail, outscored me by a close margin. He was not good enough, however, to convince me that he was doing his best.

Between the courtroom and the commanding general's compound was a small garden, kept meticulously neat and green with grass and other growing things by a Montagnard man who possessed a grin that never seemed to disappear. He squatted there with a pair of scissors and a knife cutting grass or puttering around the bushes and flowers. I looked forward to seeing him every day. He tended a crippled man or boy, probably his blood brother, who never left his side. Whenever one moved, so did the other.

The gardener carried the crippled person on his shoulders to work in the morning and home at night. They lunched together and shared conversation, punctuated by laughter, through the day. I was intrigued by these two people with practically no earthly possessions, one disabled, unable to move distances, and the other with a limited capability to make a living, both always seemingly happy! A man who probably had never been taught that it was one's duty to care for his brother, was doing so, sharing life, not as a duty or responsibility, but out of love and an instinctive feeling that all men are brothers. There was so much we could have learned from them. Even the children I had seen in Pleiku shared among themselves whatever possessions they acquired.

The first case at Camp Enari was not a difficult one, but rather typical of the hundreds I had tried in the past and was to try in the future in Vietnam. Private Rodney Spivey was charged with one specification of disobeying Captain Pat Gossard, his commanding officer, and one specification of unlawfully possessing ten grams of marijuana.

On the morning of the first alleged offense, Captain Gossard ordered Spivey to get his gear together and hop on a truck that was leaving on a combat mission. Spivey told Gossard that he had misplaced his rifle and Gossard replied that he would get another one for him. Spivey testified that he took Gossard's words to mean that he would obtain the rifle immediately, so he stood by waiting and watched as the truck departed for combat without him.

On the morning of the second alleged offense, Spivey was apprehended by Sergeant Claude Zimmer in a part of the city of Pleiku that was off-limits to American troops. As a routine part of the apprehension, Zimmer advised Spivey of his legal rights and performed a search of his clothing. A plastic bag containing ten grams of marijuana was found in Spivey's combat trousers. There was no dispute as to these facts. During the trial, Spivey denied knowledge of the presence of the prohibited substance, and testified in part as follows:

Q: (By the defense counsel) What do you have to say with regard to the marijuana?

A: (By the accused Spivey) I didn't even know I had that on me.

Q: Where had you been?

A: In a bar that never closes.

Q: Now, how long were you there?

A: I was there all night. About a day altogether.

Q: Can you account for how the marijuana might have gotten into your trousers?

A: Yes, I can. There was a *boysan* down there . . .

Q: This what?

A: This boysan . . . And he said, "I'll souvenir you something," and I guess that was it.

Q: You didn't know it was there?

A: No, I didn't.

Spivey explained that "a boysan is a young Vietnamese. He was not a real good friend. He worked around the house . . . On the day before I left, the boysan said 'I'll souvenir you something.' The boysan must have given me the marijuana but I did not see him give it to me. The Vietnamese like me. I guess the Vietnamese say they 'souvenir' you when they give you something. I guess that was it."

After findings of guilty, the prosecutor presented evidence that Spivey had been previously convicted for being disrespectful toward a superior officer and failing to obey a lawful order. He was sentenced to be dishonorably discharged from the army and to be confined at hard labor for four years.

That sentence, however, was by no means final. Like all other general courts-martial, the findings and sentence were subject to several reviews and appeals at which time they were subject to be greatly reduced or disapproved altogether.

CHAPTER FIVE

McNamara's Boys

The second case I tried in Pleiku provided my first experience with a soldier whose level of intelligence was officially considered below normal, but had nevertheless been subject to the draft. In 1966, the Department of Defense had launched Project 100,000 or POHT as it was referred to in official reports, which lowered the standards for entry into military service. POHT was, in reality, an effort to increase the diminishing number of acceptable draftees and enlistees at a time when the need for men was increasing and, at the same time, avoiding the political pratfalls of making it more difficult for college students and other privileged categories to avoid the draft.

As announced at its creation, the POHT program had altruistic motives. The project would be an opportunity over the years to rescue hundreds of thousands of economically deprived young men by providing them with the opportunity to enter the armed forces. Moreover, according to the same official sources, the project would assist young men in becoming more responsible citizens as they served their country and when they returned to civilian life.

POHT soldiers were sometimes called "McNamara's boys" or, more cynically, "McNamara's morons" because it was allegedly

Secretary of Defense Robert McNamara's idea to create the program. They had the dubious distinction of being the only service members whose limited intelligence was broadcast by the numerals 67, which preceded the rest of their serial numbers. Thus, the fact that they were officially considered intellectually inferior was known to their commanding officers and company clerks as soon as they reported for duty. Pejorative terms used to describe POHT members were undeserved. Many served with distinction, struggling through the swamps and jungles of Vietnam along with their fellow soldiers, often better. Many were decorated for valor. Others gave their lives.

Studies after the war conducted by the General Accounting Office concluded that the program as a whole was successful, but other independent studies concluded that POHT soldiers were more likely than others to desert and be court-martialed for other crimes. In my own experience, I feel that every POHT soldier who was tried by general court-martial should not have been accepted into the armed forces.

Private Roy House was charged with murder. He was drafted into the army in 1967 after the requirement of a minimum score of thirty on the Armed Forces Quotient Test had been lowered to ten. After nine months of mediocre service in Vietnam, House shot and killed a fellow soldier. The crime could only have happened because of an unfortunate combination of circumstances: House's low intelligence and low regard for himself, the availability of weapons, the heat of the night, and the intensity of a war atmosphere.

The events that resulted in Private House's court-martial occurred when units of the 1st Battalion, 12th Infantry, were located in a forward fire support base outside Plei Djerang in early June, 1968. House was engaging in conversation and drinking beer with Private First Class John Kelly and Private First Class Bob Anka when a mortar shell, fired by the enemy, landed in the midst of the fire support base, forcing most of the soldiers into bunkers. A few minutes later, conversation among the three soldiers resumed outside the bunkers, peaceably at first. House did not drink as much as his comrades. He had, in fact, given most of his ration of beer to Kelly and Anka.

For no discernible reason, an argument developed between House and Kelly. Kelly grabbed House by the collar, but released him and proceeded to his bunker, followed by Anka. House fired six rounds in Kelly's direction, killing Anka almost immediately. Kelly was not hit. After the shooting, House casually walked away and obeyed instructions to lay down his weapon.

In a pretrial statement made to criminal investigators, Kelly swore:

> Me and Bob (Anka) had our three cans of beer . . . we went near Junior's (House's) bunker to fool around and he had three cans of beer so me and Bob drank them . . . an explosion came and everybody ran to the bunker except me and Junior. I jumped behind the wheel of the howitzer and loaded my M–16 and so did he and when everything settled down, I unloaded mine and he didn't. Me and Junior got in an argument and I grabbed him . . . I was just playing with him . . . He jerked and I let him loose and he grabbed his M–16, which was still loaded, and I told him to go ahead and shoot because I thought he was just playing around . . . I was just bullshitting him!

At trial, Kelly repeated under oath substantially what he had said in his pretrial statement, but elaborated:

> I grabbed House . . . on the shirt collar . . . and I was about to let loose on him and he jerked loose and grabbed his weapon . . . I started walking toward him. I thought he was just joking around. Then he told me to come on and that he wanted me to take another step and I knew that he was pretty serious. I told him I was just playing with him. I told him just forget about the whole thing . . . it was just a joke . . . I turned around and I started walking toward my bunker . . . Anka had been following me to the bunker . . . I heard about five or six rounds go off . . . I turned around and looked behind me and Anka was laying there. He had been hit.

Private First Class Jimmy Winn, a member of the unit who was filling sandbags, testified that he saw House with the rifle and heard him say, "Don't fuck with me!" Winn was frightened by what he saw and heard, and returned to his bunker, where he heard six shots fired from the direction where House was standing. Then, "I heard Bob cry out 'I'm hit!' . . . Bob was lying on he ground, sir. He had about three holes in him that I seen."

Corporal Louis Waibel testified:

> Well . . . we were working on the ammunition bunker. We heard somebody yelling. I looked over and saw somebody shooting. I thought gooks were coming through the perimeter. House was coming toward us after the shooting . . . He seemed scared when I halted him. He seemed confused. He gave me no problems . . . I couldn't say if he appeared to know where he was. I halted him . . . and put him on the ground. He was confused. He was docile.

All witnesses agreed that House did not make any effort to conceal himself or to run away after the incident.

House testified in his own behalf, swearing that:

> After a few beers and good conversation with Anka and Kelly, Kelly approached me for no reason and said, 'I'm going to beat your ass' he says, just like that. And, I said, 'Man, why do you want to beat my ass, I haven't done nothing to you . . . I don't want to fight you' and he grabbed me. I tried to remain calm but Kelly said that he will put a bullet right between my head and then . . . the only thing I know . . . all that I can recall is that he grabbed his weapon or something . . . and the next thing I remember I was over . . . I was over there . . . and somebody threw me down on the ground . . . I do not remember firing my weapon.

A psychiatrist brought in by the defense counsel testified:

> House's intelligence placed him in the mentally subnormal population. He has an emotionally unstable personality manifested by poorly controlled angry outbursts. His angry feelings overwhelm him. House was concealing, consciously or unconsciously, the true

nature of his act because he cannot make sense out of what he did. Further, he lacks insight into his own intellectual dullness.

House's judgment, the psychiatrist added:

. . . seems defective on the basis of his being unable to integrate complex, threatening social situations into meaningful behavior patterns . . . his general intellect seems uniformly dull and he is unable to make very simple abstractions. He cannot calculate how much change he would receive after purchasing something that costs less than a dollar but paying with a dollar . . . he has experienced a lifelong pattern of being a scapegoat and inferior because of his gullibility, general dullness and speech impediment.

The psychiatrist concluded, however, that:

. . . although House's defective intelligence and emotional instability are important factors in the alleged crime, he is able to distinguish right from wrong, and adhere to the right, and therefore could be held responsible for the offense, if the court so found.

The members of the court found the accused guilty as charged. The defense counsel then introduced evidence that confirmed that House was one of the unfortunate soldiers included within statistics which indicate that the disadvantaged and minorities were disproportionately represented among those required to serve in Vietnam. As a youth, House suffered from living in poverty on the outskirts of a small city and was subjected to the whims of an alcoholic father who was a poor provider. House repeated two grades and was never capable of graduating from high school. His only employment consisted of odd jobs. He was unemployed at the time he was drafted. He had always had a speech impediment.

The court sentenced House to be discharged from the army with a dishonorable discharge and to be confined at hard labor for ten years. I do not know the final disposition of House's case, but it is my experience with similar cases that the Court of

Military Review in Washington would order additional psychiatric examinations, and would substantially reduce the sentences, or even reverse the convictions.

After the trial, I spoke a few words to House, who showed little emotion or understanding of what had transpired. His stuttered sentences and lack of understanding convinced me that he should never have been allowed into military service, even though technically qualified under the revised standards.

As I was proceeding to my quarters after the trial, I conveyed my thoughts about the case to the commanding general of the division, whom I encountered by chance politely speaking to the two Montagnard men who came daily to tend the little compound. The general replied that there were also POHT soldiers who did a creditable job. I did not disagree with that statement but did not pursue discussion of the subject. I continued to my quarters, where I packed and inquired about the next available flight to Saigon.

CHAPTER SIX

Cholon and the Lucky Hotel

After returning to Saigon from my first trip to Pleiku, I began a search for suitable quarters. I wanted to stay at the Rex, where the judges who preceded me had lived, and where Paul was living when he was in town. I was, however, assigned to the Lucky in Cholon, which I was assured would be quite suitable as it had been recently constructed. As much as I hated the task, I packed my belongings and departed from Paul's room in the Rex.

The driver who was assisting me in the move drove to a hotel in Cholon that looked very impressive. It was large and sturdy. On the inside were a reception area, dining room, and elevator. All things considered, the place appeared quite comfortable. To my chagrin, however, I was informed by the desk clerk that this was not the Lucky, but rather the Hong Kong.

I expressed my confusion but was assured that I was in the right place. The only entrance to the Lucky was through the Hong Kong, an established hotel. The clerk assigned me to the tenth floor of the Lucky, above which was only a flat roof.

I was disappointed many times during the few minutes it took to travel from the lobby of the Hong Kong to the top of the Lucky. I discovered that my new hotel was an upward extension of a building contiguous to the Hong Kong, and it had recently been built of what appeared to be cinder blocks. It rose straight into the sky and was seemingly unsupported by any solid construction above the main hotel's sixth floor. The elevator in the Hong Kong worked, but, of course, could rise no higher than the hotel itself. It was therefore necessary to walk across the roof of the Hong Kong and into the Lucky, which had neither lobby nor elevator.

With the help of my escort, I climbed the stairs to the top of the Lucky, dragging luggage I had brought from the United States and all the military equipment that I had been issued in Vietnam. There was absolutely nothing in my assigned room other than two single army cots with bedding. No closets, telephone, toilet, shower, table, or other amenity. The floor was concrete. Living here would mean that I could neither make nor receive phone calls without walking down the stairs of the Lucky, crossing the roof of the Hong Kong, and taking the elevator to the lobby on the bottom floor. I was totally depressed, and decided to make an effort to get something more convenient.

The driver and I returned to the billeting office, where I pleaded for something, anything, at the Rex, but the officer in charge was adamant in his refusal. There was nothing to be had, he said, because a group of officers from Thailand were due to arrive soon and would require all the available spaces. He did, however, tell me that there was an opening at the Brinks, which was just a block or so away from the Rex, and I was welcome to take a look at what was available there. The Brinks was the hotel that had been attacked by Viet Cong terrorists on Christmas Eve in 1964, leaving two American officers dead and about sixty injured.

The driver took me to the Brinks. The quarters offered to me there were a portion of a small living area in a two-bedroom suite. The bedrooms were already occupied. Within the living room, where I would be sleeping on a small cot against one of the walls, were a television, a multispeaker stereo system, and a conversation area consisting of three chairs and a coffee table in the center of the room. I decided to return to the billeting office.

After much cajoling, the billeting officer offered to put me on a waiting list for the Rex, giving in to my plea that it was necessary to be near a telephone and other judges. But he could not promise how long it would be, if ever, before the transfer could be made. So I returned to Cholon and made the long haul once more to the top of the Lucky. I could not unpack because of the lack of closets or furniture, so I opened my suitcases and conveniently arranged their contents according to my needs.

I lived in my new quarters about five weeks, but the actual number of nights I spent there was less, because when Paul or any other friend at the Rex left town, I moved temporarily into his room. Furthermore, I spent about four nights out of every week trying cases in other parts of the country.

Life at the Lucky was an unforgettable experience. Living on the top floor as I did allowed me to step directly outside and to the roof for fresh air. This I did every evening I spent there. From the roof, I could clearly see the Cha Tam church in Cholon about two blocks away where President Nho Dinh Diem and his brother had been captured and then assassinated on November 3, 1963, just three weeks before President John F. Kennedy was killed. Wherever I happened to be in Vietnam, I reenacted in my mind events of historical significance that occurred there, and every time I looked at that little church, I thought of Diem. I did not know then about the United States' participation in his overthrow, but I did know that his death was historically significant and responsible for the series of seven unstable governments in South Vietnam that followed his execution.

At the top of the Lucky, the residents of the upper floors usually gathered in the open air to watch the sunset and discuss the war as we listened to mortar fire going out of and coming into Saigon. The sky was brightened throughout the night by flares dropped from helicopters. When B–52s dropped their bombs in nearby areas, the Lucky was shaken and I worried that, like the walls of Jericho, the building would come tumbling down. My bed moved almost from one side of the room to the other.

Several officers at the Lucky formed a singing group and gathered frequently on the roof. Asked to join, I had to refuse because God did not favor me with a voice capable of harmonizing. Still, listening to them provided background music as I contemplated the war around me.

Whenever I slept at the Lucky, I woke up in the mornings about five-thirty, dressed as fast as I could in order to shorten my stay there, had breakfast in the officers' mess at the Hong Kong, and caught a military bus for the trip to my office, wearing a steel helmet and side arms. The bus, with windows and entrance protected by steel bars and meshed wire, passed through the main section of Cholon, affording a fascinating glimpse of life into that part of the city. There were Chinese car repair stations, food stores, dentists' and doctors' offices, shops for making jewelry, drug stores, and other businesses of varied descriptions.

People were at work in front of their shops or homes, taking advantage of the early morning air while hammering, cooking, sewing, or doing whatever else was necessary to their professions or lives. Others crowded the streets eating, squatting, reading newspapers, or just awaiting the passage of another day. In the parks, which were plentiful and beautiful, but filled with refugees, elderly gentlemen shadowboxed in total concentration, oblivious to everything and everyone around them.

Riding through Cholon on the bus, one could not help but observe that this was a city in the midst of war trying to survive in its own ethnicity. Newspapers and signs everywhere were written in Chinese characters. Before the war, Cholon was the more prosperous part of Saigon. In addition to legitimate industry, it also had the reputation of a city of iniquity with the largest whorehouses and gambling dens in Asia. Warlords had their own armies and lived in palaces connected to each other and to Saigon by a maze of alleys and underground tunnels. Chinese workers on the docks of Saigon, wracking their bodies under bales of rice and other commodities, returned to their hovels in Cholon at night to gamble away the few piasters they had earned during the day. Others sought relief from their misery in the opium dens that proliferated in the city.

After leaving Cholon, we passed the Phu Tho Saigon race track, which had been scarred by thousands of bullets. On television, I had seen some of them put there during the Tet Offensive earlier in the year when fighting raged in the area. I remembered the same beautiful track I had visited eight years previously with Colonel Durbin. Refugees now swarmed around and inside the area. Hundreds of rickety shacks were thrown together with scraps of wood and tin, but I could see no evidence of sanitary facilities or other amenities. Needless to say, the horses were not running.

CHAPTER SEVEN

The Man Who Would Be President

On the morning of July 26, while still officially living at the Lucky, but staying temporarily in a friend's room at the Rex, I phoned my office and received the good news that the case assigned to me that afternoon in Dong Tam had been canceled. I decided to use my free day to attend the trial of a Vietnamese civilian who had been receiving much publicity in the media.

Truong Dinh Dzu was a fifty-one-year-old Saigon lawyer who had run for the presidency of South Vietnam in September 1967 as a peace candidate, but was defeated in the election by Nguyen Van Thieu. In his campaign, Dzu announced that he favored a meeting with the National Liberation Front, the political arm of the Viet Cong and other anti-Diem factions, as a step toward ending the war. As the peace candidate, he had achieved attention in the world press. After the election, which was observed and declared to be fair by United States congressmen, President Thieu ordered Dzu's detention on charges of "action harmful to the anti-communist spirit of the people and the army." Since the beginning of 1968, the South Vietnamese government had been threatening to bring charges against Dzu for his campaign activities and, during the summer, it was announced that a trial would take place on Friday, July 26.

The United States government was much embarrassed about Dzu's trial because the election had been proclaimed one of President Thieu's promised reforms and a landmark for the evolution of democracy in Vietnam. Dzu had not advocated the overthrow of the Diem government, but only made a suggestion that the United States itself later concurred in by negotiating with agents of the National Liberation Front in Paris. No matter, President Thieu was determined to throw his opponent into prison.

About eight-thirty in the morning, I walked leisurely through the streets of the city to the courtroom, located in a depressing building surrounded by a large concrete wall on the banks of the Saigon River. The charges were based entirely on an interview made during the election campaign with members of the British Broadcasting Corporation and United Press International. Now, Dzu was being tried for making statements that, by Western standards, and probably even by normal South Vietnamese standards, were not treasonable.

There were few people in the courtroom, but it was surrounded by armed policemen and South Vietnamese soldiers. There were also guards within the courtroom, where Dzu's wife, son, and daughter were seated in the front row. Dzu's wife, to my surprise, was dressed in modern western style and wore what appeared to be expensive jewelry. Personally, I thought that, under the circumstances, it would have been more appropriate to wear clothes that conformed more to Vietnamese culture. A number of reporters whom I recognized on sight, a representative from the United States Embassy, and a few other spectators were scattered throughout the room. I sat next to Bernard Weinraub of the *New York Times* and Peter Kann of the *Wall Street Journal*.

Dzu was brought into the courtroom under tight security shortly before the trial and allowed to speak briefly with his family. He was accompanied by a lawyer. When the court of five young military officers entered, we all stood.

The entire trial lasted two hours. I could not understand the proceedings but there was much shouting between Dzu's lawyer and the president of the court, a South Vietnamese major. After the reading of required legal documents and much argument, the court recessed, presumably to deliberate. When they returned, Dzu was sentenced to five years' imprisonment. There was more shouting, but the court members ignored the pleas of Dzu, his family, and his counsel, and calmly walked out of the room through the door behind the panel.

As he was dragged from the courtroom by a dozen or so military police with M–16 rifles furnished by the United States to the ARVN (Army of the Republic of Vietnam) for combat action, Dzu shouted a few words to his family. He was then thrown into the bed of a truck and hauled away to prison crying, "I am not guilty!" in English, leaving his wife and children in tears. After the trial, I saw the daughter, a young lady, dressed in a mini skirt, standing alone near a wall outside the building, weeping.

The Vietnamese government announced that, because of the nature of the charges, Dzu would not be able to appeal his sentence. Rumors abounded that he would be confined to Con Son island. The infamous prison there was the home of the so-called Tiger Cages, where several persons occupied a single cell with no windows. Guards paced on cat-walks from which food and water were thrown to prisoners below. Sanitary problems were obnoxious; the cages were disinfected from above. The prison was built by the French when the island was known as Poulo Condore, and used to incarcerate the most troublesome of their political enemies.

After the trial, Weinraub and Kann invited me to join them and a couple of other reporters for lunch. On the casual walk away from the courtroom, we stopped briefly at the Majestic Hotel, where two young American women joined the reporters. I do not recall whether they were also reporters, or merely visitors to Saigon, but they seemed quite at ease in their surroundings. We continued our walk together from the hotel to the Restaurant Le Castel on Tu Do Street. The chef there was well known to the habituès of the establishment, a meeting place for reporters and important civilians.

Within a short time, I felt comfortable as a member of the group and realized that I was not leaving behind all the comforts of home when I departed for Vietnam. There was a well-stocked long mahogany bar just beyond the entrance to the restaurant. The dining room, with piped-in stereophonic music, was decorated in simple but elegant taste. We all sat together in a large booth. I was intrigued by the circumstances in which I found myself less than a month away from home, where relatives and friends were concerned for my safety and comfort. Peter Arnett, already a Pulitzer Prize winner for his reporting in Vietnam, stopped by for a few minutes to chat with his friends.

Our meal began leisurely with vichyssoise, progressing to a rabbit ragout with Côte d'Azur salad, and concluded with fresh fruit and cheese. Intermittently, we were served orange sorbet, and afterwards, espresso coffee. At two-thirty, I regretfully made excuses in order to return to my office. The reporters insisted that I be the guest of their newspapers. Vietnam would never again be this delightful, I thought.

CHAPTER EIGHT

Fire at the Rex

After lunch with the reporters and friends at Le Castel, I walked to the Rex where military phones were available. I called the office for messages and received the sad news from the Red Cross that my father-in-law in Switzerland had passed away. There was nothing I could do other than walk over to the Vietnamese Telephone and Telegraph office to send messages of condolence to my wife and her family. Afterwards, I took a lonely stroll along Nguyen Hue, the Street of Flowers. It made no sense to return to my office. I continued at a slow pace back to the hotel for a solitary meal in the open mess.

I went directly to my borrowed room after dinner and wrote several letters to the family, explaining why it was not possible to leave Vietnam for Switzerland. Then, unable to focus on written material, I mused absent-mindedly, recalling the many happy days when I was stationed in Germany and went to the Swiss mountains on holiday with my family. Before midnight, I drifted off to sleep.

At about four o'clock the following morning, I was awakened by a woman's voice calling to her friend in the room adjoining mine. "Wake up, Mildred! There's a fire in the hotel!" she shouted, banging on Mildred's door.

Nothing in the world starts the adrenaline flowing faster than the knowledge that one is in danger of being engulfed in flames! I rushed out of the door, looked down from the balcony, and saw fire rising from the office on the bottom floor where reporters attended the Five O'Clock Follies, or, more respectfully put, received daily afternoon official briefings. I rushed back into the room, grabbed my trousers and wallet, not bothering with shirt or shoes, and walked to the stairway. Fortunately, the Rex was one of the better-constructed buildings in Saigon, with concrete stairs, and it did not seem that we were in imminent danger. I walked more or less calmly down the stairs, immediately behind Mildred and the woman who had awakened her. There was no panic, even as others joined us, and it appeared that everyone in the building had received word of the fire in time to exit without harm.

The occupants of the Rex, in all states of dress and undress, gathered in the open park adjacent to the entrance of the building. No Vietnamese civilians were in sight. The fire department arrived almost as quickly as residents evacuated the hotel. There was no evidence of fire on the outside, but smoke was emerging from many windows. An effort was made to account for the occupants of the building by calling roll from a roster acquired at the downstairs clerk's desk. Most people whose names were called responded, but not everyone was present, some being away in the field, others on leave, and yet others at unknown places.

When Red Benoit's name was called, there was no answer. I could see quite clearly that a light burned in his room on the second floor, and I was concerned about him. I knew that he was not away from Saigon, so I searched the crowd and made inquiries, but without success. I then took it upon myself to approach the fire marshall, an American sergeant, to report that I knew the person who occupied the room on the second floor where a light was burning, but he had not answered roll.

Without hesitation, the fire marshall ordered two of his men to break into Red's room to search for occupants. Complying with orders, they ran into the building with pickaxes and smoke masks. They broke into Red's room, pushed open the windows, and shouted down to their chief that no one was present there. At that point, Red came from nowhere in a fit of anger ready to strangle the fire marshall.

"Get those fucking weenies out of my room!" he screamed.

"Sir, please, I'm doing my duty!" replied the fire marshall.

"I said get those damned weenies out of my room!" Red shouted again. "I've got a thousand dollars' worth of new stereo equipment in there and I don't want anyone in that room!"

"Sir, please, we're shorthanded already! Let us do our job!" pleaded the sergeant.

"You can see there's no damned fire in that room! And the door was locked, so they must have torn it down. I have no more security!"

"Sir, please, please! Let us do our job!"

At this moment, Joe Ammerman approached Red, asking him to back away from the firemen, and Red did so. I watched them as they returned to the office sedan parked nearby, where they had taken refuge upon leaving the building, accounting for the fact that Red did not answer the roll.

Sheepishly, I walked over to the vehicle and entered the empty front seat. Red was still cursing the "weenies" who had destroyed his door. "Red, I'm sorry, but I'm responsible for the firemen entering your room. You didn't answer the roll call and your light was on, so I thought there was a possibility you were in trouble. I'm very sorry," I said.

Gentleman that he was, Red did not reproach me, although he was still unhappy. He knew that his room could not be immediately secured, and his new stereo equipment had probably been ruined by smoke and possibly water.

With the fire extinguished, we tried to re-enter the building, but smoke was still seeping through the entrance. The fire marshall informed us that no one would be allowed inside until a thorough inspection of the building had been made, which would probably take twenty-four hours.

As dawn was breaking, a military jeep with a large-caliber machine gun mounted on its body came to escort us to the Brinks Hotel two blocks away. We were a ragtag bunch, marching down the streets of Saigon in the dawn's early light, some without shoes, others without shirts and yet others without even undershirts. Fortunately for some of the residents, they had acquaintances in the Brinks or other nearby quarters who were able to furnish them with additional garb, but most of us had to remain only in the clothing with which we had escaped the fire.

I ate breakfast on the roof of the Brinks dressed only in the underclothes in which I had been sleeping and combat trousers. Five other occupants of the Rex, including one woman, all wearing assorted clothing, shared the table. After breakfast, I was invited by an acquaintance to spend the remainder of the waiting period in the room of his friend, who lived nearby but was out of the city at the moment. After a few frustrating hours there, I took the liberty of borrowing a pair of ill-fitting boots and a shirt from the absentee occupant, leaving a note that I would return them as soon as possible.

Outside the building, I hired a Vietnamese cab to take me to the Lucky in Cholon, where I supplemented my clothing. I was unable to shave, though, because my toilet articles were still at the Rex.

When I returned to MACV, where Red and Joe had preceded me, I was not surprised to find a dozen or so messages, inasmuch as I had not been to the office for almost two days. I answered all of the calls. As usual, they concerned future trial dates.

While waiting for a bus to the Lucky that evening, I was delighted to hear from Red that all was clear at the Rex and we could return there. I had the most restful night of my tour in Saigon.

Ten months later, shortly before returning to the United States, I purchased a copy of an English-language Vietnamese newspaper that young boys and girls were forever hawking near the Rex. On page one was the picture of a woman who looked vaguely familiar. In a moment, I recognized her as the person who awakened Mildred in the room next to the one I was occupying on the night of the fire. She was, of course, also responsible for awakening me, a fact for which I am eternally grateful. Beneath her picture, the headline stated that she was being awarded a medal for heroic action. The article explained how, on the night of the fire, she went, without concern for her own safety, to an upper floor of the Rex Hotel for the purpose of saving the life of her friend, and then proceeded calmly down the stairs of the building, giving inspiration and courage for others to follow in an orderly manner.

CHAPTER NINE

Camp Evans

In August 1968 the First Cavalry Division (Air Mobile) was located in the bleakest place I have ever been. Not a single tree or growing thing was evident when I landed there on a hastily constructed runway in late summer. Everything in sight, mostly tents and a few prefabricated huts, had been erected by American soldiers. In March 1968, the First Cav, as it was affectionately called, had moved in to relieve the besieged marines at Khe Sanh. When their presence at Khe Sanh was no longer required, they had moved forty miles east in the middle of nowhere to a place they named Camp Evans. The site was in Quang Tri Province, and they were as close to the Demilitarized Zone as any major unit.

An escort from the legal office greeted me at the runway upon arrival, and together we walked to the office. There were a few vehicles in sight, but Camp Evans was so compact that vehicles were not needed for transportation within the immediate area. Amidst a sea of tents, we arrived at one with a wooden floor, screen siding, and the familiar judge advocate insignia designating it as the legal office. This was it. Just one tent, the kind ordinarily used to sleep eight persons. There were a few steel desks and chairs inside the tent, but no area of privacy for lawyers to speak to clients or judges to work. A new 19.4 cubic foot General Electric refrigerator stood among stacks of papers, books, and legal documents covered with sand and held in place with stones or other heavy objects. I dared not ask how the refrigerator found its way to this remote area, but was informed with pride that its main purpose was to keep beer cool and purloined steaks refrigerated.

I was told to use any desk that I found temporarily vacant and not worry about the person to whom it was assigned. Rather than compete for desk space, I unloaded my flak jacket, steel helmet, pistol, and law books in an empty corner. I planned to return after supper to prepare for the anticipated trial on the following day. Perhaps things would be less hectic later.

A few men without shirts were wielding picks, shovels, and hammers adjacent to the legal tent. They were seriously at work on the latest project of the judge advocate personnel. There, standing on a wooden platform partially completed, with his shirt off and wearing shorts, was Major Earle Lassiter, executive officer and guiding light behind the project. He informed me that they were building a sun deck above an existing bunker which was being enlarged. My God, I thought, the last thing in the world needed here is a sun deck! But Earle advised me that the personnel of his office often sunned themselves; besides, it was his policy that no member of the office would remain idle during daylight hours. Morale lagged when work diminished, he explained, and improved when the men were working on a constructive project. Better to lie in the sun than complain about the heat! All members of the office were well-tanned, and morale was as good as in other areas in spite of the lack of such ordinary basics as a shady refuge, movies, or a recreation room.

I congratulated the workers on their initiative and was invited to further inspect their accomplishment. The men were enlarging the bunker by digging to make it four feet deep and twelve yards square. The platform on which they were working was being built on posts eighteen inches above the hole in the ground. Two deck chairs were already in place on the completed portion of the deck, and four army cots, covered with plastic, were inside the bunker.

Two innocuous-looking soldiers were dozing on the deck chairs, one apparently a guard with an M–16 rifle across his lap and the other apparently his charge. No one seemed concerned. There was no place to escape and, with nothing to keep them busy or no place to keep them comfortable, the attitude seemed to be "Well, what the hell!"

After supper, I joined members of the legal staff in the office tent. We had a couple of beers, played cards, and talked about the home folks. Before a third beer, I retreated to the corner where I had previously laid my possessions to prepare the next day's case, which was alleged as premeditated murder.

We did not sleep that night in the bunker under the sun deck, which was reserved for the accused and his guard, but rather in two very simple tents with dirt floors, lighted by a small naked electric light bulb. We were prepared to dive into the bunker if necessary at the first sound of enemy fire, but fortunately we were spared that experience during the night I was there.

The courtroom was a tent near the helicopter pad, about two hundred yards from the office. Nothing resembling a witness room or deliberation room was anywhere in sight. The prosecutor informed me that we would have the use of a trench normally used as a community bunker. The courtroom contained nothing more than a couple of tables joined together for the court members, card tables for me and the reporter, two small wooden tables for counsel and the accused, and steel folding chairs behind each of the tables. The trench was to be used by court members while legal matters were being discussed inside the courtroom, by other parties to the trial when the court members were deliberating inside, and by witnesses while waiting to testify. The accused, counsel, court reporter, guard, spectators, and I would all be sharing the trench simultaneously. The situation was almost intolerable. No tree to furnish shade, no place for the accused to be with his counsel, not even a rest room.

Private Eugene Hill, the accused in the case, charged not only with murder, but with the unlawful use of marijuana, looked pathetic as he entered the courtroom. In addition to his other woes, he had apparently not slept the previous evening. His hair was disheveled, his clothes were in disarray, and he was confused about finding his assigned seat. My thoughts were briefly drawn to a family gathering back home to celebrate my mother's seventieth birthday. Well, I thought, this is war, and the trial, as well as the war, will go on. The parties took their assigned places. I waited until the noise of the helicopters diminished, although they were never totally silent, and called the court to order.

The evidence was shocking in that it revealed so unnecessary a crime. Having nothing to do on a Sunday, Private Hill and a friend spent the afternoon at the Nevada Bar in An Khe. While there, Hill consumed a few beers and some double shots of scotch. They returned together to base camp about six o'clock because Hill was assigned to guard duty that evening. After supper, he shared a marijuana cigarette with two soldiers before reporting for duty.

Private Hill assumed his duties as guard in a building near the entrance to camp at seven o'clock. While on guard, he spent most of his time sitting down, sometimes dozing, and sometimes talking to Private Philip McQueen. While thinking about nothing in particular, Hill was accosted by a friend and fellow soldier, Private Hal Cooper who, in a playful manner, "poked" the accused in the midsection of his body. Aroused from his lethargy, Hill chambered a round in his M–16.

Private McQueen, a witness for the prosecution, testified that after Cooper playfully assaulted the accused, Hill said: "I'll lay a clip on you!" before loading his weapon. McQueen thought all this was horseplay because Hill and Cooper were close friends. Cooper, however, did not take Hill's words and actions lightly and quickly ran from the scene. McQueen continued:

I took a step away from Hill and then Cooper said, "Say man, what's the matter? What have I done?" Hill came down with the

M–16 like a bayonet thrust with his right hand pulling the bolt to the rear and letting it fly forward. This told me only one thing."

Cooper started to run down the hill toward the guard house, still saying, "What did I do? What did I do?" and "What's wrong? What's wrong?" All this time, I was backing up, letting things take their course and getting out of the man's way . . . Hill was pointing his weapon in the direction of Cooper.

When the prosecutor asked McQueen what happened next, the witness answered: "I started whistling. I turned around, and got away from the action."

Other witnesses for the prosecution testified that Cooper ran into the room of a friend, frantically crying that the guard was after him with a weapon. Even before finishing his complaint, Hill entered the room, pointed the rifle at Cooper and said, "Now I got you!" Cooper tried to run from the room but accidentally bumped into Hill's rifle causing him to fall off balance in the doorway and drop into the hall. Hill followed Cooper, who grabbed the rifle, but Hill was able to force the barrel to Cooper's head and fire it, killing him immediately. When subdued, Hill fell to his knees and cried, "God, help me! What did I do?"

Hill's testimony was somewhat, but not altogether, inconsistent. He testified that:

When Cooper poked me in the back, I jokingly told him I'd put a clip on him. I then chambered a round as part of the joke, but just as I did so, was notified that my tour of duty as a guard was completed. While walking slowly to the guard house, I saw Cooper in a barracks and wanted to play around with him again. I went into the room and said "I got you now!" and we struggled . . .

He lunged and grabbed the weapon with both hands. The barrel of my weapon, in Cooper's hands, was just below his chin . . . and that's when it went off . . . I dropped the weapon, sir . . . a witness came over and I told him, "Blow my brains out for what I did!"

Evidence introduced for the defense indicated that Hill had been a good soldier, was not known to lose his temper, and had been a good friend of Cooper. When asked why he joined the army, he testified that he was married, had four children, and, "I was destitute at the time, I couldn't find any work."

Hill was convicted of unpremeditated murder and wrongful use of marijuana. He was sentenced by the court to be dishonorably discharged and to serve fifteen years' imprisonment. As he left the courtroom with his counsel and guards, Hill was the picture of dejection. He looked as if the end of the world had arrived for him, and it probably had. If he had not been able to support his family before he came into the army, there was little possibility that he would be able to do so, either from prison or after release, with the stigma of a bad discharge.

I had nothing more to do with Hill's case, except authenticate the record of trial, but years later while going through his court-martial papers, I learned that the term of his confinement had been greatly reduced and he was released from prison. I also saw a copy of the telegram notifying Cooper's parents that their son died in line of duty while stationed near An Khe, Republic of Vietnam. I remembered him sadly when I saw his name on the Vietnam Veterans' Memorial in Washington.

CHAPTER TEN

Defiant Child

One of the most exciting places in Saigon-Cholon was the great marketplace on the main thoroughfare from one city to the other. I drove by there on several occasions and entered it once. The traffic in the area seemed never to relax during daylight hours. It was here that, in a fleeting glance on one rather routine day, an enigmatic picture was etched in my memory that remains vivid to this day and will always haunt me.

The entire population of Saigon and Cholon seemed to enter into and exit from the hundred doors of the great market. There were myriads of little stalls within, where Chinese and Vietnamese peasants, farmers, artists, and craftsmen plied their trades or sold their wares. Housewives, houseboys, servants, mandarins, monks, cooks, and chefs spent a part of every day at the market. This was the heartbeat of the city, without which it could not survive. It was a fascinating place in which a sightseeing American could easily become lost.

Across the marketplace, I paused to avoid the relentless traffic. Standing and waiting there, I saw two women who had apparently emerged from the building. A dialogue totally consumed their attention. The younger, about seventeen, looked angelic and appeared fragile but determined. She wore a simple cotton sleeveless dress, not particularly clean, and sandals without socks. She held a small paper bag against her breast.

The older woman was perhaps thirty-five but looked older, weary from life and war. She was dressed in the white blouse and loose black pants that was the dress of almost every working adult Vietnamese female in the city. Her hair was disarrayed, and her eyes passively expressed an acceptance of all the misfortunes life had bestowed upon her. She carried nothing, but spoke continuously, using gestures, frequently staring at the bag in the girl's hands.

Tears streamed from the girl's eyes as she listened and tried to speak. Her eyes pleaded as she occasionally looked into the little bag. The older woman appeared also to concentrate upon the bag, but it seemed of no importance to her. She spoke animatedly, pointing frequently to the girl and her precious possession and to some place in the distance beyond the traffic. She was upset, but made no claim to the bag. The girl was resisting, but I could not determine why. Whatever words she may have spoken had no effect on the older person. Every brief attempt by the girl to speak seemed to bring remonstrance from her elder. Yet, in spite of the dispute, there appeared to be an inexplicable bond between the two. Perhaps they were mother and daughter, or sisters. All part of the enigma.

Vehicles of all description were passing by. Large trucks, small taxis, military vehicles, mopeds, and motorcycles were making so much noise that I could hear only the combined drone of all those machines. Thousands of people, concerned with their own problems, entered the market and departed with vegetables, meat, geese, chickens, pigs, paintings, and bags of all sizes. There were men and women, young and old, Hindu and Muslim, Chinese and Vietnamese, American and Eurasian, poor and rich attending the great market during the brief moment of my scenario. They passed without noticing the two women, whose conversation did not attract a single eye, except mine from a distance. Neither the crowd nor the noise, nor the war, nor heaven nor earth distracted these women from each other. Their conversation was too important, too involved, too emotional, to be a mere sales dispute. The emotion was transmitted through the crowds, through the noise and through the traffic to me. It was total.

The older woman finally made a gesture to indicate that the conversation had terminated. She turned her back to the girl and returned into the marketplace. There was no forgiveness, no agreement. Just a shrug of the shoulder, one more point with the finger, and departure. The young girl watched her vanish into the crowd, looked intensely after her, attempted to hold back more tears, and stood for a brief moment transfixed. She then looked at the bag in her hands and gently placed it on the ground. After standing up briefly, she had a second thought, bent down again and with a gentle touch of the hand, but in a mark of studied defiance, pushed over her little bag, emptying its treasure upon the ground. Then, ever so gently, but still defiantly, with tears streaming down her cheeks, she walked deliberately into the stream of oncoming vehicles.

Several people were attracted to the scene where the dispute had taken place, but only for a few seconds. That was all the time it took to dispose of what had been the young girl's bag of green beans.

CHAPTER ELEVEN

Riot at the LBJ

On the first day of September, during the noon recess of a case in Long Binh, Colonel John Douglass approached me asking whether I would like to take a ride to observe the stockade remains. "Stockade remains?" I asked incredulously. He answered in the affirmative and added that he was surprised that I had not heard about the riot on the preceding evening. Assuming that, if indeed there was a riot, courts-martial might result and I would be assigned to one or more cases, I refused.

The fact that there was a riot in the Long Binh Stockade (more commonly referred to as LBJ, or, Long Binh Jail) did not come as a surprise to me. Over seven hundred prisoners were crowded into a compound built but not suited for five hundred inmates. The overcrowding, combined with summer heat, lack of creature comforts, and harshness of discipline made the situation, in fact, a riot about to happen. The incident received wide publicity throughout the United States.

Twelve general courts-martial resulted from the LBJ riot, in which one person was killed, several were injured, and half the stockade burned. Of the six cases to which I was assigned, one resulted in acquittal and five resulted in convictions with sentences ranging from two to five years.

Much of the same evidence was introduced in each case, and was fairly summarized in the case of Private Richard Fallows. He was charged with riot, manslaughter, and conspiracy to overthrow lawful authority. Captain Clinton Paul Pappas was the trial counsel, or prosecutor; Captain Nancy Fields, the defense counsel; and I, the military judge. After almost two days of testimony, the prosecution rested and the defense counsel asked for an out-of-court hearing, which I granted. The following ensued:

Judge: Defense Counsel, what is the purpose of this out-of-court hearing?

DC (Defense Counsel): Sir, the defense moves for a finding of not guilty. We have heard lots of evidence about a group of men carrying torches, swinging bunk adapters normally used for supporting upper bunks, entering administrative areas of the stockade, releasing maximum security prisoners from the Big Max, assaulting guards and killing one prisoner. The only evidence against the accused, Private Fallows, however, is that two guards saw him in a crowd that was rioting, having a bunk adapter in his hand. There is absolutely nothing to show that he intended to use the adapter in an unlawful manner, or, for that matter, that he ever held it upright. There is no evidence to indicate that he railed against authority. I suggest there is nothing more than the fact that he was caught up in an event in which he was not involved. That's all, your honor.

TC (Trial Counsel): Your honor, Fallows was indeed a part of the crowd that was raining destruction on the stockade. Consider this, there were numerous prisoners not participating in the disturbance and indeed, running away from those raising havoc with authority. Many prisoners had, in fact, assembled at the front gate showing their intent not to get involved in the riot. Private Fallows had a choice to make and he made the wrong one. There is indeed evidence to show that Fallows remained with the crowd and picked up a bunk adapter, which is sufficient to proceed with the trial at this time.

Judge: The motion is denied. The case will proceed. This out-of-court hearing is terminated. Trial counsel, call the court.

TC: Yes, sir. (Trial Counsel enters the deliberation room and returns a moment later with the court members, three officers, and four enlisted persons.)

Judge: The court will come to order. Captain Fields, you may proceed with the case for the defense.

DC: Thank you, your honor. The defense waives an opening statement to the jury and calls the defendant, Private Fallows, as a witness. (Fallows approaches the trial counsel and raises his right hand to be sworn.)

TC: Do you swear to tell the truth, the whole truth, and nothing but the truth?

D (Defendant): Yes, sir.

DC: Now, Private Fallows, try to relax. The court is interested in everything you have to say, so speak slowly and loudly as you can. First of all, you were confined to the Long Binh Stockade on the night of August 31st, 1968, is that correct?

D: Yes, ma'am.

DC: Please tell us just what happened that night.

D: Well, I was just laying on my bunk trying to sleep when my friend Paul and a few prisoners came to my tent with a bunch of rolled up papers burning at the end. Paul came in the tent and said that the brothers were going to get revenge against the chucks for all the shit we've been taking. I told Paul I didn't want to get involved in any of that mess. I had just gotten out of maximum confinement in the Big Max, which was a living hell, and didn't want any more trouble. Well, there were eight white dudes sleeping in the tent with me and they all ran away and I was left alone and I didn't know what was going on so I went with Paul and a few of the other prisoners who were with him.

DC: Where did you go?

D: I did not know where we were going or what was going on. I was just afraid to be left alone, so I joined the brothers and only did so to protect myself. I did not want any trouble. Well, when I got out of the tent, I could see a bunch of guards lined up with rifles about fifty yards away from us and I could hear sirens coming toward the stockade and I was real scared.

DC: Did you pick up a bunk adapter?

D: Yes, ma'am, but I never wanted to use it. In fact, I never did use it. I just held it in case I needed to defend myself. For all I knew, maybe some Viet Congs were attacking the stockade. Everything was confusion.

DC: How did it all end?

D: Finally, a battalion of soldiers arrived to assist the guards. The stockade commander told all the prisoners near the gate to go outside and sit on the grass across the street. They left us brothers inside while the fire brigade was putting out the fires. When the fires were out, they locked us inside and we stayed there for two days. They threw C-rations over the fence and that's all we had to eat.

DC: Private Fallows, why were you in the stockade?

D: For selling grass, ma'am.

DC: How long had you been in the stockade?

D: Seven weeks, the last one in maximum confinement.

DC: Tell us about that.

TC: I object, your honor. Being in maximum confinement before the disturbance has nothing to do with this case.

DC: It does indeed, your honor. It bears upon the state of Private Fallows' mind. The conditions in the Big Max, as it was called, were enough to drive anyone to lose his ability to think rationally.

TC: I object again, your honor, defense counsel is testifying.

Judge: All right, Captain Fields, let the witness do the testifying, but I will overrule the prosecution's objection. You may continue with your examination.

DC: Thank you, your honor. Now, Private Fallows, tell us about maximum confinement.

D: Well, as you said, everybody called it the Big Max. There were these big conex containers, big steel boxes they used to ship things to Vietnam, and the stockade was using them for punishment. There is only one little hole in each side for light and air, and I guess it gets about one hundred and forty degrees in there during the daytime.

DC: Why were you in the Big Max?

D: For smoking grass.

DC: How were you treated while living in a big steel container?

D: Terrible, ma'am. There was no seasoning in our food. We only got out twice a day to go to the bathroom and exercise for half an hour. The guards, especially the chucks, were real nasty. I was in there for seven days.

DC: And how long had you been out of Big Max on the night of the riot?

D: Just three days.

DC: Now, just once more, Private Fallows. Did you intend to hit anyone with that bunk adapter, or join in a riot, or do anything to overthrow lawful authority in any way?

D: No, ma'am.

DC: Or do anything at all that was unlawful?

D: No. When Paul came to my bunk and everybody left, I was alone in the tent with him, and I was scared, so I just joined the group outside. I didn't know what was going to happen. I didn't plan anything.

DC: OK. Now, I'd like for you to tell the court something about your life. Where were you born?

D: Selma, Alabama.

DC: How long did you go to school?

D: About seven years, ma'am, but I never did finish anything.

DC: Are you married?

D: Yes, ma'am, and I have two kids.

DC: Does your family have any means of support other than your army allotment?

D: No, that's all they have.

DC: How long have you been in Vietnam?

D: Five months, ma'am. I spent two months of that time fighting the Viet Cong with the First Division.

DC: Do you know who the Viet Cong are?

D: Not exactly. All I know is they are communists and bad people.

DC: Do you know what a communist is?

D: No, ma'am

DC: Did you know where Vietnam was before you entered the army?

D: Well, everybody was talking about it. But I did not know where it was.

DC: Do you know where it is now?

D: No, ma'am. I just know it's where I am now and far away from home.

DC: Speaking of home, did you ever have a job there?

D: Not exactly. I just did little odds and ends. I swept floors and pumped gas, but that's about all.

DC: (To the military judge.) Your honor, the defense and the prosecution will now offer a stipulation of fact as follows: Private Fallows volunteered for the army under the Project 100,000 program, which lowered the standards for entry into military service. Before that program was in effect, he could not have qualified for service because of his low IQ and his lack of education.

Judge: Private Fallows, do you understand the stipulation?

D: Yes, sir.

Judge: Very well. The stipulation is accepted and the court members may consider the facts stated therein as evidence in this case.

DC: Why did you volunteer for the army, Private Fallows?

D: Well, ma'am. I wasn't making any money to speak of in civilian life and my wife was never feeling well. She washed a few clothes for other people now and then, but her mother had to take care of the kids most of the time. We just couldn't live decent, so I volunteered for the army.

DC: Thank you, Private Fallows, that is all.

Judge: Trial counsel, do you wish to cross examine?

TC: Yes, sir. Private Fallows, no one forced you to come into the army, is that right?

D: Yes, sir.

TC: You went through basic training, right?

D: Yes sir, but I was recycled, and it took a long time.

TC: But you did finish, and were sent to Vietnam, is that correct?

D: Yes, sir

TC: What have you been doing since coming to Vietnam?

D: Like I said, I was in the field fighting the Viet Cong for two months, and the rest of the time, I just hung around.

TC: You just hung around. You also went to the village pretty often to buy grass for your buddies, is that right?

D: Just a couple of times.

TC: And you were court-martialed and sent to the stockade, is that right?

D: Yes, sir.

TC: And in the stockade, you did not behave very well. You smoked a lot of grass in there, did you not?

D: Everybody smoked grass. I smoked some.

TC: And it was only after the second time you were caught that you were sent to the Big Max, is that right?

D: Yes, sir.

TC: Now tell me, on the night of the riot, no one forced you to join that group burning buildings and assaulting guards, is that right?

D: No one forced me, but there was no place to go.

TC: Why didn't you run away with the white dudes in your tent?

D: It just wasn't the thing to do.

TC: Why didn't you run to the front gate where most of the prisoners, including some brothers, had gathered?

D: I can't say. I guess I thought we would eventually get there.

TC: Now you were in the group that entered the administrative building and the kitchen to set them on fire, is that right?

D: I never went into those buildings.

TC: But you stood outside watching.

D: Just watching.

TC: You were with the group that attacked and killed one of the prisoners, is that right?

D: I didn't see that. I didn't even see anyone get hit. They only told me later that someone was killed.

TC: Now, Private Fallows, there were at least two large groups of prisoners. Why did you stay with the group that was raising hell and making most of the noise?

D: It was just natural, sir. I didn't hit anybody. I didn't set anything on fire. I didn't let any of the prisoners out of the Big Max. I was just there.

TC: But you did pick up a bunk adapter. What were you going to do with that?

D: I don't know, sir. Everything was happening so fast.

TC: When your friend Paul came to your tent, he had a burning torch made out of rolled up newspapers, did he not?

D: Yes sir.

TC: And there were a few brothers outside the tent waiting, is that not also right?

D: They weren't waiting. They were just there. I don't know what they were doing.

TC: Private Fallows, let me try to sum things up. Correct me if I make any mistakes. Your friend Paul came to your tent with a flaming torch and asked you to join him. Eight of your tent mates got scared and ran away, but you joined Paul's group, some of whom were yelling "Kill the chucks!" You picked up a bedpost. You watched while members of the group entered and set fire to the administrative building and the kitchen. You were in the group when someone killed another prisoner, although you say you did not see or know about this. Is all of this correct?

D: Yes, sir.

TC: Why didn't you leave the group?

D: Well, sir, them guards in the stockade were fuckin' with me for so long I figured there was nothing in the world I could do to save myself.

TC: Thank you. I have no further questions.

After arguments by the trial and defense counsels, I instructed the members of the court on the law of the case and their responsibility to make findings of guilt or innocence. I advised them that the accused's family background, his lack of education and all other matters which may have influenced his behavior must be considered. One of the requirements of the case was that the accused actually intended to override lawful authority. Did he have that specific intent? Did he have even the ability to form that specific intent?

Fallow's case was the fourth of the alleged rioters in which I participated. In my opinion, he was no worse, and probably less involved, than the others. Although technically he was guilty of some offense by remaining in the group that participated in the disturbances, I believed that he had not personally performed any of the acts of destruction or homicide that had occurred. But that was for the court to determine.

In less than an hour, the court members returned from the deliberation room and the president announced:

"Private Fallows, it is my duty as president of this court to inform you that the court, in closed session, by secret written ballot, two thirds of the members concurring, finds you: Of all specifications and charges: Guilty."

The defense then had an opportunity to present matters in extenuation and mitigation. Fallows testified in his own behalf, repeating substantially what he told the court before findings, adding a few details about the poverty of his family and the health of his children. He continued:

"I tried to join the army a long time ago but the recruiting sergeant said I was not qualified because I did not have an education. A year later, that same sergeant came to my house and told me that the rules had changed. He wanted me to enlist and promised me a lot of good things. I could even get an allotment of money for my family. So I joined the army and was sent to the infantry. Look where I am now!"

The defense counsel offered the following statement in the accused's behalf:

"The system that allows a person as unqualified as Fallows to join the army and be sent to Vietnam is unjust. Moreover, there is an inherent inequity in placing men like Fallows closest to harm's way without an understanding of what other options are open to them.

"In his lifetime, Fallows did not have good advice from any person who really cared about him or could have given him an opportunity to improve himself. Finally, I beg you to consider all of the unfortunate circumstances of the accused's life and to be lenient in your sentence. The army should bear some responsibility for recruiting young men who are totally unqualified to perform the tasks of a soldier."

I then had the responsibility of advising the court members with respect to the appropriateness of a sentence. In the three cases involving the riot in which I had already participated, the courts had imposed sentences of dishonorable discharge, total forfeitures of pay and allowances and confinement at hard labor. Two years confinement in one case, three years in another and five years in the third. In all of those cases, the accused had been seen, as a minimum, lifting bunk adapters or other dangerous objects, and shouting obscene epithets. Paul, the prisoner who had appeared at Fallow's tent and encouraged him and others to join the riot, was considered to be the ringleader. He had received a sentence including confinement at hard labor for ten years in a case tried by my fellow judge, Lieutenant Colonel Wayne Alley, who had come to Vietnam as a replacement for Dick Snyder. I could not advise the court members of those other sentences or that, in my opinion, the accused was the least guilty of all the prisoners charged with crimes. One soldier yet to be tried had been seen actually throwing a fireball into the chapel, and another not yet tried had committed an assault that resulted in the death of another prisoner.

After advising the court of the maximum sentence that could be imposed in Fallow's case, and giving a few other standard instructions, the members retired to the deliberation room to consider punishment.

As the court departed, the defense counsel spoke for a while to the accused, then joined a few of the spectators in the rear of the courtroom smoking cigarettes. Fallows returned to the defense table seeming not to comprehend what had happened. From the bench, I looked at him, totally dejected and alone. I decided to approach Fallows, stepped down and joined him at the defense table. He did not seem to resent my intrusion on his presence but said nothing until I spoke.

"Private Fallows," I said, "whatever happens will not be pleasant but I promise that I will try to help you. Do you have any brothers or sisters?"

"A brother and a sister," he answered, "but they're not much help."

"What about your father?"

"He lives in Detroit somewhere. I only saw him once or twice when he came to visit his relatives and dropped by to see my mama. He didn't talk much to me."

"Do you know if he ever gave money to your mother?"

"I don't know."

"Private Fallows, you don't have to answer this, and I really don't have any business asking, but just for my information, have you ever in your life been happy?"

"Not real happy. A couple of times my cousins came around when some people brought Thanksgiving stuff and we were laughing and horsing around. My wife and mama were feeling good. but, it didn't happen often."

After a long, awkward silence, the members returned to the courtroom and all participants resumed our proper places. Fallows reported to the president, who announced:

"Private Fallows, this court, voting by secret written ballot, two thirds of the members concurring, sentences you: To be dishonorably discharged from the service, to forfeit all pay and allowances and to be confined at hard labor for eight years."

Fallows was stunned. With gentle prodding, his counsel led him back to the defense table where both sat in absolute silence. After a pause, he asked to speak to me.

"What about money? What does forfeit mean?" he asked. "How will my family eat? Will they still get an allotment?"

I hesitated, but could only be honest.

"They will for a time," I answered, "but one day the money will stop."

He looked directly into my eyes, his lips quivering and tears rolling down his cheeks.

"Can your brother help you?" I asked.

"I don't think so," he mumbled. "Mama says he got a pretty good job after his discharge from the army, but I never saw him. I think he went to meet our daddy in Detroit."

Neither of us could think of any other thing to say. There was nothing in the world I could envision in Fallow's future that might be considered encouraging. He was going to jail, he was losing money, and he would eventually be sent into the world with a punitive discharge.

The general who convened the court in Fallow's case reduced the confinement at hard labor to five years, but otherwise approved the findings and sentence. I knew from experience that the reduction of confinement would not be very meaningful, so I took an unusual approach in an attempt to help Fallows.

For the first time since becoming a military judge, I wrote a letter to the Court of Military Review in Washington on behalf of a soldier in whose case I had participated. I emphasized that Fallows entered the army as a Project 100,000 soldier, and, although many of the men recruited under that program made considerable contributions to the armed forces, Fallows was one who did not have the ability to do so. He could barely read or write. Of the two hundred or so prisoners who participated in the riot, Fallows had the misfortune of being one of twelve recognized by guards who would be able to identify him in court.

Most important, I wrote to the court, Private Fallows would never have been involved if others had not encouraged him. He was a follower, not a leader. The evidence in all the cases already tried indicated that some prisoners were planning the riot at least three days before it occurred, and Fallows was never implicated in the plotting. Although he had indeed used marijuana in the stockade, so did at least fifty percent of the other prisoners. Serving more time in prison would be useless. Going into the world with a dishonorable discharge diminished all chances of his future success. I asked the court of review to seriously consider reducing the sentence.

Several months after leaving Vietnam and reporting to my new duty station in Munich, Germany, I received the appellate decision in Fallow's case. It was very short. The findings of guilty were approved in their entirety. I was pleasantly surprised, however, to read that the court acknowledged receiving a letter from the military judge who participated in the appellant's case, recommending clemency. The court then reduced Fallow's confinement to that which had already been served and changed the dishonorable to a bad conduct discharge.

Thus Fallows had returned into the world he left, not better or wiser, but under more distressing circumstances than when he volunteered for the army almost three years before.

CHAPTER TWELVE

Rape and Murder at the Americal

In the appellate decision of the case of *United States v. Captain Robert Cole,* one member of the Court of Review, referring to the evidence of record, quoted General Douglas MacArthur's words when he confirmed the death sentence of Japanese General Tomoyuki Yamashita, as being "shamefully applicable here":

> Rarely has so cruel and wanton a record been spread to public gaze. Revolting as this may be in itself, it pales before the sinister and far reaching implication thereby attached to the profession of arms. The soldier, be he friend or foe, is charged with the protection of the weak and unarmed. It is the very essence and reason of his being . . . This officer . . . has failed utterly his soldier's faith. The transactions resulting therefrom as revealed by the trial are a blot upon the military profession, a stain upon civilization, and constitute a memory of shame and dishonor that can never be forgotten.

The facts that gave rise to Captain Cole's case occurred in a place known as Dragon Valley in the District of Tam Ky, not far from My Lai, scene of the massacre that bears the name of that village. On the rainy afternoon of June 2, 1968, Cole was commanding officer of Company B, 1st Battalion, 52nd Infantry, 198th Infantry Brigade, 23rd Infantry Division (Americal), which was involved in a combat mission sweeping through several small villages. As the men of the First Platoon of that unit were marching in staggered formation, Sergeant Warren Butcher, a highly regarded squad leader, was shot and killed by enemy fire while voluntarily acting as point man. His body was carried away by helicopter, but the men of the platoon continued the mission and captured several enemy suspects in one of the villages.

The circumstances which led to the trial of Captain Cole and four others concerned only three of the captured detainees: two Oriental females, both presumed to be medical personnel affiliated with either the Viet Cong or the North Vietnamese Army, and one Vietnamese man presumed at the time of his capture to be sympathetic to the Viet Cong. The females were clearly distinguishable from each other by every witness who later gave sworn statements or testified at the trials. One, known as Que, thought to be about seventeen years old, was identified as the taller and older of the two. The other, known as Yen, presumed to be about fourteen years old, was repeatedly referred to as the smaller, or younger nurse. One witness thought that these women were "unusually better looking than the ordinary Vietnamese female." The male, who later testified in one of the trials, was identified as a local villager named He Nhai, but was referred to by witnesses during the investigation and at the trial as The Old Gook. He had no known connection with the enemy.

When the members of Company B and the detainees reached the area where they were to spend the night, the two nurses and He Nhai were taken to a place set aside for interrogations near the helicopter landing zone. The other detainees were tied to trees, or escaped. Sometime during the questioning, two Vietnamese interrogators, one named Phan and the other Lun, apparently obtained some hearsay evidence that the younger nurse had knowledge of a small hidden cache, consisting of one or more small-arms weapons.

During the interrogation of the nurses and He Nhai, which lasted about an hour, they were beaten with sticks, hands, and knees. Several members of Company B, including the executive officer, Lieutenant Steven Sales, observed the questioning and physical abuses. The commanding officer, Captain Cole, stopped by, but there was no direct evidence of record that he observed the beatings. Sergeant Alvin Muller of the First Platoon not only observed, but participated in the interrogation and ripped open the girls' blouses. When Phan hit the detainees, causing them to fall backwards, Muller caught them and shoved them back to Phan, who continued the assaults. During the interrogation, Sales said that the girls would be shot the next day.

When interrogation of the three suspects was completed, He Nhai was tied to a tree and Captain Cole gave Muller permission to take the girls to the area designated as a bivouac for the First Platoon. Word of that fact soon spread among the troops. Within minutes, rumors were rife throughout the entire company that the girls would be raped by members of the First Platoon in retaliation for the killing of Sergeant Butcher. Muller led the nurses, with their clothes torn and breasts exposed, to the area where members of his platoon had already begun to prepare for the night.

Corporal Ralph Clayton, a grenadier in the unit, met Muller and the nurses on their arrival at the First Platoon area. An agreement was made that Muller would take Que and Clayton could have Yen. Two or three soldiers standing by agreed that they would take Yen when Clayton was finished with her.

As Que stood by, Muller borrowed Clayton's poncho liner, joined it with his own and fashioned a place for himself and Que to spend the night. It was not yet dark, but the weather was misty, the ground was wet, and overall conditions of the area were miserable. Muller immediately had sexual relations with Que against her will, then departed temporarily.

Corporal Clayton took Yen a short distance away from the meeting place with Muller and forcibly had sexual intercourse with her. He then left her unguarded, knowing there were soldiers waiting for her, walked over to a nearby foxhole, sat on its edge, and, within minutes, observed the girl he had just raped performing oral sodomy upon Specialist John Fulton and Specialist Carroll Burroughs. His (Clayton's) testimony:

"Fulton had the girl perform oral sodomy on him. He forced the girl to perform oral sodomy. He took a knife and held it behind the girl's head, and used profane language describing what she should do."

The prosecutor asked: "Did anything else happen that night?"

Clayton continued:

"Yes, sir, it did . . . when Specialist Fulton got through with the girl, Specialist Burroughs tried to have intercourse with Yen but he said the girl was too small. As he got off, the girl leaned up so nobody else would get on her . . . When she got up . . . Burroughs already had his penis out, and when she moved her head, he held her head and forced her to commit sodomy . . .

"Fulton advised Burroughs to use a knife, it was better that way, but Burroughs did not take Fulton's advice. A third soldier, waiting in line, then forced Yen to commit the same act upon him."

The records do not clearly establish what happened to Yen the rest of that night, but when Clayton last saw her, she was with two other members of his platoon in a foxhole. Evidence did establish that, at a minimum, two soldiers had intercourse with Yen against her will later that night and enough noise emanated from the First Platoon area to warrant a warning about observing night discipline. Sounds of a girl crying were heard throughout the night.

Although not firmly established, there was evidence that at least one and probably two soldiers had intercourse with Que between the time Muller first had intercourse with her and the time he returned to his prepared sleeping area about nine o'clock.

Clayton joined Sergeant Muller and Que in Muller's makeshift bed and went to sleep, with Que between the two soldiers.

During the night, Que began to cry, toss, and turn. Muller ordered her, in Vietnamese, to be silent and announced to Clayton that he was "going to get him some more of that," whereupon he pulled the poncho liner completely off of Clayton, covered himself, and proceeded to have intercourse with Que, once again against her will. When the act was completed, Clayton had intercourse with Que without her consent. Her reaction during the act was "just like a log. She did not make a move."

Clayton awoke the next morning to find blood on his person, his clothing and the bedding. His poncho liner was so stained that he threw it away. Que herself was covered with blood on the lower part of her torso and appeared to be in a state of shock. Muller told Clayton that the girls would be shot.

Early in the morning of June 3, before breakfast but during daylight, events occurred in the First Platoon area that were still not perfectly clear after the interrogation of more than one hundred witnesses by criminal investigators. Nevertheless, certain events of that fateful morning are without dispute.

When Clayton removed himself from Muller's makeshift bed, he noticed a "bunch of people" standing around laughing about something. Closer inspection revealed that Corporal Dave Bellow was having sexual intercourse with Yen. Testimony established that she was "out, unconscious, with her legs in the air over the guy's shoulders." While Bellow was laughing and having intercourse with Yen, she was, according to Clayton, "limp as a wet rag. It was more like torture than sex."

In addition to members of Company B, wandering soldiers from a contiguous unit watched Bellow's activities for a period of at least forty minutes. Sergeant Paul Boxer from Company A testified that he "sat on the ground and cleaned my weapon and watched what was going on." He further testified that the bystanders ". . . were making noise, like a bunch of GIs together, having a bullshit session . . . I would say Bellow was not having sexual relations . . . he was more like torturing her . . . she was about like a dishrag when you throw it against the wall."

When Bellow had finished with Yen, he stood up and walked over to Que, who was huddled in a foxhole weeping. He grabbed her by the hair, looked into her eyes, and announced to the bystanders that he did not think he would take her.

When Que removed herself from the foxhole after Bellow's abusive behavior, Sergeant Ralph Porter saw that she was in pain, clutching her stomach, moaning. In his written statement, he swore:

"Her stomach was very distended looking, and swelled out . . . I pulled her pants down to look at her stomach. And it was swelled out like she was pregnant or something, really all distended and distorted. I pressed on it to see if it was hurting up there internal, they told me she had been raped. I used the flash suppresser of my rifle when I was pressing up against her. I just didn't want to touch her with my hands. She was just sloppy looking and had blood on her."

Sergeant Porter regarded himself as sympathetic to the girl, even though he refused to touch her with his hands, except to pull down her pants. He also swore that he had seen both girls beaten for a period of about forty-five minutes the night before, that he saw Muller assist in the beatings, and saw Lieutenant Sales witnessing the interrogations and beatings. During the morning, he tried to remonstrate with Muller as the soldiers were watching Bellow and Yen, but Muller merely replied that the girls had already been raped between ten and twenty times each. Porter replied:

"I hope they . . . all catch the clap!"

And Muller responded:

". . . that is impossible because the girls were both virgins."

During most of the time the young women were being sexually abused, Captain Cole was at his command post, about a hundred meters away. There was no evidence that he actually witnessed the misconduct, although it was common knowledge, even among members of the adjoining company, what was going on.

Lieutenant Sales was in the area when the assaults were taking place during the morning. At about ten o'clock, when Yen and Que were both lying on straw mats, exhausted, Sales ordered Muller to "bring the girls and The Old Gook" to the command post.

The procession of Muller, He Nhai, and the bleeding girls with their breasts exposed was witnessed by several persons. They halted about six feet from the command post, where Cole was sitting. At the command post, a decision was made by Sales and Cole to take the girls and He Nhai to the landing zone about forty meters away. Sales and Burroughs accompanied Muller and the Vietnamese to the landing zone, which could be seen from the command post if one looked carefully.

Captain Cole remained in the command post during the entire episode that followed, but there was no direct evidence that he witnessed what was happening at the landing zone, although his radio operator, sitting beside him, did.

When the group of soldiers and detainees reached the landing zone, there were about twenty persons awaiting them, including both American soldiers and Vietnamese detainees. Sales announced that a decision had been made to execute the younger girl. He asked Phan, the interpreter, to kill Yen but Phan refused. Someone from the crowd suggested that The Old Gook shoot the girl. Sales agreed.

Although He Nhai knew nothing about shooting a rifle, Sergeant Robert Ivy handed him an M-16 with one bullet in the chamber. Ivy then put his own M-16 to the back of He Nhai's neck to insure that he would not turn against his captors. At this point, Sales requested and was granted permission from Cole to report to nearby American units that there would be a brief period of test firing. The report was duly made by one of Cole's aides and all Americans in the area took necessary safety precautions.

He Nhai fired the M-16 in Yen's direction; the single bullet tore off a portion of her neck and chin, but did not kill her. Lieutenant Sales approached the wounded girl, gasping and bleeding on the ground, and with his own M-16, completed the execution. A witness to the act stated:

"The first round made her head jump . . . The second round hit her head . . . It spread her brain matter all over the ground in the area."

Two soldiers dragged Yen's body away to a nearby road, where bodies of two Vietnamese casualties from the previous day also lay. Corporal Ted Baxter, the radio operator who was with Cole in the command post when the shots were fired, went immediately to the landing zone. He returned in minutes and reported to the Captain: "The girl has been shot by the gook."

After the shooting, Sales also returned to the command post, where, in bloodstained clothes, he exchanged glances with Cole, and after a pause, reported: "The gook shot the girl with an AK 47."

Captain Cole did not report the incident to headquarters, even after he saw Yen's body by the side of the road. He did, however, tell a corporal to keep Que in the unit for a while. This was done, although all of the other detainees were either released or taken to an intelligence gathering unit for further questioning. One sympathetic soldier brought food to Que for a few days and furnished her with a blanket, sleeping space, and other small necessities.

On the day after the execution, Cole's battalion commander came to the area where he noticed Yen's body, as well as those of the other dead Vietnamese, and demanded an explanation. Cole answered that they were suspected Viet Cong who were shot by other Vietnamese the previous day. Cole did not report the non-battle death or other atrocities in his organization as he was required to do pursuant to MACV regulations.

Four days after the incident, Company B's medic thought that Que could not "make it anymore" as she was sick and still bleeding. Because of a misunderstanding and without the consent of Captain Cole, he arranged for her to be transferred to the rear area for medical attention. A soldier testified that when Que was put on a helicopter to be transported to the rear, Cole saw her and remarked: "If she's taken back to Military Intelligence for interrogation, and she tells what happened in the field, we'll all swing for it!" At least one soldier had already made the remark that Que should not be sent back to G-2 because Cole would be hanged if she were.

Specialist Ralph Porter provided most of the information concerning the last days of Que among the American forces. After the events of June 2 and 3, he told Captain Cole, his commanding officer, that he was fed up with what he had heard and seen, and that he was not going to fight the war in such circumstances. Cole told Porter to catch the next chopper and, if he could find a job in the rear, Cole would release him from Company B. Porter departed the next day, June 4.

Porter remained at a place called LZ Bayonet for about eight days, and was successful in finding a position with the 11th Infantry Brigade, another unit of the Americal Division, effective June 10. On June 6, he reported the incidents of June 2 and 3 to a chaplain who, in accordance with Porter's wishes, promised not to make a further report, at least until he had spoken to Captain Cole.

On the morning of June 10, just before the scheduled departure for his new assignment, Porter went to the mail room at LZ Bayonet, but it was locked, which was unusual. When he met the mail clerk a short distance away from the mail room, the latter explained that he placed the wrong lock on the door by mistake the evening before, but he would get Porter's mail for him before his departure. A few minutes later, still concerned about his mail, Porter returned to the mail room and noticed a side door partially opened. In his statement to the criminal investigators, he swore:

"I stuck my head in the door and the supply sergeant was in the mail room. There was also a Vietnamese girl in the mail room with her back to me and the sergeant pushed me, acting very strange and telling me that the mail clerk would be back to get my mail for me."

On June 11, Porter chanced upon Specialist Ray Hornung, who had been in Dragon Valley on June 2 and 3 and had also, by chance, been infused into the 11th Infantry Brigade with Porter. Porter continued his statement:

"Hornung asked me if I had seen the North Vietnamese nurse in the supply room at LZ Bayonet and I began to piece together why the mail room was locked and why the supply sergeant had acted so strange. Hornung told me they couldn't take the North Vietnamese nurse to S–2 because Cole would hang if she were interrogated."

On June 12, Porter made a return visit to the mail room at LZ Bayonet and noticed a cot in the small room where no one usually slept; the room was empty although it had "that lived-in look." He was directed to get his mail from the adjoining supply room rather that the mail room. Porter asked the supply clerk: "Hey, what did you do with the dink?" To which the clerk replied: "We took her home."

"All the way to Tam Ky?" Porter asked. Stammering, the clerk replied: "I don't know, I just work here."

Porter then made a second trip to the chaplain's office, which led to the official report of the incidents of June 2 and 3. Records introduced at the trials reflected only that Que disappeared into a hostile area and was unable to be located for investigation or trial.

Lieutenant Sales was originally charged with premeditated murder, but psychiatrists determined that he was mentally incompetent to stand trial, and he was returned to the United States for treatment. No disciplinary action was taken against him.

Captain Cole was charged with failing to report a non-battle death of a female detainee who was killed while in custody of his unit, and failing to enforce safeguards to protect female detainees in the custody of his unit. He was convicted of violating a lawful general regulation, which was framed in the words of the Geneva Convention pertaining to the protection of civilians in time of war.

After findings were entered, the defense counsel introduced evidence to the effect that Cole was twenty-seven years old, had graduated from a prominent American university, and that all members of his family were successful in their own professions.

Records reflected that he had earned Parachutist and Ranger ratings, as well as the Combat Infantryman's Badge. He had come to Vietnam with Company B in October 1967, had much combat experience, and on the day before the alleged offenses, he returned from R&R in Hawaii. The court sentenced Cole to be reprimanded and to pay a fine of $2,500.

Sergeant Muller was tried for two offenses of raping Que, once on the evening of June 2 and once during the early morning hours of June 3. He was convicted only of the latter offense. After findings of guilty, upon questioning by the Defense Counsel, Muller testified:

"I just feel like my whole life has gone down the drain . . . Sergeant Butcher got killed, and I guess everybody like Lieutenant Sales [who had been found mentally incompetent], everybody was in a state of shock . . . I didn't care if I got killed or not . . . Well, the witnesses against me committed a crime as bad as mine or worse . . . They're going back to their families . . .

"I want to go home worse than I ever wanted to go home before . . . I just wanted to live. Now, I don't know. What's there to live for? . . . I didn't give a damn if . . . the VC killed me. I just wanted to get back on them a little bit. For all the trouble they've caused me, for all the guys I've seen die."

Muller then testified that he had been in Vietnam for eight months and had been on many long-range combat patrols, some when his buddies were killed. On the afternoon of June 2, his friend and leader, Sergeant Butcher, was killed before his very eyes and he couldn't believe it. His testimony continued: "I guess in a way I wish it would have been me instead of him, Butcher. I knew his girlfriend. He would have been married when he got home. I seen Sergeant Butcher get hit. I couldn't believe he was dead."

Muller was sentenced to be confined at hard labor for a period of two years but the time was later reduced to one year.

Ten days after Muller's conviction, Specialist Fulton was brought to trial on charges of committing sodomy with Yen, and assaulting Yen with a knife, with intent to commit sodomy. He was convicted only of the sodomy charge. He explained to the court his feelings in the following words:

"I'm sorry; might as well say that I let myself down. We walked into an ambush, Sergeant Butcher was killed.

"He [Butcher] quit school when he was in the eighth grade to help his parents. He was just great. You could drop him from a chopper; you could go anywhere with him . . . you just wouldn't think twice about doing anything [for him]."

Fulton then explained how upset the entire First Platoon was about Butcher's death and continued:

". . . our company commander gave us the detainees, and not an order given to rape them or anything, but gave them to us to secure for the night. Everybody was upset, one thing led to another . . .

"I, doing such a crime, I just can't see it. Like just animals, there is no cause for doing it even though we were upset. Come to find out after the detainees were interrogated by our interpreter, they knew the ambush was set up there. They let us walk into it; wouldn't say anything. I could have shot them right there. When you see people like Butcher get shot down, excuse me, their guts blown all over, you want to go out and get revenge. Maybe you don't, but I do."

At this point, Fulton broke down in tears and was given time to compose himself. There was no cross examination. He was sentenced to be confined at hard labor for one year.

Specialist Bellow was charged with the rape of Yen. At the end of the prosecution's case, the defense counsel argued that the prosecution failed to show that Yen did not consent to the act, and the only act proven by the government was intercourse with Yen, which was no crime. Based upon those arguments, he made a motion for finding of not guilty. The military judge granted the motion. Bellow was free without having to put on a case.

Specialist Burroughs was charged with sodomy but was found not guilty.

Specialist Porter was granted immunity from prosecution in exchange for his testimony against those who were tried.

Charges against others allegedly involved in the offenses were dropped after the acquittal in Burrough's case and the favorable ruling on the motion in Bellow's case.

No member of Company B was separated from the service as a result of acts committed against He Nhai, Que, and Yen.

CHAPTER THIRTEEN

The Animal Fair

Lieutenant Colonel Bob Jones loved animals. In fact, Bob himself was gentle as a puppy but sharp as any lawyer in Vietnam. He was the staff judge advocate of II Field Force, which was located not far from Long Binh. A collection of dog memorabilia decorated his office. A calendar on the wall guaranteed Bob pictures of different poodles each month. A shelf on another wall displayed little toy dogs he had collected and brought to Vietnam. And his desk was smothered with plastic, ceramic, china, and glass dogs of all pedigrees.

On the first occasion when I was assigned to hear a case at Plantation, Bob surprised me by calling in advance to say that he would himself pick me up at the Lucky Hotel and bring me to the site of the trial. I was happy with this arrangement because, previously, I had traveled away from Saigon only by plane or by helicopter.

When Bob arrived on the scheduled morning, we met in the lobby of the Hong Kong Hotel. As we walked out of the door, I spotted his jeep immediately because, as in some other legal offices, the legend "Here come de Judge!" was painted on the panel below the windshield. Inside the jeep were the driver in his assigned place and Bob's sergeant major sitting in the rear seat, cuddling a fluffy little dog with black spots on its body in places were there should have been hair. Unknown to Bob, the spots had been painted with a chemical by the vendor in order to sell the dog at a higher price with the explanation that this was a rare breed, indeed, found only in Vietnam.

It became immediately apparent to me that the reason Bob wanted to come to Saigon was to buy a dog to substitute for the poodle he had left behind in the United States. The animal he purchased was a friendly little thing and the occupants of the jeep vied for the privilege of holding "de Judge," as the dog had already been named. They offered me the opportunity to take a turn, but I declined with the explanation that "de Judge" had not had a rabies shot. "No matter," they replied, "he's just a puppy!"

Within a few days, two incidents happened that changed the course of events in the legal office of the II Field Forces. First, men who loved the animal built a little doghouse for their mascot surrounded by little sandbags as protection against mortar fire, and put a sign that identified it as being the home of "de Judge." No one could deny that that was the cutest thing at Plantation.

Secondly, "de Judge" expired of rabies. Although this was a shock to all men of the unit, some of them refused to take the series of painful rabies shots recommended by the medics. Most, however, considered the advice wise. So, on several occasions during trials, the court was required to recess in order for one of the court officers or the court reporter to report for his rabies shot. Happily, those who refused to take the shots had not been tainted by "de Judge."

I had not refused to touch Bob's little dog because of a dislike for animals, but rather because of an experience at our office in MACV headquarters. Sergeant Al Dugas was determined to have a squirrel for a pet and went down to the animal market in Saigon to purchase one. The one he selected, however, did not appreciate the gesture of its prospective new owner and bit Dugas, who then refused to buy that or any other squirrel.

When Sergeant Dugas returned to the office, he related the story of the squirrel that bites, pleased that he had discovered the bad habits of his intended pet before purchasing it. He was not pleased, though, when another sergeant advised him that he should indeed have purchased the squirrel in order for the medics to determine whether the animal was diseased. Frantically, Dugas rushed back to the market and made a firm offer to purchase the animal. Sadly, the vendor informed him that he could not keep any pet that bites, and he therefore threw the squirrel into the river. Sergeant Dugas underwent the series of rabies shots.

The incidents of the dog and the squirrel aroused my interest in the animal market. I persuaded Sergeant Dugas to give me a tour of the place when I next had an opportunity to take a few hours off. It came shortly after I received the happy news that a small room at the Rex Hotel was available and mine. I accepted without either thinking about the offer or looking at the room, and arranged to take the following Sunday off, when I would spend the morning moving to my new quarters and the afternoon visiting the animal market. Dugas came to the Rex Hotel in the early afternoon and we began our excursion.

The market was located along the Saigon River, just a few blocks from my new home. We walked there to find something quite unlike anything I had ever seen. The vendors sat in their allotted spaces on the crowded sidewalks selling virtually every kind of animal to be found in Vietnam smaller than a tiger.

Snake peddlers kept most of their wares in baskets, but at least four or five wrapped the reptiles around an arm or leg, or even their entire bodies. An Indian merchant kept a cobra in a hypnotic trance by playing a flute.

Dog vendors had canines of all descriptions and sizes tied on leashes to an overhead wire. Some were fat, but most were thin and mangy except for the puppies, which were easier to sell. Several of the dogs were chemically painted with spots or small circles to give them an exotic look. All seemed to be barking at the same time. The dogs offered for sale as pets were separate from those sold as food.

Small-animal dealers were grouped together. Their wares, intended mostly for sale as pets, included an amazing variety of rodents and other species of animals that I could not identify and whose names I did not learn. Most were confined to old bamboo or screen cages that apparently had been in use for many years. We saw several varieties of monkeys, some tied on ropes and jumping all about, others in cages. Cats, like dogs, were sometimes burned with spots and circles to increase their value.

Continuing down the street, we came to that part of the market where live animals intended to be used exclusively for food, such as goats and pigs, were sold. Chicken sellers were doing a brisk business and seemed to have the easiest time disposing of their wares.

The market sold more than animals. There were special foods available for exotic animal consumption, and others for human consumption thought to have special therapeutic value. Reputed aphrodisiacs made from horns, ears, eyes, or other parts of specified animals were also available.

The animal vendors were interspersed with ordinary country fair–type booths, hawkers selling trinkets or their own hand-crafted specialties. The market did not seem to attract any particular category of person. There were male and female, healthy and lame, old and young, all seemingly enjoying themselves. Many of the little ones carried balloons; others attempted to play with the more friendly monkeys, dogs, and cats. None were afraid, and apparently rabies was not a cause to hinder any of the children or adults from taking their pleasure on a sunny Sunday afternoon.

CHAPTER FOURTEEN

Kathy

I first met Kathy at the steakhouse on the roof of the Rex one evening after returning from a trip to Lai Khe. She was having dinner with a captain from Long Binh with whom I had associated frequently in court. He invited me to join them and I did. Kathy was an attractive woman, about thirty-three, I presumed, although she appeared younger. She had short hair, a perfect complexion, a round face with large brown eyes. Her most remarkable features, however, were her constant smile and her ability to listen. People looked at her constantly.

Kathy was a toucher. Her hands seemed always in motion as she gently touched the arm or the hand or the shoulder of the person to whom she was speaking. On the occasion of our meeting, we shook hands and later during the meal she frequently touched my arm or hand to emphasize a point as she spoke. At the same time, she held the hand of the young captain. She was a secretary for the United States Agency for International Development (USAID), one of many American agencies in Vietnam. After dinner, Kathy invited me to join her and her friend for a drink in her apartment.

Kathy lived in that conglomeration of buildings across from the Rex that bordered on the two parks. We walked along Le Loi

Street and turned left on Tu Do Street for fifty yards or so, where we stopped in front of an entrance directly across from the Continental Palace Hotel. We paused before entering when Kathy pointed to a wizened, crooked man crossing the street toward us on his hands and feet under his body as fast as a young boy can run.

The man, whom I had seen several times, had a special place in his heart for Kathy. When he reached us, he looked up and gave her a great, almost toothless grin. It was apparent that he was happy to see her. His legs were frozen in right angles at the knees, with his bare feet flat against the pavement. His back was parallel to the sidewalk, supported at times by one or both arms, but he forced his head in an upright position. Kathy bent down, gently touched his face, smiled at him, and dropped a few piasters into the calloused hand lifted towards her. His smile broadened. The captain and I added a few coins before proceeding inside the entrance to the elevator, which took us up to Kathy's apartment floor.

There was a small kitchen to the left as one entered Kathy's apartment. Directly forward was a dining-living room combination about forty feet long and fifteen feet wide. It was completely furnished, including pictures on the wall, plants, and curtains. To the left, beyond the kitchen, was the door to her bedroom, in which there were a king-size bed, tables, lamps, and other bedroom furniture. A door from her bedroom led to the bathroom, complete with bidet and a combination bath and shower. It was all air-conditioned. "Do members of President Thieu's cabinet have such apartments?" I asked, half joking.

"Oh, this is nothing!" replied Kathy. "There are a dozen apartments in this building alone that are much nicer than mine, with outside views. My boss and a roommate who works for the United States government share a villa you wouldn't believe."

"Do you work for the head of USAID?" I asked.

"Far from it. My boss only handles one section of the agency. And, he has a gardener and a housekeeper to keep the house, which is surrounded by a large wall."

"Where does the big boss live?" I asked.

"You wouldn't believe that, either. I think some famous French general lived there. The last time I visited, a combo entertained and I danced with Ambassador Bunker."

Now it was becoming clear to me that the government was taking very good care of its civilian employees. Kathy had a good selection of liquor and beer, but she herself did not drink except in restaurants with meals. We sat in comfortable chairs and spoke of inconsequential matters with background music provided by the Armed Forces Network.

I was disappointed when I noted the clock on Kathy's wall indicated that the eleven o'clock curfew was fast approaching. I could get to the Rex in a couple of minutes, but there was no way the captain could return to Long Binh in that amount of time. For a moment, I toyed with the idea of inviting him to my room, where I had a folding cot, but quickly realized that the idea might not appeal to him. I stood up, thanked them both for a lovely evening, and excused myself. The captain did not seem concerned about curfew.

As time went by, I saw Kathy frequently, mostly in the company of one or more men, some of whom I knew, and at other times in the company of one or more women. People seemed to gravitate to her.

There was no consistency to Kathy's dress. Frequently she wore miniskirts; at other times, slacks or dresses of various lengths. Once she wore an au dai that she had purchased as a souvenir. She was always smiling, never outwardly depressed. She ate frequently at the open mess or the steakhouse at the Rex, and used the swimming pool there.

One evening in late November, Colonel Tom Edwards and I were sharing a meal in the open mess when Kathy and a woman friend joined us. I had, as the months passed, developed a friendship with Tom, whose room was next to mine and with whom I frequently shared the evening meal. He was about my age, very proper in all respects, and, by army standards, an intellectual. He was in his element when speaking of Herodotus, Tacitus, or

Thucydides and the ancient civilizations about which they wrote. He did most of the talking when we were together but I encouraged him to do so because it was a learning experience I enjoyed. I think Tom enjoyed having someone willing to listen to him.

The conversation with the women at the meal was pleasant, Kathy being her usual ebullient self, and Tom more restrained in his historical orations. Before dessert, Kathy's friend excused herself, leaving only the three of us at the table. We lingered a while, until Kathy asked us to escort her to her apartment. I excused myself because I had work to do and an early flight the next morning. Tom was a bit embarrassed but felt comfortable enough with Kathy by this time to walk home with her. I bid them both good night.

When I returned from Cu Chi the following evening, I showered, changed into comfortable clothes, and went to the open mess. Before I reached the end of the serving line, Tom, who was already in the room, came quickly to me saying that it was very important we talk alone. He excused himself from his former companions and went over to an empty table for two, reserving a place for me.

"What's up, Tom?" I asked when I arrived at the table. "You look a bit troubled."

"Sit down, and listen carefully," he replied. "You won't believe what I have to say."

"Try me!" I offered.

"Well, last night after you left, I escorted Kathy home as she requested. But it didn't end there."

What I am about to hear is not possible, I thought.

"So what happened?"

"Jack, you know I'm no Lothario. I'm forty-five years old and have never had an affair during my married life. I have a son at West Point and a daughter at Bennington. I was president of the PTA at the American High School in Ludwigsburg, Germany. I was . . ."

"I know these things, Tom. What happened?"

"Well, she invited me up to see her apartment and I accepted. You know I looked upon her as a friend . . . "

"Yes, I know you did." At this point I began to suspect Tom more than I did Kathy.

"Really, I did. When she offered me a drink, I accepted a Coke but only to be polite. Then, we sat down to watch a TV program and before I was aware of the time, it was past curfew."

"Please continue. I'm sure you haven't finished."

"Not nearly. She said quite calmly that I'd have to spend the night in her apartment. She went about rummaging for sheets and things to make up the divan in the living room for or me. I was trapped, really. But Kathy had no designs on me. She insisted that I use the bathroom before she got ready for bed. My wife would never believe this."

"I presume you then said good night and went to sleep," I said.

"Not I, but she did. I couldn't help thinking that there was only an unlocked door between the living room and her bedroom. I twisted and turned and got up to walk around. I took milk from the refrigerator. Not only was sleep impossible, but I couldn't even sit down comfortably. Finally, I had to go to the bathroom, passing through her bedroom. I didn't know whether to dress or go in my underwear, but decided to take a chance."

"Did she wake up?"

"Not at that time, but she did when I put on the light in the bathroom. Then, when I left the bathroom she startled me by putting on her bedroom light, asking what was the matter. She really was understanding, what with me stuttering in my shorts, she could see how uncomfortable I was. 'Look,' she said, 'you're all uptight. I know you're married and I'm really not interested in sex if that's what you have on your mind, or if that's what you think I have on my mind. It's three o'clock in the morning. Come in my bed and I'll give you a Seconal and we'll both get some sleep.' Now, how in hell do you think I could calm myself in her bed when I couldn't do so in the living room?"

"Don't stop now," I said. "There must be more!"

"I can't understand how or why, but I took her suggestion."

"You went into her bed and she gave you a Seconal?"

"Yes, but it didn't do much good. I kept turning and twisting."

"Until daybreak?"

"No. Then, I think she got a little irritated. She gave me another Seconal and that did it. When I woke up, she was gone; there was daylight all over, and I missed the bus to work this morning."

"That's some story!" I said. "But, it's over now and nothing happened, so you shouldn't be concerned. Your conscience is clear."

"Would you believe the story of an older man being invited into a younger woman's bed and nothing happened?"

"Probably not. At least, if that's all I heard."

"Do you think I'm going to tell any part of what happened to any person?"

"Look, really. No one is going to hear about it. Kathy certainly won't think twice about what happened. You've had an emotional experience. That's all it was. It's passed. The whole PTA in Ludwigsburg would believe you if they heard the whole story."

He did not appreciate my attempt at humor. He sat a while longer, still disturbed. Then, he stood up without finishing his meal, complaining that he was tired and had to go to bed.

A few nights later, I saw Kathy sitting alone in the open mess and joined her for dinner. She was happy and gregarious as usual. I hoped that she would bring up the subject of Tom spending the night at her apartment, but it was apparent that that had been an event of little consequence to her. I knew what an emotional experience it had been for Tom but curiosity prevailed over propriety, causing me to pursue the matter.

"I'm sorry I couldn't escort you home the other night with Tom," I said. "I hope everything was all right."

"Oh sure!" she answered. "He was very nice. If I'd have known how uptight he was, though, I'd have sent him home before curfew."

"I'm sorry you were inconvenienced."

"I wasn't really, except that he kept me from getting a good night's sleep. I'll say this for him. He's the only guy who ever slept in my apartment without trying to make a pass at me. He was so concerned about his wife. Actually, I left before he woke up and I haven't seen him since. I'd like to, because he is quite nice."

"You will, sooner or later," I replied. "He eats here most of the time. I think he's away now because I knocked on his door tonight and he wasn't in."

"Well, I wish more men were like him."

"I think tonight is the first time I've seen you alone," I said, changing the subject.

"I won't be for long. I'm waiting for a friend who will meet me here after dinner. I met her at a party last night and she doesn't have a place to live. Right now, she's sharing a small room with an older American woman and it's not a satisfactory arrangement."

"Is she going to move in with you?"

"No way!" Kathy responded quickly. "But I know an American civilian who says he works for an oil company and has a villa all to himself. I think he'll let her stay there. I called him today and we're going to see him about nine. Why don't you come with us? I'd feel safer walking home with someone in uniform, anyhow."

I hope it'll be before curfew, I thought, then responded: "Sure, I'll go along. Kathy, you have more friends than anyone I know. You're almost never alone. Do you ever get lonesome?" I asked.

"You bet I do," she answered. "I can't stand to be alone."

"But you always seem to be happy."

"That's how you see me. I always try to be in the company of others, even in my apartment. Before curfew, that is."

"You have so many friends."

"I know a lot of people, but I don't really have many friends. Almost every man I meet wants to go to bed, except your friend

Tom, of course. About three weeks ago, I met a doctor who was here on a fact-finding mission of some kind, and he was no exception. I like people, I really do, and I like to be with them, but the men who visit me all try to use the curfew as an excuse to stay at my place overnight. Sometimes I let them, but I insist they sleep on the divan in the living room."

"Haven't you made any serious attachments since you've been here?" I asked.

"No, and that's a pity. I'd marry tomorrow if the right man came along. But, the men here are either married already or looking for a good time. A lot of married ones are looking for good times, too, I might add."

"I've always had the impression you were quite content. I've seen you with men who were married and men who were not married."

"I don't mind being with married men, as long as we're having fun. I see nothing wrong with that. Of course, I'd prefer to be with single men, but here in Vietnam, it seems they have no desire to get serious."

I pondered a moment about the line of demarcation between having fun and having a good time.

"I guess I know about as many men as anyone around here," she continued, "I have friends in the army, navy, air force and Marines. And even civilians, as you'll find out tonight. One day I'll get marred to a man younger than me. I don't count my years chronologically."

"Vietnam is hardly the place to find a suitable man according to your specifications. If you do want to marry, it might be a good idea not to exclude older men."

"Listen!" she said. "There's something wrong with any man older than me who has never been married. I'm thirty-five, you know."

Perhaps she had a point, but I gave her my advice for what it was worth. "Be practical, Kathy. Don't exclude a whole category of men."

"I'm not conceited, really I'm not, but I do look young. I could have dates with young guys every night. They're all over the place."

"I know they are, and I'm sure they'd like to go out with you, but from what you've said, they're not interested in marriage. Things may not be different in the real world." Since she seemed to have a pretty thick skin, I decided to push on just a little further.

"By the way, what ever happened to you and the captain from Long Binh who was with you the night we met? I still see him occasionally, but never the two of you together."

"Oh, him! He was just like all the others, even worse. He can't be trusted. We had dinner together several times before I met you. We were pretty close, but I also told him I wouldn't go to bed with him or anyone else until I knew they were serious. I'm a perfectly proud Catholic. He didn't believe me."

"What do you mean?"

"Remember that night you just mentioned? You came up to my place with us. I knew he couldn't return to Long Binh so I let him stay in my apartment. We talked a long time after you left; then I fixed a place for him to sleep on the divan. Well, he sat down and was reading a magazine when I went to the bathroom to get ready for bed. When I came out, he was in my bed leering at me, and I knew what his interests were, even though I had forewarned him. We had a fight and I haven't seen him since."

Before I could indicate a reaction, I noticed an attractive young woman standing in front of our table smiling at us. Kathy seemed happy to see her friend and introduced me to Dianne, who sat down to join us for coffee and dessert.

From the ensuing conversation, I understood that Dianne had gone to Hong Kong to meet a boyfriend on leave from Vietnam, but things hadn't worked out very well. Not wanting to return immediately to the United States, she took a part-time job in Hong Kong at a hotel doing business with Americans. The pay there, however, was not sufficient to support her, so, at the suggestion of another American on leave from Vietnam, she decided to come to Saigon to look for work with the American forces. She had no luck up to that time, and was still looking around. Meanwhile, she needed a place to live and Kathy seemed to be her guardian angel.

I do not remember the name of the man whose home Kathy took us to, but he lived about a mile from the center of town. The residential area was the finest in the city, previously reserved for French and then American families. To get there, we walked past the Continental Palace Hotel and several official buildings surrounded by barbed wire and guarded by Vietnamese soldiers.

Kathy's friend lived in a white stucco house surrounded by a concrete wall except for an iron gate at the driveway. We rang a bell at the gate and, at the sound of a buzzer set off from within, we were admitted into the premises. The yard was large enough for trees, a sizable lawn, servant's quarters, and a bed of flowers.

The two-story house was approximately nineteen hundred square feet. The furniture was sparse, but adequate for a single person. We did not go upstairs but were told that it consisted of three small bedrooms and one bath. The house and furnishings had been provided to the occupant by his company and he apparently had no particular desire to make them more attractive.

Our host was polite, but not exceptionally so. My impression was that he thought Dianne much too young to have as a house mate, especially since she was unemployed. He served drinks and snacks, but showed no enthusiasm about the proposed living arrangement. We left the house at ten-thirty, the parties having come to no agreement, which both Kathy and Dianne interpreted as a negative reaction.

The walk back to Kathy's apartment was exciting. At that time, the curfew started at eleven o'clock, and would begin in about thirty minutes. Traffic was minimal and there was a strange silence in contrast to daylight hours, with the exception of an occasional mortar blast in the distance. As we passed along the guarded buildings, the Vietnamese soldiers armed with M–16 rifles stood up and shouted, "Numbah One!" when they saw the two women. No hassles, no problems. In the middle of Saigon, whose datelines filled the papers back home with reports of agony, assassinations, and mortar attacks, we witnessed only peace and quite except for the happy shouts of indigenous soldiers.

We arrived at Kathy's apartment with sufficient time remaining for Dianne and me to return to our respective hotels before curfew.

CHAPTER FIFTEEN

Lai Khe

Big Red One, as the First Infantry Division was commonly known, had fought bitterly in and around Saigon during the 1968 Tet Offensive and other major campaigns. It's mission was partially to defend the approaches to Saigon and the border regions between Vietnam and Cambodia. While continuing to fight Viet Cong and North Vietnamese army forces, the division also participated in pacification activities and training South Vietnamese Army (ARVN) forces. The division headquarters was located at Lai Khe, about thirty miles west of Saigon on what had previously been part of a French rubber plantation. The only remnants of colonial days were a run-down mansion and a broken-down swimming pool.

The garrison at Lai Khe was on alert status during my first visit there. Mortar shells from enemy forces struck the compound almost nightly and frequently during daylight hours. The men of the staff judge advocate section had constructed a bunker next to their office sophisticated enough to accommodate eight sleeping persons during the night. There were two raised wooden platforms against each of the walls for the lucky few who turned in early, but others slept on the ground, usually in sleeping bags.

Inasmuch as the bunker was only seven feet wide, four feet deep and ten feet long, the operation of extricating oneself from a sleeping bag, trying to avoid others sharing the bunker, and negotiating the ladder to the outside in the dark was a delicate operation. There was also the problem of undressing and finding a place to lay one's clothing.

I was invited to spend my first night at Lai Khe in the judge advocate bunker. Because of the obstacles involved, I slept with my clothes on and made no effort to leave the bunker until daylight.

On the morning after my first night in the bunker, I asked several members of the legal staff if they had known anyone sleeping above ground at Lai Khe who had been hit during the nighttime mortar attacks. To my surprise, no one knew of any such casualty. Then and there, I made a decision to forgo the safety of the bunker. On subsequent nights, I joined those brave souls from the office who shared a tent as their quarters and spent the nights on a simple cot above the ground.

My first case at the Big Red One was typical of incidents that happened hundreds of times in Vietnam, as well as other places where troops were stationed. The court-martial could have been avoided, in my opinion, with mature initial guidance and perhaps a mild punishment. A frustrated soldier, perhaps exhausted from combat or under the influence of alcohol, released his emotions in one brief moment of passion by throwing caution to the winds and offering violence to anyone who tried to control his actions or happened to be in the vicinity when the offenses occurred.

The incident began when the soldier refused to comply with the orders of his sergeant to get out of bed. The sergeant was quite willing to forgive the initial disobedience, but after a second refusal by the accused, the sergeant called in his platoon leader to repeat the order. Another refusal, and the platoon leader called in the company commander. Another order given and another refusal to obey. While all three were still present, in addition to a few spectators who happened by, the accused, in a fit of passion, leaped out of bed, grabbed a chair and threw it in the direction of all parties present. As a result, he was charged with disobeying three orders, as well as offering acts of violence to the spectators.

The soldier was sentenced to one year's confinement at hard labor, but no discharge. The staff judge advocate later told me that after three months, the soldier returned to duty.

The second case involved typical military-type offenses that might be expected in a combat zone. The accused was charged with three specifications of desertion. As generally understood, desertion requires proof that the accused departed from his unit with intent never to return. There is, however, another type of desertion, which is absence from one's place of duty, no matter how long, with intent to avoid hazardous duty. In this case, the accused had, on three separate occasions, gone away from his unit after having been assigned to night combat patrols, but returned shortly after the patrols had departed. This case was more serious than the first because it involved three separate incidents of misbehavior. The accused was convicted of all offenses charged and sentenced to five years confinement at hard labor in addition to a dishonorable discharge.

The third trial involved the type of case that sometimes occurred in Vietnam because of unfortunate prevailing circumstances and attitudes under wartime conditions. On the evening of July 29, Miss Than Thi Hong, a nurse employed in Company C, 1st Medical Battalion, sought additional employment at the local noncommissioned officers' club. She was immediately put to work and, at closing time on the same evening, was told to count the money in the cash register. After completing her chores, the sergeant in charge of the club arranged with Corporal Robert Horan, who had a three-quarter-ton truck at his disposal, to escort Miss Hong to Lai Khe Plaza, a central location in the village.

Several American witnesses testified for the prosecution about events preceding and following the alleged offenses before Miss Hong took the witness stand. The evidence tended to show that she entered Horan's vehicle about 10:30 p.m.; that she appealed for help to Americans on duty at a small outpost about

1:30 a.m. the following morning; and that she again reported two alleged incidents of attempted rape at the break of dawn.

Miss Hong was called to give evidence at the trial. I was doubtful whether she should testify in English or in Vietnamese, using an interpreter. I preferred that she testify in English because, while reviewing the pretrial papers, I noted that her English, although faulty, was superior to that of the 1st Infantry Division's interpreter, with whom I had previously spoken.

As Miss Hong entered the courtroom, she was accompanied by the interpreter. Before anyone else spoke, I gave her an opportunity to demonstrate her ability to speak English. I asked a few simple questions, including her name, place of employment, and residence. Although she answered in fractured sentences, she was, in my opinion, capable of conveying her thoughts. I advised her that she should make an effort to testify in English, but if, during her testimony, she did not understand a question or was unable to express her thoughts, she should request an interpreter. Somewhat to his surprise, I directed the prosecutor to proceed without an interpreter. He apparently had never spoken to the witness in English.

After being sworn, Miss Hong answered the first few questions without hesitation but began to falter when the prosecutor used words such as "accused" and "court-martial." When those and other relatively difficult words were explained to her, however, she seemed quite capable of understanding them. I was fully aware of the importance of her testimony because the outcome of the case would largely depend upon her credibility.

In my opinion, her own words in English would express her thoughts better than if funneled through an interpreter. Miss Hong testified in part as follows:

Q: (by the prosecutor): Miss Hong, where do you work?

A: (by Miss Hong): I work for Charlie Med. I am a nurse.

Q: Please explain what you mean by "Charlie Med."

A: Company C, 1st Medical Battalion.

Q: When the NCO Club closed on the evening of July 29, please tell us what happened.

A: Sir, when club closed about 9:45, I must stay in the club and count money and after I count money, I hear the club manager tell me, "You go home. You have a ride now."

Q: Did you get into a truck?

A: Yes, I did.

Q: And who was driving the truck?

A: Horan.

Her testimony was given in halting sentences, but graphic detail. She sobbed sporadically, but continued:

Q: Please continue.

A: When I get in truck, this GI he take me and go for ten minutes, and he stopped, and he told me, "truck has broke" and he forced his hand under my legs. I say, "No, I don't want to do that". . . he hold my neck, I try get out, I fall on right side, it is very difficult to tell this story, he try take off my pants first . . . and this road have many water and wet and I guess we get fight, I don't know. He take me and he go over to tree . . . he force his hand on my mouth, he force me to lie down and he try take off my pants. About twenty minutes later he take down my pants but not all the way and he lie over my body, on my belly I feel his body. He try fuck with me . . . he say he love me and I say "If you love me, you don't do that, because I am not whore and also I am not your animal." And I hit him . . . I try and go away. I run on the road and then he force me back, he say he will kill me if I run, and I . . . Sir, I forget my story.

After a few calming words, a drink of water, and a few moments of silence, she continued:

And I talk with him. "I can't stay in the woods all this night. If you love me, tonight if you want to, I stay with you." He take me back to the truck. He take me to the motor pool and I call loud, but nobody hear me . . . he take me to a small room, he close door and take off my pants because they are easy for him to take off. He try same as in the woods. I called and nobody came and I am very sad, but I try something. I force my finger in my mouth and I make vomit and he don't let me out. He say "We fuck first, and then you go," and I say "I must go now, please, and you let me out" . . . he force me to lie down on bed. And I say, "Now I want to go bath and I am very dirty, my stomach very hurt now. If you don't take me, I don't know where to go. If you keep me, I smell very bad."

At this point, Miss Hong began to cry uncontrollably. I permitted a recess to allow her to compose herself. When we reconvened, she was able to continue her testimony:

A: Oh, I forgot. Inside, he say if I want to go out, I must take off all my clothes first. And I take off my clothes and put them in my bag. And I hold my bag and I go out. He not see my bag because I hide it close to my stomach. I run away, but I fall down in hole same as bunker, and I wet all my clothes.

Miss Hong further testified that she left the hole, put on her wet clothes, went over to a small unit where men were on guard and asked them to phone the military police. One member, acting as a medic, cleaned her arm and neck but told her she could not stay there because she might be a Viet Cong or a whore. Again she asked that the MPs be called but was told that there was no phone. The medic said he was sorry but she could not stay with the soldiers because they would get in trouble. Miss Hong then went out into the night, sat down by some trees, and waited until daylight when she reported the incident again to a different American unit.

On cross-examination, Miss Hong admitted that, when Horan told her to take off all her clothes if she wanted to go outside to the bathroom, she herself removed her blouse. Horan started to go out with her, but she managed to run away with her clothes hidden in her purse, and he could not catch her. When defense counsel asked if Horan ever made love to her, the response was that he tried but she was able to prevent him from having intercourse. She explained that, in nursing school, she learned that if a woman stops breathing, a man could not penetrate her, so she tried that as long as she could. Then she crossed her legs. She was more or less able to achieve success in defending herself against being raped because Horan appeared to be drunk.

She smelled beer and whiskey on his breath. That completed her testimony.

Several witnesses called by the prosecutor confirmed Miss Hong's testimony with respect to complaints and her physical condition following the alleged offenses. The sergeant in charge of the unit to which she reported at daybreak testified that Hong was in a state of emotional distress; her clothes were wet and disheveled; she had apparently been crying a lot because her eyes were red; her hair was messed up; and her neck and left arm were bruised. The prosecutor then rested his case.

The case for the defense was based solely upon the testimony of Corporal Horan. In the initial stages of questioning, the defense counsel elicited testimony that Horan had attended school only for a period of eight years and that his intelligence quotient placed him in the lowest mental category possible to be accepted into the army at the time he enlisted.

Concerning the alleged offenses, Horan testified that between five and nine o'clock in the evening of the incident, he went in and out of the noncommissioned officers' club several times and had about six or eight beers. Just before closing time, he informed the club manager that he had transportation that could be used to take the girls home, if there was such a need. There was, in the case of Miss Hong, who was working late, and the club manager accepted his offer. The record of trial reflects Horan's additional testimony as follows:

> Miss Hong got in the truck and I drove on. She was sitting in the middle of the passenger's seat. I stopped and I asked, well, I sat there and talked for a few minutes and then I asked her, I said, "You make love?" and she said, "No." And, I believe that I kissed her a couple of times. I'm not sure, but then I asked her, I said, "Let's go out there and make out," and I believe she said, "No." I can't say for sure. Anyway, I got out of my side and went around and opened the door and got her by the hand and led her out to the woods . . . And put my arm around her and kissed her a couple of times, and then the next thing I knew, we were on the ground. It was sort of damp. It really wasn't muddy but it was dirty enough out there . . .

It was rough, a lot of weeds and all, a lot of thorns. And, I told her, I said, "Come on. Let's make love," and she says, "No, carry me back to Charlie Med." I said, "then you make love?" and she said "Yes, if we go back." I says, "I have a place in the motor pool. We'll go down there," and she says, "Okay." So we got back and I did not drive her to Charlie Med but to the motor pool.

Well, in my room at the motor pool, we were both sitting down on the bed and I said, "Make love?" and she said "No." I said, "Come on, let's do it?" and she says, "No." And then she asked me if I had any water. I told her, "Let's make love, and then I'll give you some water," and she said, "No." And by that time she acted like she had vomited or something. Then she asked me if she could go outside to use the bathroom, and I said, "Yes, just go outside by the grease rack in the woods there." Anyway, she never did return and I walked outside and looked around for her, but I didn't see her. So I returned to my room and went to sleep.

On further examination, Horan denied ever having taken off either his or Miss Hong's clothes, ever having demanded Hong take off her own clothes, and ever having attempted to have intercourse with Hong against her will.

When the prosecution and defense concluded the presentations of their cases, I instructed the members of the court on their responsibilities with respect to findings. I spoke at length about the issue of credibility. The members of the court had the awful responsibility of making that determination. A finding of guilty would adversely affect Horan for the rest of his life. An acquittal would mean that they were not totally satisfied with Miss Hong's testimony. Whatever the findings, someone would be hurt.

The court members found Horan guilty as charged. They were then informed that Horan had been twice punished for minor disciplinary infractions within his unit. He was sentenced to be dishonorably discharged from the army and to be imprisoned for five years.

I have thought about Horan's case on many occasions during the years following his trial. I have never changed my opinion that his conviction was warranted, but I feel that Horan was not altogether lying. Perhaps he was shading the truth a bit, but not intending to deceive. Perhaps, with his limited intelligence, he did not believe that he was committing criminal offenses on the night of the incidents. There was nothing wrong in asking a girl to make love, he may have thought, and a mere negative response would not necessarily constitute a refusal. Horan may have reasoned to himself that he was innocent because Miss Hong did tell him, after the incident in the woods, that she had no alternative other than to spend the night with him.

At the time of Horan's trial, I regretted, as I do now, that the standards for acceptance of young men into the army were as low as they were during the Vietnam War. If men were indeed needed, the practical approach might have been to call up reserve and National Guard units, to make the draft equally applicable to all young men, and to tighten draft legislation. But no president or Congress was about to make those politically dangerous decisions.

After the trial, I read a letter Horan wrote to the commanding general pleading his innocence. Simple words, such as "rape" and "guilty" were misspelled. He was of the opinion that he had been convicted of the offense of rape, rather than attempted rape. Corporal Horan's letter assumed that, as an American man, he should be believed rather than a Vietnamese woman. I had previously observed a situation where a total disregard for the dignity of Vietnamese women had been expressed. During a training session for personnel bound for Vietnam that I attended at Fort Bliss, Texas, a sergeant lectured to us in graphic detail how to search Viet Cong if we had the opportunity. It included delving into all orifices of the body. Furthermore, he wanted us to know that, if he were present and there were women to be searched, he would be the one to do it. Many of the officers and soldiers laughed, accepting the obscenity of the remark as ordinary conversation about matters taken for granted. Perhaps Horan had been taught certain things in basic training that led him to believe that Vietnamese women were subject to his desires.

❧

A sad note from Lai Khe

Major General Keith L. Ware, commanding general of the 1st Infantry Division, and seven other occupants in his helicopter were killed when his aircraft was shot down near the Cambodian border on September 13. The tail section close to the tail rotor of the helicopter was penetrated by a number of .51-caliber rounds fired by the enemy.

The body of the helicopter began to rotate causing the pilot to lose control. It crashed and burned. The division G–4, Lieutenant Colonel Hank Oliver, who shared a trailer with the staff judge advocate, and whom I had visited on several occasions, was in the aircraft. Ten days before the tragedy, on September 3, I had been in Lai Khe and spoke at length to both General Ware and Colonel Oliver.

General Ware was a quiet, dignified gentleman, fifty-two years old, who worked himself up to his position through the ranks. During World War II, he had been awarded the Congressional Medal of Honor for valor. Away from home, lonesome like everyone else, he adopted a dog named Rex who failed to meet the requirements of the K-Nine Corps but not the affection of the general who kept him by his side at all times. They died together.

General Ware was buried at Arlington National Cemetery shortly after his death. The president of the United States attended his funeral.

CHAPTER SIXTEEN

Election 1968

I did not vote in 1968. Sitting with about ten members from the legal office in Dong Tam, huddled around a small black-and-white television, we watched and listened to the presidential election results. Some of the group supported former vice president Richard Nixon, thinking that he might succeed in his promise to end the war with honor. Others felt that the Peace Conference in Paris would have a better chance of success with the election of Vice President Hubert Humphrey. President Lyndon Johnson, a lame-duck president, had little influence in Paris, but perhaps Humphrey, if elected to the high office, would be more effective. Personally, I did not favor either. I was a skeptic. In my opinion, there was no way to end the war with honor, regardless of who won the election.

I began to doubt the possibility of success in Vietnam during 1967 when the number of United States troops there was growing exponentially with no evidence we were winning the war or approaching a peaceful settlement. Early in 1968, with those doubts growing, I was called out of a courtroom at Fort Polk, Louisiana, and told that I was being considered for an assignment to Vietnam; unless someone else volunteered for the position, I would have no choice.

I could have resisted going to Vietnam. I was eligible for retirement; was stationed in Texas, where I had previously made my home; and was a member of the state bar. I had good prospects for employment and was still young enough to begin a second career. I seriously considered retirement.

During the period of my doubts about accepting an assignment to Vietnam, the United States Marines were besieged at Khe Sanh and the Viet Cong achieved a psychological, if not a military, victory in the Tet Offensive. I watched the fighting on television nightly, witnessed General Loan executing a suspected Viet Cong soldier without trial, and heard prominent newscasters questioning the wisdom of America's presence in Vietnam.

More disturbing than all the headlines and graphic pictures, though, were the changing attitudes of some of the president's closest advisors. Secretary of Defense Robert McNamara, an architect of the war, disappointed the president by his actions, which reflected a feeling that there could be no victory in the war. He was replaced by Clark Clifford, once an advocate of our policies in Vietnam and an adviser to all Democratic presidents since World War II. He, too, grew disenchanted with the possibility of success, and could no longer encourage Johnson to continue his aggressive policies. Wise men from the past were called on to advise and comfort the president, but they could not agree on what their leader should be told except that his policies were untenable.

In the years preceding 1968, there had been much dissent in the United States. Martin Luther King, Jr., was vociferous in his denunciation of the Vietnam War; civil strife and protest marches were increasing; Dr. Benjamin Spock and Rev. William Sloan Coffin, Jr., were indicted for conspiracy to counsel young men to violate the draft laws. In late 1967, Democratic Senator Eugene McCarthy announced he would be a candidate for president in the following year, advocating a negotiated settlement of the war.

Some of us in the military, who had taken an oath to defend our country, and did so when called upon, were beginning to question the wisdom of its Vietnam policies. Sadly, some officers in the United States, who accepted their roles without question, were misinformed about daily occurrences in Vietnam. I heard a Lieutenant Colonel at Fort Bliss, Texas, express surprise to learn that Rolling Thunder, the operation that authorized the constant bombing of North Vietnam, was still in effect in February, 1968.

I called Washington to let my superiors know that I would accept orders to Vietnam, no need to look for a volunteer substitute. I cannot, even now, be certain whether it was a sense of patriotism, duty, or curiosity that compelled me to do so. The army had been my profession for twenty years; I felt that I could not refuse even what I interpreted to be a request. On the other hand, I am sometimes troubled by the thought that my motive might have been curiosity. The opportunity to observe Vietnam firsthand was attractive because my job as a senior military judge would take me to all sections of the country, from the Demilitarized Zone to the Mekong Delta. I would be able to witness for myself the experience of Vietnam.

In March, Senator McCarthy made an impressive showing in the New Hampshire presidential primaries. Robert Kennedy entered the same race soon thereafter as a peace candidate. President Johnson, in effect, acknowledged that he could not lead the country to victory when he announced on March 31 that he would not be a candidate for re-election. In the same month, Richard Nixon, out of office, pledged that a new administration would "end the war" in Vietnam. War protests and peace marches increased. It appeared to me that the average American's assessment of the war was beginning to change.

Those were my thoughts even before the 1968 campaign began. Disturbances since March had added to my apprehension. Martin Luther King, Jr., and Robert Kennedy were murdered; the riots in Chicago during the Democratic Convention were unprecedented for such an occasion; the number of troops in Vietnam increased by ten thousand but the Joint Chiefs of Staff had requested an additional two hundred and five thousand. Young men were fleeing to Canada or seeking legal methods of avoiding the draft.

The campaign did not change my mind. Richard Nixon, as vice president during the Eisenhower years, had certainly concurred in the momentous decisions concerning Indochina in 1954 and thereafter. It was President Eisenhower's decision to replace the French after their defeat at Dien Bien Phu and subsequent departure; to establish, in fact, the nation of South Vietnam; to support Ngo Dinh Diem as the miracle man of Asia; and to send American advisers and treasure to build up the South Vietnamese army.

Nixon believed in the war's necessity. Out of office, in the early 1960s, he did not hesitate to express his opinion that the war in Vietnam must be won, or that the Communist Chinese must be prevented from entering Vietnam by whatever means necessary.

During the campaign, it was widely believed that Nixon had a secret plan to end the war, and he did not discourage that belief. He spoke constantly of ending the war "with honor," but did not explain how that could be done. Perhaps he reasoned that his campaign oratory would have the same effect on the voters as Eisenhower's promise to visit Korea and end the war there if he was elected in 1953.

I did not believe that there would be peace with honor. It was unrealistic to think that Ho Chi Minh could be bombed into submission or that he would accept even an offer of mutual withdrawal of fighting forces from South Vietnam without a promise from the United States to withhold all support to the South Vietnamese government.

Nixon had always advised negotiating from strength. With over half a million American servicemen and women in Vietnam, in addition to a navy and air force second to none in the world, how much more could we be strengthened there? Did he anticipate incursions into Laos, Cambodia, and North Vietnam? Or the use of nuclear weapons? If so, those were not viable alternatives, in my opinion.

Vice President Hubert Humphrey was an unknown insofar as the Vietnam War was concerned. I could only make assumptions.

Although he promised the president not to stray from the path set by him, I assumed that his true liberal feelings would prevail, and, if elected, he would act in accord with his party's original platform to end the war quickly. I could not anticipate how his feelings, whatever they might be, could be translated into extraction of our forces while simultaneously preserving the integrity of the South Vietnamese government.

Convinced that neither party could end the war without being humiliated in the process, I explained to my colleagues in Dong Tam why I had not voted. They did not seem to care. There was neither a mood of elation nor depression when Humphrey conceded. Now what would happen? I wondered. Will Nixon's "secret plan" work? Would we have peace with honor? I did not think so because I did not think anyone could achieve the impossible. But, I said a prayer that somehow, in some impossible-to-predict way, peace would come to the United States and to Vietnam.

CHAPTER SEVENTEEN

Silent Night

Johnny Abadie was a smart cookie. He knew all the answers. Never at a loss for words, he commented about everything in his company. The platoon leader was pretty stupid; he should never had been allowed into Officer Candidate School from which he had graduated only a few months before coming to Vietnam; the commanding officer was not much better; the chow was bad and the first sergeant had his favorites. Johnny spoke louder than any of his fellow soldiers, but he was not offensive, except when discussing officers. He did have a way to get the things he wanted of his fellow soldiers, especially marijuana, and he wasn't bashful about using it or passing it around to his friends.

Johnny had graduated from high school in New York City and boasted to his friends that he played football, basketball, and baseball, and was a general all-around big man on campus. The girls loved him and he loved the girls. He began smoking cigarettes when he was twelve but he had the will power to quit during sporting seasons. When army recruiters came to his school, he volunteered immediately, saying he wasn't afraid of any Viet Cong. He was not unpopular among most of the soldiers, but his officers hated him. Although he managed to avoid serious trouble, he did receive company punishments twice for being late at formations. His record as a combat soldier was as good as any-one's in the unit.

Something happened one day, however, that reversed the tide for Johnny. He purchased a few ounces of marijuana from an outsider and sold some of it to three of his buddies. His offense was reported to the commanding officer, and Johnny was threat-ened with a court-martial. "Not for me," Johnny confided to his buddies, "they will have to catch me first!" With those words, he departed from his company without permission.

Frustration and the threat of a court-martial were not the only causes of Johnny's departure, although they provided the turning point that pushed him to the decision he made. Johnny was in love. He knew that Kim Hoa, whom he called Kim, would give him the refuge he needed in Saigon.

Kim was not an ordinary girl like those who worked in bars and had formed liaisons with some of Johnny's buddies, but a pharmacist in one of Saigon's largest Western-style drugstores on Tu Do Street. She had come to Johnny's attention on his first trip to Saigon where he had been officially dispatched to pick up supplies. He unofficially extended that trip, however, to visit a pharmacy for the purpose of purchasing what his fellow G.I.s referred to as "beetle juice," a drug that was legal on the Viet-namese market, but forbidden to American soldiers by the Uni-form Code of Military Justice.

Johnny was entranced when he first saw Kim, delicate and beautiful, with face and body perfectly sculpted. Her long black hair fell gracefully past her shoulders to her waist. She weighed less than a hundred pounds, but her smile reflected the charm of a Renaissance painting. She spoke English with a fractured but engaging accent. Her au dai flowed gracefully as she moved about. Johnny tried with all his skills and talent to arrange a later meeting, but had no success.

On his second visit to the drugstore, Johnny detected in Kim's attitude what he assumed to be a slight interest in his pres-ence. He followed his instincts, and persuaded her to take a short walk with him. Without touching, they strolled leisurely up and down tree-lined Duy Tan Boulevard to and from Notre Dame Cathedral in the center of the city.

From that day, Johnny thought and dreamed only of Kim. He sneaked away from his unit near Long Binh as often as he could to share Cokes with her on the terrace of the Continental Palace Hotel, which was across the street from Kim's pharmacy.

Within eight weeks after their first meeting, Johnny and Kim were living together in a small room near the large market between Saigon and Cholon, although Kim had never before shared her life with a lover. She was aware that her parents had long ago promised her to a young man in their village, but after three years at the university in Saigon and one year as a pharmacist in a large city, there was little chance that Kim would return home to live.

When Kim insisted that Johnny meet her parents, he managed to get a four-day pass from the first sergeant, convincing him that he deserved a break at the rest and recuperation (R&R) center in Vunc Tau. Indeed, at that time, Johnny had not even taken his authorized week of R&R, after having been in the country for six months. On the way to Vunc Tau, it was nothing at all for Johnny to make a detour to Saigon. From Saigon, he and Kim took a regular Vietnamese bus to Phuoc Vin and from there walked to the village where Kim was born and her family lived.

Kim's parents were not pleased with the idea of their daughter bringing home an American soldier, but they reluctantly consented. They were pleasantly surprised, however, when they met Johnny, who was able to gain their friendship with his congeniality and thoughtfulness for bringing gifts to them and their children. He was respectful at all times and gained favor with the children by teaching them how to play American games. He seemed at ease coping with Vietnamese customs, and enjoyed the food they served. The visit ended with all-around good feelings.

As the weeks progressed following the home visit, Johnny and Kim's love grew deeper and they promised each other that one day they would be married. That was the situation when

Johnny was threatened with a court-martial and departed from his unit.

When Kim saw Johnny at the door of their room with a full duffle bag, she surmised that something was wrong. She welcomed him, however, and when he promised that they would never again be separated, Kim suggested that they be married in her village. The thought of marriage had occurred previously to Johnny, but he had been hesitant to ask because of the possibility of rejection and moreover, there was not a chance in the world that permission to marry would be given to him by any United States official. But now that he was free of military restraints, Johnny eagerly accepted Kim's proposal, encouraging her to arrange a date in the village as soon as possible. She gained her parents' consent and a marriage date was settled with the proper officials.

On the afternoon before the wedding, the couple again went to Kim's village via the local bus. Upon arrival before dusk, most of the villagers (but probably not the young man who continued to hope that one day Kim would be his own bride) were waiting excitedly near the community well, gossiping and playing children's games. Some escorted the couple to Kim's parents' house where a wonderful smell radiated, a sign of preparations for the feast that was to follow the wedding. Kim's mother and her friends had spent a week cooking delicate Vietnamese meat and vegetable dishes as well as traditional sweets. Kim's father and some friends were outside watching a whole pig being roasted over a smoldering fire.

On the evening of their arrival, after a modest meal including rice wine, the entire family and Johnny visited the concrete structure (in the form of a woman's womb) on the outskirts of the village where Kim's ancestors had been buried for centuries. This was a custom more common during the Tet holidays than at weddings, but Johnny himself requested the visitation since he had never before had the opportunity to do so. Later that evening, one of Kim's relatives brought Johnny to his house, where he spent the night.

A traditional Vietnamese marriage is not a simple matter. There are customary notifications, promises, and preparations to be made by the families, first at the time of engagement and later in preparation for the marriage. Kim's parents agreed to forgo all but the essential parts of a wedding, including the acceptance of Johnny's traditional offer of money to compensate them for the education of their daughter.

On the morning of the wedding, Johnny dressed in fashionable shirt and trousers, his latest acquisitions from the Cholon Post Exchange, which he had carefully chosen for this special day. Then, again accompanied by his host, he went to Kim's home where dozens of relatives, friends, village officials, and several Buddhist monks in saffron robes were already assembled. The house was festively decorated with candles in the shape of dragons, Chinese lanterns, red roses, yellow mums, and small lilac flowers.

In all his dreams, Johnny was not prepared for the beauty of his bride, radiant in a completely white au dai, embroidered with likenesses of traditional village flowers. Together with Kim, he was taken to the family shrine where pictures of recent ancestors were honored. Reverently, they joined hands, said silent prayers begging for future blessing, and then turned to bow in respect to Kim's parents.

During the ceremony that followed, performed by the village chief, Johnny respectfully responded to instructions concerning the expected responses of a bridegroom. The villagers who attended were impressed with Johnny's attentiveness to his bride throughout the day, which was spent in feasting and celebrating, accompanied by traditional wedding and popular music. Late in the evening, after the last of the guests departed, Johnny and Kim retired to a small room especially prepared for them in the parents' home. Early the next day, a farmer gave the couple a ride in his hay wagon to Phuoc Vin, whence they took the old bus back to Saigon and a new life.

The first few weeks of marriage were the happiest time of Johnny's life: no money worries; a beautiful, tender, and compliant wife who loved him; a nice enough place to live; and best of all, no one to give him orders. He did not regret his decisions to leave the army and marry Kim. They awoke before dawn each morning and embraced each other until the silence of the night was shattered by the curfew's end, indicating the beginning of a new day. They went to market early in the morning to purchase supplies for the evening meal. Then, as Kim dressed for work and carefully brushed her hair, Johnny looked at her lovingly, wishing there would never be another day in his life without her.

During the day when Kim was at work, Johnny joined a group of American deserters living in the area. They were all young men, barely old enough to vote but living by their wits as outlaws in a war-torn country. They taught Johnny how to obtain illegal ration books to use in the Cholon PX. Radios, television sets, tape recorders, and cameras purchased there would bring enormous profits on the black market.

Johnny was not ashamed of his unlawful transactions. He rationalized that the United States government sent provisions to Vietnam for the Americans, and the bottom line for the Americans was to fight a war. He had already participated in more than his share of combat. His conclusion, therefore, was that other American personnel and their allies, including civilians, who had the freedom to use the PX but had never seen combat, were less deserving of its luxuries than he was.

When not engaged in illegal activities, Johnny and his new-found friends played card games and spent endless hours in idle conversations. Unlike his companions, who drifted along under the influence of drugs, Johnny did not even smoke marijuana, an old army habit. There was no pleasure for him greater than dreaming of Kim and anticipating her return from work. He used some of his time making their little room more comfortable. He bought a large mirror for Kim, a nicer wash-basin than had been furnished with the room, more mellow tapes for his new recorder, and a few inexpensive paintings to hang on the walls. Every evening when Kim returned, Johnny had a gift for her. A doll, a handkerchief, perfume, or any little thing to let her know that he loved her very much. Although his friends cavorted about at night spending money on fancy food and good times, not once did Johnny and Kim leave their own little piece of the city.

Johnny watched in silence as Kim cooked the evening meal. Her lithe body shunted about quietly as a kitten. Sometimes, they did not speak, but took pleasure only in being alone in each other's presence. After dinner, when traffic died down because of the curfew and all was quiet except for the distant rumblings of mortar shells, they embraced and made love in the stillness of the night.

Early one morning, less than a month after their marriage, the little world of Johnny and Kim was shattered. They were awakened by a bullhorn from a vehicle announcing that the location of several American deserters in the area was known to the military and Vietnamese police. The booming voice demanded that all illegal residents come outside to surrender. Preferring to accept the risks of not complying, Johnny hid under the bed but within half an hour, the door to his room was torn apart. When he looked up, American and Vietnamese police in uniforms were staring down at him. Johnny attempted unsuccessfully to resist, but was forced out of the room as Kim cried aloud, powerless to interfere. He was then unceremoniously carted off to the holding stockade in Saigon where he remained until the next day when armed guards from his unit picked him up. Johnny's commanding officer immediately confined him to the Long Binh Stockade, where he was held pending further action.

Court-martial charges were prepared against Johnny alleging that he sold marijuana to his fellow soldiers; deserted the United States Army; stole a .45-caliber pistol that was in his possession when he left his post; and resisted arrest on the morning he was apprehended. The pretrial Article 32 investigating officer recommended that Johnny be tried by a general court-martial on all the charges. The commanding general of the 1st Infantry Division at Lai Khe concurred, and ordered that the case be referred to a general court-martial to be convened on December 24th at Di An.

On the morning of Christmas Eve, 1968, I was taken by helicopter to Di An to preside over the court-martial of Private John M. Abadie. I was met at the helicopter pad by a legal officer who escorted me to the place of trial. All these years later, today it seems incredible that a simple canvas structure could serve as a suitable courtroom. Like many other venues of trial in Vietnam, it was nothing more than a tent originally intended for other purposes, with side flaps rolled up, and a few chairs and tables arranged to make it resemble a place where a trial could take place. We called it a courtroom.

As we approached the courtroom, Johnny was the first person to come to my attention, a fact made obvious by two armed guards who accompanied him. More interesting, however, was the young Vietnamese woman, well groomed, weeping, and holding his hand. All officers of the court had taken their assigned seats before my arrival, at which time the defense counsel motioned Private Abadie and his guards to enter and take their assigned places. The prosecutor informed the witnesses that they must remain outside, or take shelter from the sun in a nearby legal office until they were summoned.

The presentation of evidence to the court consisted of testimony by three members from Private Abadie's unit who testified to the sale of marijuana before Johnny left his unit without authority; the company clerk who proffered the necessary documents to show that Abadie departed and returned on the dates alleged; the first sergeant who testified that the pistol assigned to the accused was missing since the date of his absence; and two military policemen who assisted in apprehending him in Saigon. Johnny testified only that he intended to return to the army one day, and that he intended to return the pistol. The defense counsel offered nothing else in his behalf on the merits of the case. The court found him guilty of everything of which he had been charged and then, about seven in the evening, recessed for dinner, to reconvene an hour later.

In extenuation and mitigation, Johnny swore that he had never been in trouble in civilian life; that he performed his combat duties well, having gone on eight long-range patrols, each lasting more than two days; that he had done nothing in his company that might be considered serious misconduct before his departure. He begged the court to be lenient, especially since he was now happily married and convinced that he could be a good soldier. One of the members of the court, who appeared a bit cynical to me, asked whether Johnny knew he was not legally married, and furthermore, how could he perform combat duties efficiently in the future if he had to be concerned about a woman in Saigon whom he presumed to be his wife.

When Kim Hoa took the witness stand to testify in Johnny's behalf, at about nine-thirty, the entire compound was relatively quiet. Christmas music, dedicated by the Armed Forces Network to homesick Americans, drifted into the courtroom from almost every radio in Di An. Kim looked delicate and fragile as a porcelain doll, even though she had spent the long day in and out of the sun. She described how she had met Johnny at the pharmacy; how their acquaintance had grown into deep affection; and how affection progressed to love and marriage. Even her parents, who were devout Buddhists, respected Johnny for his good manners and the example he gave to the villagers. Most of the members of the court seemed impressed by Kim's background and behavior, but the one who had earlier appeared unsympathetic wanted to know why she had been living with the accused even before she could even presume they were legally married. She simply said that they were in love. Kim pleaded for the members to be lenient as possible with her husband because of her absolute certainty that one day they would be reunited and she wanted that day to arrive as soon as possible. When she completed her testimony, crying softly, the prosecutor touched her gently, pointing to the exit. I felt that even he was a bit sympathetic, but he nevertheless asked for a severe sentence appropriate to the seriousness of Private Abadie's offenses. The court then recessed to determine what sentence would be imposed.

During the deliberations on sentence by the members of the court, I sat alone in the grass on an incline overlooking the courtroom. There were lights in many of the tents on the compound. Cigarettes burning like fireflies indicated that some people were walking about. Johnny and Kim were sitting not more than twenty yards from me, their hands tightly clasped, with guards permissive enough to allow an occasional show of deeper affection. As sentimental as I wished to be about my own absence from home, I could not dismiss thoughts about the future of the accused and his wife. From experience, I knew that Johnny would be sent to prison, leaving Kim alone with her memories in Saigon. Since the marriage had not been sanctioned by American officials, it was doubtful she would be able to immigrate to the United States any time soon, if at all. Yet, I assumed that, in her innocence, Kim was trying to console her husband with thoughts of being together in the near future. Although I knew this could not be, I believed that Johnny had become a more mature person because of his recent experiences.

When the court reconvened, the president announced that Private Abadie was sentenced to be dishonorably discharged from the army and to be confined at hard labor for five years. Johnny had apparently been prepared by his defense counsel because he remained stoic, but Kim's tears reflected emotions that could not be contained.

After adjournment, the court members, spectators, and witnesses departed from the area. At my suggestion, Johnny and Kim remained alone in the lighted courtroom for a few minutes, discreetly observed by the guards outside. When the couple returned to the guards, they embraced, crying softly, until interrupted by an officer who had accompanied Kim from Saigon that morning and was to return her there in a military sedan that was not bound by the curfew rules. Johnny was handcuffed and taken to a waiting jeep that would return him to prison and Kim was led to the sedan that would bring her to an empty room. Their eyes focused on each other until it was impossible to communicate further. The vehicles drove away in different directions as music from the Armed Forces Network concluded its Christmas eve program with the prayerful "Silent Night."

CHAPTER EIGHTEEN

A Hometown Boy

Private Ben Rasteau had a reputation among members of his unit as a loner with no record of misconduct. On the afternoon of the alleged offenses, he had been assigned as a guard in the defense of his company's perimeter. With three other members of his unit, he sat in a bunker, silently separated from the others, who played cards, spoke of home, and drank beer.

Without warning or reason, Rasteau picked up his M–16 and sprayed the bunker with rifle fire, killing all three of his comrades. He then went out into the open where he continued to shoot indiscriminately until he himself was shot in self-defense by his first sergeant. Those were the facts and there were a dozen witnesses to prove them. For the defense, there was only the report of a psychiatrist who believed that, at the time of the alleged offenses, the accused was not capable of forming a specific intent to kill, although he did know right from wrong.

While reviewing a report of the case in the courtroom at Dong Tam early on a Sunday morning, I was distracted by the arrival of a jeep containing the first participants of the drama that was about to unfold. In addition to the driver, there were two armed guards escorting Rasteau whose chest, hips, and entire left leg were enveloped in a white cast. The accused, with great difficulty, and the guards dismounted from the jeep, entered the courtroom, looked around, and departed almost immediately after seeing me. For a while, I watched from my bench, thinking that I had never seen a more innocuous-looking defendant. The three stood outside, probably sharing the same thoughts, but hardly speaking. I decided to join them.

The guards were relieved when they saw me approach. Members of Rasteau's unit, they knew him at least casually, and seemed uncomfortable guarding their fellow soldier. There was no mood of hostility among them. They shared cigarettes and matches, seemingly aware of each other's unpleasant situation.

Rasteau smiled ruefully when I introduced myself, but did not speak in response. I commented upon his obvious physical discomfort and told him that he might remain seated throughout the proceedings. When I asked about his hometown, his reply startled me.

"Lafayette, Louisiana, sir."

Lafayette, the heart of Cajun country, is my own hometown. My reaction to his reply apparently conveyed this information to him. We had spent our youths in the same environment. The thought that we had experienced other Sunday mornings in the same surroundings, although twenty-five years apart and in another world, provided a spirit of kinship between us. He looked into my eyes and spoke with emotion as he talked about the long walks he had taken in woods that I had loved as a child. We fished in the same bayous and spent weekends in the same scout campgrounds. I had seen his father on numerous occasions in the department store where he had worked for thirty years. Rasteau spoke of familiar playing fields, schools, and churches. He sadly mentioned the hospital where his mother died and the cemetery in which she was buried. Before he was drafted, Rasteau worked in a service station where I had often purchased gas. Perhaps I had seen him there while on leave from the army. The landmarks of the cathedral, the courthouse, and the college were as important to us as the familiar mountains and ancestors' tombs were to the Vietnamese.

Although there was a separation in time between us in Lafayette and in job assignments in Vietnam, we nevertheless felt an attachment to each other because of common bonds. He did not attempt to speak of his alleged crimes or other matters between judge and accused that must be left outside the courtroom. The level of his voice remained constant although he knew that after the trial there was nothing but hospitals and probably prisons to look forward to. I knew that I would be returning to an air-conditioned room in Saigon and looking forward to a reunion with my family in Hawaii in a few weeks.

As we stood there looking into the distant fields and mountains, I realized how fortunate I had been. Twenty-five years before, when I was Rasteau's age, there was another war in which I had participated. It was easier then; we knew who the enemy was. Pearl Harbor had been attacked and the Germans had declared war. The issues were clearly drawn. Even near the battlefield, spirit was generally high. We wrote letters to our girlfriends back home who were proud to hear from the boys overseas, listened to the patriotic songs of George M. Cohan and Irving Berlin, took pleasure in trying to devise methods of keeping cool our daily ration of two bottles of beer. No drugs to speak of then. No doubts about our cause. No dissidents calling the president a killer. No one back home suggesting that we were wasting our lives. It was all so different in Vietnam.

Finally, the other participants in the trial began to arrive. The prosecutor, with a sheaf of papers in his hand, called me aside to ask routine questions about seating arrangements and recess times. He tried to steer me away from the court members and the witnesses. Having no privacy, the defense counsel sought out a corner of the courtroom to converse with the accused until time for trial.

I quietly walked over to the judge's bench, avoiding contact with members of the court. A shuffling of feet and the voice of the prosecutor made me aware that the participants were seeking out their assigned seats. Somehow, my mind was not on the pending proceedings. Maybe it was the thought of Sunday morning in

Lafayette, or was it the thought of Sunday morning in Dong Tam? Church bells there, mortar fire here. The prosecutor cleared his throat:

"Your honor, we are ready to proceed."

I looked around quickly, checked the seating of the court members and other participants. I checked Rasteau once more to insure that he was as comfortable as possible under the circumstances, then looked at the president of the court for the first time and finally said:

"The court will come to order!"

CHAPTER NINETEEN

Farmers

Flying in a helicopter over land ravaged by war is never a routine experience. As the experience repeated itself, however, the noise of the engines tended to lull me into a state of unconsciousness, especially in the early morning hours.

Flying to Dong Tam on a Sunday morning in March, I was the sole passenger in a small OH–6 Cayuse helicopter when the pilot nonchalantly disturbed my reverie. He pointed to a much larger UH–1 Huey which had been hit by enemy fire and was rapidly descending in our general direction. There were other helicopters of various sizes and capabilities within our range of vision going about the business of waging war, but we were nearest to the falling craft. "Colonel," the pilot said, "we're going down to assist the chopper that's been hit. Grab that M–16 rifle behind you, just in case."

Strange that this should be happening to me, probably the only officer in Vietnam who, except for one occasion on a rifle range in Korea, had never fired an M–16.

The stricken aircraft landed in a rice paddy without apparent injury to any of its occupants. We hovered nearby for a few moments until the arrival of several larger and better-equipped helicopters. The members of the downed craft indicated that our help was not needed and expressed thanks with a thumbs up sign. I replaced the M–16 on the back panel with a sigh of relief, but before we were on course again, I observed a simple pastoral scene that jolted me into a new perspective of the conflict in which I was participating.

Not fifty yards from where the stricken Huey had alighted, a group of about fifty Vietnamese farmers, bent over with faces to the ground, were working in the fields, apparently oblivious to the circumstances surrounding them. The rhythm of their bobbing heads and hands, and their short steps forward, were not interrupted by the fortuitous circumstances of war. They did not seem even to communicate verbally among themselves. Not one had attempted to offer assistance to the occupants of the damaged craft. They had, it seemed to me, become detached from the war, over which they had no control.

My first reaction was disbelief and anger. How could these people remain indifferent to the misfortunes of a friendly helicopter crew? Was it worth fighting to assist people who were not willing to help in their own defense? The behavior of these workers probably reflected the behavior of most Vietnamese farmers in similar circumstances. I could not offer myself a satisfactory explanation. If I could not understand the behavior of these farmers, who were the heart and core of the Vietnamese people, how then could I understand the rationale for our presence in Vietnam?

As I thought about the farmers, my anger began to fade. There had been few rewards for them in the past, and they could anticipate even fewer in the future. The toil of planting and harvesting rice in the midst of a war offered little satisfaction. A peaceful night's rest near the graves of their ancestors offered the greatest consolation for a hard day's labor. These farmers had only recently witnessed the alien influences of French, Japanese, Vietminh, Americans, and one or more of the religious sects having their own private armies, which were endemic to the area surrounding Saigon. Elected and unelected governments had imposed repression upon them. Their lives, they must have reasoned, could not possibly be improved by assisting foreign visitors. How could Americans who came by day, even from the sky in strange machines, offer more than brown-skinned political agents who visited them by night?

The farmers knew that the Americans would not react adversely to their lack of assistance, but more importantly they knew that the Viet Cong would retaliate if they did assist the Americans. Perhaps there were Viet Cong working with them in the fields. So, there was nothing to be gained and much to be lost by interrupting their labors. They continued to work, therefore, hoping only that a long day's journey of toil might dissolve into an evening of peace.

By the time we landed in Dong Tam, I began to comprehend why the farmers offered no assistance to the endangered soldiers. The answer to a more fundamental question, however, continued to disturb me. If the farmers refused to help us, why should we help defend them against people we presumed to be their enemies? Was it possible they preferred a way of life alien to that which we offered? I could not be comfortable with these questions, so I put them aside to be resolved another day. That day has not arrived.

CHAPTER TWENTY

I Want a Body Count

On the afternoon of November 22, 1968, near the village of Phu Loc, not far from the ancient Vietnamese imperial city of Hue, trouble was anticipated in an area where members of A Company, 2nd Battalion, 505th Infantry, 3rd Brigade, 82nd Airborne Division were on a tactical mission. The company officers were attending a meeting atop a small hill overlooking the surrounding woods when Sergeant Benjamin Martinez, a member of the organization, interrupted to say that four Vietnamese men had been observed walking down a trail from the village toward the hill. One of them appeared to be carrying a pack on his back.

All of the officers stood up to observe the moving group. Captain Calvin Karpov, the Commanding Officer, ordered his Forward Officer, Captain Clint Roberts, to plot artillery targets, but to hold fire for the moment. When the Vietnamese men disappeared into the woods, the meeting resumed.

A few minutes later, the meeting was interrupted a second time when Sergeant Martinez reported that apparently the same four Vietnamese men had been observed again, this time walking toward the village, none apparently carrying anything on his back. Captain Karpov, suspicious of what might be happening, ordered Captain Roberts to plot artillery targets again, where the group had last been seen and ordered another of his officers, Lieutenant Ralph Thompson, to pursue the men. The captain remained in his position on the hill, as did Captain Roberts. There, they could observe Thompson who, together with a radio operator, Corporal Herbert Stall, and a medic, Corporal Rob Rigsby, began to pursue the Vietnamese men.

The evidence as to what happened thereafter, as it appeared in the pretrial investigation, was not entirely consistent, but certain facts were incontrovertible. A member of Thompson's group spotted the Vietnamese men, fired, and hit one of them in his left hand. The wounded man dropped behind some bushes, but came into the open a short while later with his hands raised, one of them bleeding. He approached within ten meters of Lieutenant Thompson. Meanwhile, the radio operator, who had lagged behind talking to Captain Karpov on the hill, approached Thompson, saying that "Sixer" had ordered him to kill the Vietnamese man. "Sixer," as everyone knew, was the radio call signal for Karpov. Thompson took the radio from Stall and reported to his commanding officer that the prisoner was wounded, unarmed, in the process of surrendering, and, apparently had some kind of identification. Karpov replied:

"Dammit, I don't care about prisoners. I want a body count!"

Lieutenant Thompson would not shoot and told his radio operator not to shoot. Stall disregarded the order and discharged a burst of automatic fire from his M–16, killing the Vietnamese man instantly.

When Thompson advised Captain Karpov that he had his body count, he was told to bury the corpse as well as he could. Thompson returned to the unit with the dead man's possessions, which did not include a weapon, but did include South Vietnamese identification.

Captain Roberts, who had been ordered to direct mortar fire in the direction of the Vietnamese men, stood near Karpov on the hill, and substantiated all of the radio conversations between

Karpov and members of Thompson's group. He also heard the shots from Stall's rifle that killed the wounded man.

Approximately thirty minutes after the incident with Thompson's group, Karpov received a radio call from another member of his company who was on patrol in the area saying that a second prisoner had been captured. Karpov directed Sergeant John Bowles, one of his noncommissioned officers, to check the man out. When Bowles asked what to do if the man had identification, Karpov replied: "Are you shitting me?"

When Bowles reached the captured man, whose hands were tied behind his back, he pushed him to his knees and reported this fact to his commanding officer. In reply, Karpov stated: "He's a gook or a dink, and you know what to do with him!"

The prisoner, while kneeling with his hands tied, was summarily executed by Bowles. The rope that bound the hands of the deceased was removed and his body rolled into a ditch. This prisoner was also unarmed and had South Vietnamese identification.

No one reported the incidents to higher headquarters immediately except for the body count. Captain Roberts and Lieutenant Thompson, however, were bothered by the events and sought counsel from a chaplain who advised them to report the matter to their superiors at battalion level. An investigation was conducted, resulting in two charges of premeditated murder against Karpov and one charge of premeditated murder against Stall, the radio operator. Bowles, who killed the second Vietnamese man, drowned three days after the incident before charges against him could be investigated. When I was appointed military judge on the cases, only charges against Karpov and Stall were pending.

At Captain Karpov's trial, Lieutenant Thompson testified that he countermanded Karpov's order. He insisted that Stall not shoot the Vietnamese man. Captain Roberts testified that, while standing on the hill, he heard all of the radio conversations between Karpov and members of Thompson's group, and personally witnessed the second execution.

Some of the personnel from Karpov's unit testified for the prosecution that A Company had a reputation for not taking prisoners; others, however, testifying for the defense, had never heard even a rumor of such a reputation in the company.

With respect to the first killing, the medic, Corporal Rigsby, testified that Thompson told him to check out the man with the bleeding hand who was trying to surrender but, in attempting to obey, he slipped into a gully and dropped his weapon. Almost simultaneously, he heard a voice shouting "Watch out, Doc!" and a burst of rifle fire coming from Stall's weapon. The Vietnamese man fell dead at his feet.

Thompson testified that, after seeing the wounded and unarmed man coming toward him, but before the shooting, he called "Sixer" to report these facts but was rebuffed with: "I don't want any prisoners. Shoot him!" Thompson made a request to spare the man's life, but the captain replied: "I don't care about prisoners. I want a body count! I want that man shot!" Disregarding the captain's request, Thompson would not shoot, and ordered Stall not to shoot the wounded man, who was making an attempt to reach in his back pocket, apparently in an attempt to obtain identification.

After the shooting, Thompson demanded of the radio operator: "Why the hell did you have to shoot a defenseless man?"

Stall replied: "'Sixer' said we had to kill him!"

In explaining his action during the trial, Stall testified that when Rigsby slipped, the Vietnamese man made a suspicious move as if to grab the medic's weapon. He, therefore, opened fire to protect his buddy.

Captain Roberts testified that he quite clearly heard "Sixer" give an order to kill the second man. Roberts then picked up a pair of binoculars and witnessed the shooting of the Vietnamese man, who was kneeling with his hands tied behind his back, making an effort to reach for something in his back pocket.

In his defense, Karpov testified that he never said a word about either killing, but rather only told his subordinates to "pursue the situation." He admitted that Thompson did tell him something to the effect that "you have a body count!" but was shocked by that report. He further testified that Thompson was not a very good platoon leader, but one who had to be "chewed out" every day.

Two men from the company testified that they thought Thompson had a funny attitude toward combat because he did not like to kill people. Another testified that Roberts was "OK" but was not a disciplined officer.

Captain Karpov's brigade commander, a brigadier general, and his battalion commander, a lieutenant colonel, testified that the accused was one of the best company commanders they had ever served with. Several enlisted men from the company, especially those peripherally involved in the incidents, echoed the praises of their commanding officer. Karpov had previously served a tour in Vietnam and had been awarded several medals.

It did not take long for the members of the court to make up their minds. In less than thirty minutes, Karpov was found not guilty. Charges against Stall were dropped as a consequence of his commanding officer's acquittal.

I have no personal knowledge of what happened immediately after the trial. I did not see Captain Karpov again after he fled the courtroom, shielding his face from photographers representing the news media. I was informed by authoritative sources, however, that within his unit, there was great rejoicing at Karpov's acquittal. The defense counsel informed me later that, while celebrating the victory with a party in A Company, the participants were wearing buttons which read: "WINE WOMEN AND BODY COUNT." Hardly able to believe this, I asked him to secure evidence for me, and he did. Among my files, I still have the button, a story of the case as reported by the *Overseas Weekly,* and an article from *Time* magazine quoting the words about body count spoken at the trial.

Three years after the trial of Captain Karpov, while attending a meeting of judge advocate officers in Berchtsgaden, Germany, I was in the audience when a new Department of Defense movie on the Law of War was previewed. The scenario unfolded on a hill overlooking a battlefield, obviously in Vietnam, on which a captain stood giving orders over his field phone: "I don't want any prisoners, dammit! I want a body count!" This was portrayed as an example of an officer disregarding the Law of War. That's not the way the court saw it.

CHAPTER TWENTY-ONE

Sergeant Mika's Headaches

Sergeant Michael Mika was the most sophisticated member of the MACV judge advocate office: tall, smart, handsome, neat, and polite. Hollywood could not have improved his image. He spent free daytime hours visiting the monuments of Saigon and improving his knowledge of Vietnamese culture. Mika was courteous to everyone, military and civilian, regardless of rank. He was admired by everyone who knew him. In short, Mika was as perfect a soldier and gentleman as could be expected. But, Mika had a problem. He had headaches.

It was impossible to avoid knowing about Mika's headaches. His only fault, if it was a fault, was letting people know about them. When they first began, he went to the dispensary at MACV but the medicine prescribed there did no good; he then went to a personal friend who was a doctor in Dong Tam but received no help there; he tried the United States Army Medical Dispensary in downtown Saigon, but again no relief; finally, Joe Ammerman made arrangements for Mika to be admitted to the 3rd Field Hospital near Saigon for tests. He returned to the office three days later still complaining of headaches.

A few days after his return from the hospital, Le Kim Hoa, a young secretary in the office, suggested to Sergeant Mika that he visit a Chinese doctor in Saigon. He ridiculed the idea saying that if American doctors with all their sophisticated paraphernalia could not help him, how could a Chinese doctor unaware of modern technology assist him? Hoa patiently explained that her mother, who once had headaches as bad as Mika's, was cured by their doctor; her father, who had arthritis so bad he could hardly bend his arms, was cured; and she herself, who many times had high fevers, was cured by the same Chinese doctor. "What can you lose? You tried everything else!" she pleaded. Mika was persuaded to try again. He agreed to see Hoa's doctor provided she make all the arrangements and accompany him as his interpreter.

Late one afternoon, I returned from Hotel 3 to the office where I found Sergeant Mika sitting alone at his desk holding a piece of paper that appeared to be torn from a brown paper bag, with Chinese characters inscribed on it. He told me that he had visited Hoa's doctor and was holding a prescription given to him. He would be going to a Chinese drugstore the next morning to have it filled. "This is the end!" he remarked. "I never thought I'd see the day!" Having nothing scheduled the next day, I asked if I could accompany him and he agreed.

Mika met me at the Rex the following morning and we walked to a large Chinese drug store on Nguyen Van Sam, just a few blocks from the hotel. It was crowded and Mika's first inclination was to return to MACV. I encouraged him to stay, promising that I would remain with him. We took our places at the end of the long, snakelike line.

Behind a long counter were two druggists, and behind them a giant desk with at least two hundred drawers, each with labels in Chinese characters. The drawers contained herbs, chemicals, spices, ground-up parts of animals, roots from trees, and whatever else might be called for as ingredients in prescriptions written by Chinese doctors.

Each customer presented to the druggist a piece of ordinary wrapping paper, similar to Mika's, on which Chinese characters were inscribed. Without even a glance, the druggist reached into the drawers behind him with one hand, removed pinches of the prescribed substances, and placed them into the prescription paper resting on the counter under his hand. He wrapped the ingredients into the same paper, weighed the bundle, and exchanged it for a few piasters. It took less than two minutes to fill a prescription, although the ingredients might come from a dozen different drawers. When we arrived at the counter, the druggist followed exactly the same procedure, not for a moment acknowledging that we were the only Americans in his presence, except to write the amount of money we owed. It wasn't much at all.

The most distinguishing feature between the Chinese drugstore and other stores in Saigon was the lack of argument and limited conversation between seller and buyer. The price requested was promptly paid without question, and the transaction was completed without written evidence that it had taken place.

Leaving the drugstore, Mika expressed the opinion that "There must be something to this Chinese medicine, seeing so many apparently satisfied customers!" I think that fact alone made him feel a little better. Certainly, he was satisfied because he suggested that we go for lunch at the International House on Nguyen Hue, the Street of Flowers, where he was a member. Mika was the only person I knew who belonged to the exclusive club, but that did not surprise me, knowing his love for fine food.

The International House was a combination club-restaurant, restricted to persons associated with the American forces and their allies. The initiation fee and monthly dues excluded the ordinary soldier or officer, but Mika was a well-heeled customer. He had no family to support or other obligations. He once told me that, in all his life, he did not pay a penny in interest to anyone.

I was surprised to find such luxury in Saigon. The entrance foyer led to an elegant waiting room, and the dining room beyond was comparable to that of a fine restaurant in a large American city. Brunch was being served, buffet style, and a string quartet provided background music. Waiters in uniform served coffee and drinks. For a moment, I forgot about the masses of hungry people surrounding the building and the war surrounding the city. The contrast between affluent customers dining in the club and troops serving in the field did not seem to be a matter of concern to members. Sergeant Mika mixed the prescribed portion of medicine he received from the Chinese drugstore with a bit of water and swallowed it without blinking. We then proceeded to the line for brunch.

Mika was feeling so much better after brunch that he suggested we not return to the office, but visit a couple of places he had not yet seen in Saigon. We began to stroll aimlessly until we reached a Hindu temple that I recognized immediately from my visit in 1960. A man with a twelve-foot snake writhing around his body stood near the entrance. We joined the small audience that had gathered around him for a moment but Sergeant Mika said he had seen a lot of this type of thing before and preferred to see the inside of the temple. We walked slowly within its enclosure, looking at the pictures of Hindu saints. There was no one inside to explain the meaning of the things we saw. That was the only time I had ever seen Mika at a loss for words to explain something.

From the Hindu environment, we walked to the An Quang pagoda, which I found more interesting because the monks, in saffron robes, were quite willing to chat with us. Several of them spoke excellent English. It was from this very place that the elderly Buddhist monk, Thich Quang Duc, had come to have himself immolated in the center of Saigon in 1963, a highly publicized act that caused much of the Western world to become more concerned with our presence in Vietnam. It was also from this temple and others like it that so much political opposition to past and then present governments had been directed. But our quiet conversation with the monks was more philosophical than political. They did not hide their sympathy for the refugees who, at that very moment, were sleeping, or resting, underneath the outside staircases and around the temple.

From the temple, we took one of the ubiquitous little blue-and-white Renault taxis, which roamed the city like bumper cars at a county fair, to the gardens that bordered on the zoo. We rested on a bench for awhile admiring buildings in the style of ancient pagodas and monuments. They were much as I had remembered them, but sorely in need of repair. A short walk through the zoo convinced us that the animals that remained there were in need of nourishment.

As the leisurely and pleasant day came to an end, I noticed that Mika seemed to be feeling very well. I did not ask about his headaches, afraid to remind him of them, and hoping that they had been permanently relieved.

CHAPTER TWENTY-TWO

Love's Labor Lost

First Sergeant Robert Allen was nearing the end of his third Vietnam tour in the latter part of 1968, hoping that his request for extension would be approved. He was one of the army's most respected first sergeants: handsome and tall, with the voice and military bearing of a soldier who could easily be recognized as a person of authority.

On his first tour in Vietnam, before the influx of American soldiers in 1965, there was time enough for members of the army to spend leisurely hours on the sandy beaches and visit the bars of Nha Trang, where Sergeant Allen was stationed. It was there in the New Saigon Bar that soldiers, including Allen, spent lazy afternoons, drinking beer and playing childish bar games with the working girls. From the time of his first visit to the bar, Allen played the games with Nguyen Thoa Thuc, his favorite companion, whom he called Tam for convenience. She was the daughter of a village official not far away and worked to help support her brothers and sisters. She lived in Nha Trang, however, close to the bar and returned to her village one day each week.

As time went by, Sergeant Allen, thirty-seven years old and never married, fell deeply in love with Tam. He persuaded her to quit working at the bar to take a job that he arranged for her at the Quartermaster Storage Depot in Nha Trang. She began as a general helper but was promoted quickly to filing clerk as her English and typing skills improved. Allen continued to visit Tam at the depot, and frequently drove her home in the evenings.

Sergeant Allen wanted desperately to take Tam as his wife, but the army forbade solders to marry indigenous women. Tam, through her father, could probably have arranged a Vietnamese wedding, but Allen, model soldier for seventeen years, refused to violate the military code. He wanted, however, to have Tam as his common-law wife, and perhaps, when the world was at peace, be legally married and bring her to the United States. Allen's love was reciprocated, and Tam agreed to the arrangement, with the reluctant consent of her parents.

During the Tet holidays of 1965, Allen and Tam, alone in a small Buddhist temple, vowed that they would be faithful to each other until the end of their lives. It did not matter to them that neither the United States nor Vietnam recognized the marriage. They moved into a small apartment and thereafter referred to each other as husband and wife, even to their acquaintances.

After serving eighteen months in Nha Trang, Allen was ordered back to the United States. Six months later, he volunteered successfully for a second tour in Vietnam and was assigned to the 25th Infantry Division in Cu Chi. By the time of his arrival there, Tam had become proficient in her job at the depot in Nha Trang and received praise from her superiors. The chief of staff of the 25th Infantry Division, encouraged by the recommendations of Sergeant Allen, arranged to have Tam transferred as a clerk to that headquarters. Allen and Tam lived together in Cu Chi for a year, after which time he returned again to the United States. Allen did not request a second overseas extension because the unexpected illness of his mother required his presence at home.

While stationed in Nha Trang earlier, Sergeant Allen's military qualities had impressed a young colonel who, since that time, had become a general. In 1968, he was assigned to USARV headquarters in Long Binh. The general arranged for Allen to be transferred from Fort Benning, Georgia, to Long Binh, where he began his third Vietnam tour. The general was also influential in having Tam transferred within the military structure from Cu Chi to Long Binh. Together again, with their combined income, Allen and Tam were able to rent a small house in a village not far from Long Binh.

Long Binh had the largest concentration of American troops in Vietnam, assigned to three division-size units and numerous smaller ones. It was not unexpected, therefore, that Sergeant Allen would meet numerous senior noncommissioned officers with whom he was already acquainted. He frequently had lunch with some of them at the Chinese restaurant or one of the many mess halls on post. Allen invited the best of those friends to attend a regular Friday night poker game at his home. Among those poker players was Master Sergeant Will Morris, an acquaintance of many years.

As the weeks passed, Morris became an even closer friend of both Allen and his wife, visiting them frequently, even on nights when there was no poker game. The men drank beer, and sometimes, when Morris became inebriated, he remained the entire night. He was a trustworthy friend.

When Sergeant Allen's mother died suddenly in June, 1968, he was given two weeks leave to attend her funeral. Sometime during the second week of Allen's absence, Sergeant Morris visited the noncommissioned officers club where he began to drink heavily. At about nine-thirty, he decided to visit Allen's Vietnamese wife. Although Tam was able to detect the odor of alcohol on his breath, she invited him inside, thinking that perhaps he had news of her husband. Morris asked Tam for a drink and she shared one beer with him.

When Tam suggested that Morris leave because she was tired, Morris approached her in an unusually friendly manner by placing his arm around her waist. Tam resisted but Morris persisted. His intentions became more apparent as he tried to loosen Tam's blouse. She begged him to desist, but to no avail. Morris continued his aggressive behavior and succeeded in removing Tam's blouse completely. She screamed, an act which enraged him to further violence. He threw her to the floor, removed her trousers and demanded that she have intercourse with him.

Tam's terrified screams, as Morris continued to assault her, brought neighbors, including two United States enlisted men and the lone village policeman, to her rescue. All together, they were able to restrain Morris. Another neighbor contacted the military police at Long Binh, who answered the call immediately. They arrested Morris, duly noting in their report that Morris had apparently been drinking, had to be forcibly restrained from committing even more violent acts, and was angry and shouting that Tam was a whore who should have acquiesced in his wishes. They brought Morris to his company commander, who assumed responsibility for him until he sobered up.

At the end of his leave, Sergeant Allen was met at Ton Son Nhut airport by his company commander, who thought it best that he personally inform Allen of the assault upon his Vietnamese wife. The captain then drove the sergeant immediately to his home, where Tam was waiting. Allen was shocked to see his wife's condition and to find her so distraught that she was unable to speak coherently. She had not returned to work since the assault because of bruises about her face and body. He treated her with compassion and sympathy, consoling her by promising to remain by her side no matter what further indignities she might be subjected to. Allen told his wife, and he sincerely meant it, that he would have killed Morris then and there if it were in his power to do so.

After Tam had regained her composure, knowing that her husband would not forsake her, Allen went to the Engineer Command where Sergeant Morris worked. His first priority was to find out what, if any, disciplinary action had been taken against his wife's attacker. He was infuriated, therefore, upon arrival at the Engineer Command, to see Morris performing his usual duties in the command headquarters, apparently unconcerned that anything unusual had occurred.

Allen restrained himself for the moment but went directly to Morris' company commander, demanding an immediate explanation for what he considered to be an injustice. The captain explained that he handled the matter himself by reprimanding Morris for his behavior and contemplated no further action, considering Morris's many years of exemplary service to the United States. Allen informed the captain that the action he took was, in his opinion, totally inappropriate and that he was taking the matter directly to the inspector general of the Engineer Command.

In less than thirty minutes, Allen was in the presence of the inspector general, informing him that an injustice had been done to his wife. He insisted that Morris be treated no differently than if he had sexually assaulted an American Red Cross female worker. Allen had enough experience with military justice to know that proof of the crime was easily available through the testimony of his wife and the witnesses who had come to her rescue, including the nurse from the village who tended her on the night of the incident. If no one else would prefer charges, Allen said, he himself would prepare and sign the charge sheet and force an official Article 32 pretrial investigation.

The inspector general knew that, considering Allen's good standing in the community, his complaints could not be dismissed lightly. He, therefore, ordered an investigation by members of his own office, which ultimately resulted in the preferral of charges against Morris alleging assault with intent to commit rape upon Nguyen Thoa Thuc. The commanding general decided that the charges would be tried by General Court Martial.

Sergeant Morris knew most of the senior noncommissioned officers in each of the three legal offices at Long Binh, and sought their advice. They agreed that Morris could do no better than seek the services of Captain Samuel Arkow, who was regarded as the best defense counsel in the area. He was thorough, tough, smart, and never overlooked the slightest possibility of a defense, or matter favorable to his client in mitigation. He fought in court with the tenacity of the best counsel in the United States.

Captain Arkow accepted Sergeant Morris's case. His first demand of Morris was to obtain the names of as many persons as he could who, at any time, present or past, knew Sergeant Allen's Vietnamese wife.

A break for the defense came when Morris located a sergeant who knew Tam in 1964 when she worked at the New Saigon Bar in Nha Trang. He had seen her a few times on the compound at Long Binh but had never spoken to her there. When Arkow questioned him, the witness reported that not only he, but two other soldiers he knew in Nha Trang at the time, had spent the night at least once with Tam before she obtained employment with the United States Army. This information would allow the defense counsel to question Tam about her past life, the matter being pertinent to her credibility.

When the case was brought to trial, Sergeant Allen sat alone in the rear of the courtroom, listening intently to the proceedings. When Tam testified under gentle questioning by the prosecutor, every word she spoke increased her husband's compassion for her and hatred of Morris. Tam explained the circumstances under which she allowed Morris to enter her home while her husband was away; then she described the attack upon her person and her resistance to the assault in even greater detail than she had ever spoken to her husband.

Sergeant Allen was aware of the humiliation that his wife was experiencing and shared her deep sense of embarrassment. He looked at Morris sitting at the defense table with even more contempt in his heart. When Tam completed her testimony for the prosecution, Captain Arkow began his cross-examination.

Defense Counsel (DC): Now, Miss Thuc, you testified that on the night in question, Sergeant Morris attacked you against your will.

Tam: Yes, sir.

DC: You knew Morris quite well, did you not?

Tam: Yes, sir.

DC: And on other occasions when he visited your home, you kissed him, did you not?

Tam: I did not really kiss him, but we said goodbye in a friendly manner.

DC: Did you kiss him on the lips?

Tam: No, sir.

DC: What about New Year's Eve when you were all drinking together?

Tam: Well, maybe on that one occasion.

DC: Did you enjoy his kiss?

Tam: I don't remember.

DC: Well, you did kiss him on the lips. Do you not think this might have made Sergeant Morris feel that his advances were welcome?

Tam: Only that brief time on New Year's Eve.

DC: And you continued to see him afterwards, even until your husband left for the United States?

Tam: Yes, sir, but my husband was always there.

Sergeant Allen was now beginning to feel an intense dislike for the defense counsel as well as Morris. Captain Arkow became even more aggressive on the issue of consent.

DC: Miss Thuc, do you know Sergeant Paul Meany?

Tam: I do not recall the name.

DC: Do you know any servicemen whom you met before you met Sergeant Allen?

Tam: I'm sure I met some.

DC: You met some. Could it be that you met them while you were working at the New Saigon Bar in Nha Trang?

Tam: It is possible.

The anger building up in Sergeant Allen was now obvious to Captain Arkow, but he continued the pursuit.

DC: If I provided you with the name of one of them, would you remember?

Tam: I don't think so.

DC: Did you at any time take any of the soldiers you met at the bar in Nha Trang to your home?

Tam: That was a long time ago.

DC: A long time ago, yes, but do you remember whether you did?

Tam: Maybe one or two.

DC: Could it have been eight or ten?

Tam: I don't think so.

DC: But it was at least three or four, was it not?

Tam: It could be.

DC: And Paul Meany could have been one of them?

Tam: I don't remember.

Sergeant Allen was now enraged with his Vietnamese wife as well as the defense counsel and the accused.

DC: Now, Miss Thuc, I do not mean to embarrass you, but I do want to be specific, because it is very important to the defense of this case. Did you at any time sleep with a soldier other than Sergeant Allen in Nha Trang?

Tam: Yes, sir.

DC: Would I be correct in assuming that you slept with at least three or four.

Tam: Yes, sir.

Tam had assured Allen on several occasions that her employment at the New Saigon Bar was only to help support her family. Unable now to contain the anger against his wife, Sergeant Allen quickly and silently departed from the courtroom. After Tam was temporarily excused as a witness, she could not locate her husband; nor could she leave the area as she had been excused subject to recall.

The case continued with presentation of testimony by witnesses who came to Tam's assistance on the night of the assault, including the nurse who cared for her and the military police. Morris testified that he had assumed Tam was consenting to his advances and did not resist beyond making mere expressions of disapproval. The court, dismissing the protestations of the accused, but believing the testimony of Tam and the other prosecution's witnesses, found Morris guilty and sentenced him to be dishonorably discharged from the army.

That evening, when Tam returned to her home, all of her husband's possessions were missing. He had departed without even a message. She was unable to contact him at his unit and, to her surprise, she was informed that Sergeant Allen had withdrawn his request for an extension of duty in Vietnam.

CHAPTER TWENTY-THREE

Tragedy in White

On January 3, 1969, I received a call from Colonel Tom Reece, telling me that he would arrange ground transportation for my trip on January 10, from Saigon to Long Binh, where I was to be the judge on a premeditated murder case. I was pleased by the travel arrangements because it was more convenient to be picked up at my hotel and delivered to the courtroom in one vehicle than having to schedule my own transportation by military taxi, helicopter, and pickup at destination. I looked forward to the pleasure of having a relatively late and leisurely breakfast for a change.

The promised army sedan arrived at the appointed time and place. Colonel Reece had not informed me, however, that the vehicle would also pick up witnesses for the trial. After leaving the Rex, the driver proceeded to the San Francisco Bar on Tu Do Street, where three Vietnamese hostesses, dressed in colorful national dress, and one Vietnamese man were also waiting for transportation to the trial. I would have preferred not to be closely associated with witnesses, but it was too late to avoid the arrangements with which I had been confronted.

I moved from the rear to the front seat of the sedan and the four prospective witnesses piled into the back seat, chattering excitedly as they did so. The driver then, again to my surprise, proceeded to a hospital where a Vietnamese doctor, who had also been summoned as a witness, was waiting for the military vehicle. I slid into the middle of the front seat and, with the doctor on my right, we proceeded to Long Binh. The little French I spoke restricted conversation with the doctor, who had been educated in France, to the simplest pleasantries. I could not speak Vietnamese.

When we arrived at the building in which the courtroom was located, counsel for the prosecution and defense were peering from the windows, quite amused at the combination of passengers in an official army sedan. I allowed the witnesses, accompanied by the American driver, a few minutes to precede me to the courtroom.

Corporal Eugene Casey was charged that day with the murder of Miss Huyng Le Anh at the San Francisco Bar on Tu Do Street in Saigon on October 20, 1968. The alleged murder was no mystery. Its circumstances did not require the resolution of complicated facts or issues. The case, however, did generate much interest in the English and Vietnam press because it dealt not only with the lifestyles of soldiers who had deserted their units and lived on the fringes of the underworld, but also the famed hostesses of Tu Do Street, who did not differentiate among customers, so long as they were financially solvent.

When Casey departed from his unit without permission and arrived in Cholon on October 6, he moved into the Han Lan Hotel where other AWOL soldiers, some of them acquaintances, lived. While free from military control, Casey led a life of luxury, eating in good restaurants, traveling in borrowed automobiles, meeting women, using drugs, and visiting other absentees from the army. Frequently, he walked about Saigon and Cholon in his military uniform carrying his issued M–16 rifle to mingle inconspicuously with other soldiers. He made illegal purchases in the commissary, PXs, and army liquor stores. He consorted with Filipino and Chinese persons of questionable character.

Casey spent most of the day on October 20 in the hotel drinking with friends, but took leave of them at about four-thirty in the afternoon to visit another absentee soldier, Private Ron Howard. They spent thirty minutes together, during which time Casey consumed two Immenoctal tablets, a barbiturate normally recommended for sleeping disorders and available without prescription in any Western-style drug store in Saigon. It was common knowledge that two of the pills, taken together in the dosage Casey consumed, would make almost any person begin to hallucinate.

When I observed Casey for the first time, standing outside the courtroom with his guard, I was impressed only by the fact that he looked so ordinary. He was tall, neat, nice looking, wore black horned rimmed glasses, and outwardly expressed no sense of emotion. He acknowledged no one and seemed disinterested in his surroundings. I knew from a review of the pretrial papers that his parents had separated when he was quite young and he remained with his father, who showed no interest in the boy except for providing the bare necessities of life. He had grown up as an adequate high school student but without any recorded achievements, or infractions with the law. During the trial, he was courteous when addressed, but otherwise remained silent, even during recesses. I did not see him in conversation with anyone, including his attorney.

Private Ralph Primera, a former resident of the Han Lan Hotel, was the first witness called by the prosecutor. He was wearing one combat boot and one slipper as he entered the courtroom. Primera testified that, after drinking with Casey most of the day on October 20, they met some friends, including a Filipino who owned a car. The group ate at a restaurant and then proceeded to the Mekong, Suzie Wong, and San Francisco bars on Tu Do Street, arriving at the last one about nine thirty. Casey sat in the first empty booth accompanied by a hostess, and his friends scattered about.

The San Francisco was one of many bars on Tu Do, a street famed in novels and history, when it was formerly known as Rue

Catinat. It was only a few blocks long but known to everyone who lived in or visited Saigon because of its fame for bars, night clubs, dance halls, good restaurants, and cheap hotels. In addition to a bar, the San Francisco had about a dozen tables and booths where the hostesses brought their clients. For themselves, the customers ordered whiskey or beer, and for the ladies, champagne, the latter being nothing more than a nonalcoholic mixture commonly referred to as "Saigon tea." The customers were aware that the champagne was tea but accepted that fact as the price of companionship.

Upon arrival at the San Francisco, Casey and his friends were greeted with enthusiasm by the hostesses. All the men appeared happy, were joking, and sat in separate booths. They bought Saigon tea for the hostesses. At about ten forty-five, Primera heard a commotion from the booth adjoining his. When he looked in that direction, Casey was "cocking that little three-inch .22-caliber Astra pistol which he borrowed from the Filipino." The prosecutor continued his examination.

Q: Could you hear it cock?

A: Yes.

Q: Could you see the pistol?

A: No. It was covered by his hand.

Q: What did he do then?

A: He turned and shot the girl. He just turned and pointed it and I think she said "you shoot me," or something.

Q: And what happened then?

A: He shot her again.

Q: How far away was his pistol from the girl?

A: About three feet, three or four feet.

Q: How many times did he shoot her, do you know?

A: I believe about three times, maybe four. He shot her once from a sitting position and the rest from a standing position.

When asked about wearing a slipper, Primera explained that one of the bullets fired from Casey's weapon at the San Francisco hit and damaged his little toe. He did not seek medical attention.

The first Vietnamese witness, Miss Nguyen Thi Nghai, testified through an interpreter that, while sitting at the bar with a customer, the people in Casey's party were joking around. She saw Miss Anh, who was sitting with Casey, return to the bar three times for drinks. Miss Anh then told her that Casey asked her to go out with him, and she agreed but only as a ploy to get him to buy another drink. Casey bought that third drink but when Anh asked for yet another, Casey asked whether she was playing him for a sucker. He then shot Anh four or five times. "Why you shoot me?" Miss Anh cried as she reeled backwards into Miss Nghai's arms.

The second Vietnamese witness, Miss Lam Thi Lan, who was also a hostess at the bar on the night of the shooting, insisted on testifying in English. She was able to embellish on the testimony given my Miss Nghai. Lan was helping her mother who was in charge of the bar when she noticed Casey immediately upon his entry into the bar. He looked "like very nice." The prosecutor continued:

Q: Did anything unusual happen after Casey sat down with Miss Anh?

A: He act very good. Good mood.

Q: How long did Miss Anh sit with this man?

A: About half hour.

Q: What happened then?

A: They talking and laughing. Nothing look like angry.

After half an hour, Miss Lan said that Anh took money from Casey, went to the bar for more drinks, returned to Casey's booth, and again sat down with him. A few minutes later, Anh returned to the bar and told Lan that Casey was a "cheap Charlie" because he would not buy her another drink. She nevertheless returned to his booth. Lan continued:

A: She not sit down. Then I saw him pull the gun and shot Miss Anh. And he shot one shot. Then Miss Anh said: "Why you shot me?" the man stood up. "I shoot you, you know."

Q: Then what did he do?

A: This time, he shot more shots, then he run, go outside.

Q: Did he appear drunk to you?

A: No. He not drunk. He can walk, he can run very good. He no argue. No nothing. Acting very sober. I know sober and drunk.

Doctor Tran Dai Quay, with whom I had shared the front seat of a military sedan earlier in the morning, was called as the next witness and presented us with problems we did not antici-pate. He insisted on testifying in French because that was the language of his medical school. There was no French-English interpreter in Long Binh, but there was an old employee who had worked for the French as a Vietnamese-French interpreter.

The language problem was partially solved by allowing the doctor to testify in French and having his testimony translated into Vietnamese by the old French employee. The appointed court interpreter then picked up the testimony, translating it from Vietnamese into English. This was a terrible problem, cre-ated by the double translations, the use of medical terms, and the fact that the defense counsel, who had studied French in high school, kept objecting to the way the doctor's French came out at the end of the line in English. Each objection was exhaustingly resolved with the use of French, Vietnamese, and English medical and ordinary dictionaries.

The gist of Doctor Quay's testimony was that several bullets entered Miss Anh's body and one was imbedded in the surface of her skin but fell out when he removed her clothing. He did not attempt removal of the others due to severe internal bleeding. Miss Anh died at five minutes after midnight on the morning of October 21. In Doctor Quay's opinion, death was the result of internal bleeding caused by the cutting of arteries and veins within her body.

The bartender, Huynh Than, who was Miss Anh's uncle, tes-tified that after hearing the first shot, he looked up and saw Casey shooting his niece with a small gun. He did not count but he heard "many more shots" and Casey did not appear to be drunk while firing. After the shooting, Than "took care" of Anh but did not give her first aid because he did not think she was bleeding very much. He and the hostesses were weeping and kneeling beside his niece, not knowing what to do. He later accompanied Anh in the ambulance that took her to the hospital and remained with her until the end. He was not allowed in the room where Anh was being treated, but through the door, he could hear her crying, saying repeatedly that her life was about to end.

Foster Boyd, an American engineer was sitting on a stool at the bar when he heard a noise that sounded like a firecracker. He turned to see Casey fire a few shots at a girl "wearing a white dress" from a small pistol that was almost entirely concealed by his hand. Boyd did not see what he considered to be blood on Anh's dress but only a few red spots that appeared to be a part of the fabric.

Immediately after Casey ran out of the bar, three American patrons followed. They attracted the attention of a United States Military Police patrol consisting of Sergeant Joe Mazarek, Sergeant Donald Hansen, and the driver of the jeep in which they were riding. Sergeant Mazarek ordered the driver to stop, jumped out of the jeep, and ran into the San Francisco to investigate the disturbance. Sergeant Hansen ordered the jeep driver to follow some Vietnamese policemen who were running down Tu Do Street blowing whistles at a taxi. The jeep pulled alongside the taxi, forcing it to stop. Hansen dismounted from his vehicle and opened the rear door of the taxi. Inside, he saw Casey wearing sunglasses, with a small pistol in his hand. Casey pointed the weapon in the direction of the military policeman, but Hansen grabbed the pistol, which he suspected was only a toy. He apprehended Casey and returned him to the San Francisco, where he was immediately identified.

Sergeants Mazarek and Hansen both observed Miss Anh lying on the floor, with the long folds of her white au dai spread out beside her body, and a few red spots in the area of her abdomen. Hansen radioed for an ambulance, which arrived about thirty-five minutes after Miss Anh had been shot. She was taken to a Vietnamese hospital eight blocks away.

As it's final witness, the prosecution called Private Robert LeBlanc, who had previously known Casey from the Long Binh Stockade and was being held in the Saigon detention cell for his own transgressions on the night of the shooting. When he saw Casey being admitted, his first question was: "What did you do this time?" The record of trial contains the following dialogue:

Q: What did Casey say?

A: He told me that he shot a broad. I asked him why. He told me that she was hanging over him, wanting him to spend money on Saigon tea. She just kept hanging on him driving him crazy, I guess. I don't know.

Q: Did he tell you what he shot her with?

A: He said it was a small Astra .22.

Q: Did he tell you how many times he shot her?

A: Four, he thought. He said he pushed her back, and she came at him again. He said he pulled out the gun and shot her.

The defense counsel, in his opening statement, admitted that Casey shot Anh but argued that, because of alcohol and drugs, it was impossible for him to form a specific intent to kill, an essential element of the offense of premeditated murder. The defense counsel also contended that the cause of death was negligence of others in not caring for such a frail person as Miss Anh. Specifically, the delay in taking her to the hospital and the lack of sophistication of the Vietnamese doctor were independent intervening causes that negated Casey's responsibility for the death. I thought these latter statements were specious but did not hinder the defense from proceeding.

Captain Herbert Hall, a United States Army medical doctor, testified that if Miss Anh had been treated within ten or fifteen minutes after the shooting with methods frequently used on the battlefield, there would have been an excellent chance that she could have been brought out of shock. Thereafter, the chances would have been excellent for the performance of a successful operation to stop the hemorrhaging, thus saving the life of the patient. The doctor also made the observation that, since the weapon used had such a low velocity projective, it was unlikely that the bullets would have killed a person stronger or heavier than Miss Anh, who weighed barely eighty pounds, or even killed Anh herself, if she had been more than six yards away.

Casey chose to testify on his own behalf. He admitted everything other witnesses had said about the time spent at the hotel on the day of the incident, the fact that he consumed two Immenoctal tablets at Ron Howard's rented home, and, upon further questioning, replied:

> We departed in a car belonging to a Filipino who worked in Saigon. We ate at the My Canh floating restaurant in Saigon and continued to drink there. By the time we reached the San Francisco Bar, I was in a pretty intoxicated state, even though I was still in control of my senses. A girl was sitting down alongside of me and I bought her three or four Saigon teas. I asked her if she would come with me, and she said yes. I told her not to ask for any more drinks, but she went and asked me for another. I pulled out a gun from under my shirt. I pointed the weapon at her. I thought I was just playing around. Next thing I knew, that weapon went off and she was clutching her stomach and I just sat there. Somebody started yelling, "Get up and run to the car!" I stood up and went for the door. I fired twice more. I ran down the street with the weapon in my hand, got in a taxi and told the driver to take me to Cholon.
>
> I saw a jeep pulling up, and a door of the taxi was pulled open. The military policeman took the gun out of my hand. The only intention I had in the bar was scaring her a little bit for asking me to buy her that other drink, the last drink.

In answer to the prosecutor's question on cross-examination concerning the weapon, Casey responded: "Well, sir, I borrowed it from a Filipino worker that I had known in Saigon. I considered it necessary to carry a weapon around there."

The court found Casey guilty of unpremeditated murder and sentenced him to be dishonorably discharged from the army and to be confined at hard labor for thirty years.

A few days after Casey's trial, two young army lawyers from Nha Trang were visiting Saigon and asked me to accompany them on a stroll in the city. As we walked down Tu Do Street, I pointed out the San Francisco, scene of the then notorious case of Private Casey. All three of us peeked into the bar with hands clasped to our faces against the window for a better view of the inside. Miss Nghai and Miss Lan saw us and recognized me. Both, deserting their customers, ran outside, jumped up and down like children, saying in broken English how happy they were that justice had been done. My friends and I were invited in as guests of the house, but I declined for all of us because of my association with the case. My friends were quite disappointed.

The girls then became serious as Miss Lan explained what happened two days after Miss Anh's death. All employees of the bar contributed to the purchase of a new white au dai in which their friend would be buried. The bar was closed for an afternoon during which they spent the time beside the body of Miss Anh. Lan was in tears when she concluded by saying that Miss Anh looked just like she did five minutes before her murder, dressed all in white with no red spots on her dress.

The case of Private Casey was duly reported in the *Overseas Weekly*, a paper designed and published for United States troops abroad. The story concluded:

> Saigon's English-language papers played the murder up as a jealous lover's spat when they reported the shooting at the San Francisco. "Bullshit," said Miss Nhgai in her cute, original English when an OW reporter asked her about it. "Miss Anh never see boy before in her life."

CHAPTER TWENTY-FOUR

Dinner at Le Castel

Events impossible to foresee frequently happened during my tour in Vietnam. One that I recall with delight occurred on an evening when I was dining alone in the open mess at the Rex with no particular problems. I was startled to see a woman's figure in a gold lamé pantsuit standing before me. Looking up, I saw that it was Kathy, smiling as usual, her short hair messed up a bit, and her large brown eyes staring down at me.

"Hi! May I sit down?"

"Of course!" I replied.

"I've been stood up!" she said, "or maybe the guy had to go off to bomb a village or something. I don't know. Maybe he had another date."

"Probably not," I said. "Well, you're here now. Have dinner and I'll sit with you."

"I wouldn't go through the mess line dressed like this for a million dollars. Take me to Le Castel and I'll pay for dinner."

"I'd be happy to, but I've finished dinner!"

"You can have a glass of wine or something. I've gone to all the trouble of getting dressed and everyone here is staring at me. I'd really appreciate the favor."

"I'm dressed in fatigues, but I guess that's all right."

"As long as we have money, they don't care."

I was a little embarrassed about escorting Kathy because of the combat gear and hat I was wearing. For some odd reason, judges took it upon themselves to look different from other officers in Saigon by wearing hats that looked like World War II fatigue caps. Extended borders ran about two inches entirely around the center and fell over our ears and eyes. Although practical for rainy weather, they looked horrible.

People everywhere stared at Kathy, dressed as she was. It was not unusual to see Vietnamese women, just as attractive and in clothing perhaps even more stunning, but an American woman in a gold lamé pants' suit was something hardly to be expected in Saigon. Everyone seemed to admire her, and if there was one thing Kathy enjoyed, it was being admired.

The attention Kathy received on Tu Do Street was mild compared to that which she received when we entered Le Castel. The long bar near the entrance was crowded with people whom I assumed were civilian contractors, war correspondents, investigators for congressional committees, or those other characters whose presence I always noticed but whose duties I could never determine. It is safe to say that they were among the most affluent in the city because Le Castel was not inexpensive, even for those who changed American Military Payment Certificates (MPCs, or scrip) into piasters on the black market, which I assumed many, if not all, of the patrons did. In deference to the circumstances, I removed my funny hat and soaked up the ambiance, which gave me the courage to give a smug look toward the men sitting at the bar.

A uniformed waiter led us to a booth, rather than sitting us at an open table. Perhaps it was because he wanted to keep the sight of my fatigues away from his more prosperous patrons. I ordered a bottle of wine for both of us and dinner for Kathy. She wanted everything, from soup to dessert with sorbet in between.

While waiting for service, we chatted about nothing in particular. Kathy never inquired about my family except to ask whether she was younger than my wife. There was soft music in the background, mostly from American musicals. But when an Irish tenor crooned "Danny Boy" in a melancholy voice, she stopped speaking and stared into space with eyes wide open and a faint smile on her face. Memories, I thought. Probably some past love.

"I used to have an Irish boyfriend named Danny," she said softly. "We were both quite young and I think that was the only time in my life I was ever really in love, or I thought I was in love. That was over a dozen years ago, when I was nineteen. Danny is probably married now with a house full of kids. But he was beautiful."

"Why didn't you marry him?" I asked.

"He was a medical student and wasn't ready, he said. I was living in St. Louis near the medical school on Grand Avenue, and he was living nearby in a small apartment with other students. We saw each other, at least for a little while, almost every day. At first we were just good friends, and maybe, as far as he was concerned, that's all we ever were. But I fell in love with him. One weekend he asked me to go away with him to Chicago, which was probably as far away as he could afford to go. My parents would have disowned me if they knew the reason I left, so I didn't tell them. Just disappeared for a couple of days. They never forgave me for that."

"What happened while you were away?" Why not ask, I thought, she brought up the subject.

"Well, I know this sounds crazy and a lot of people around here wouldn't believe me, but we didn't make love. At least, not really. We slept in the same room, though. Well, that's the way it was. We walked along Michigan Boulevard, sat in parks and ate in cheap diners during the day, but it was the nights that were so beautiful. It was the nicest weekend of my life."

Tears came to her eyes. Considering the fortune this dinner was going to cost, I was hoping for more than tears and an old love story. Fortunately, the waiter returned with the appetizer and Kathy returned to her outwardly happy self. I continued to sip wine as the meal progressed. People passing by continued to look at her. I was not ordinarily the subject of civilians' envy.

When the waiter brought the bill, I looked at the amount in disbelief. He must have multiplied instead of added, I thought. The moment of truth arrived for me when I remembered that I did not have enough Vietnamese money even to pay the gratuity, because I seldom used it except for things like taxis and newspapers. The waiter would gladly have taken MPCs but, even if I had enough, I would not have made the offer. I had previously rendered several opinions in cases involving illegal money transactions. Not to worry, though! True to her word, Kathy was good for the bill. From her purse, she removed a great roll of piasters, which caused me to believe for a moment that she, too, might have gotten them from someplace other than the finance office. But that was impossible! No, I convinced myself, she just legally exchanged about three hundred American dollars for piasters in case of an emergency such as this.

With the bill and gratuity paid by Kathy, we exited Le Castel, receiving the same reaction from patrons as we did when we entered. Outside, we began a slow walk to Kathy's apartment across from the Continental Palace Hotel. She enjoyed every step of the way. When we arrived, she invited me in. I checked my watch. Half hour to curfew. It wasn't difficult to figure that, allowing five minutes to walk from her place to mine, I'd have twenty-five minutes to spare, so I accepted.

I did not sit down immediately after entering the apartment and am sure that I looked as awkward as my friend Tom must have looked a few months earlier. Kathy asked me to wait a minute while she changed into something comfortable. When she returned, she was wearing a cotton robe. Her shoes and large earrings had been removed.

"Would you like a drink?" she asked with ease and without hesitation, and I am sure with no intent other than to prolong the evening until curfew.

I thanked her but declined. I could not believe that I was alone with a single woman in her apartment and she wasn't even wearing shoes. Or earrings. I walked over to the large window that faced other apartments across the way. Rain began to fall and adrenaline began to flow.

"Don't worry about curfew!" Kathy said, "You can sleep here on the couch and we can talk a while longer."

Think now, I said to myself, you can make it through the night. Well, maybe I could, but I knew it wouldn't be easy and I had a flight scheduled early the next morning.

Kathy stood in her robe smiling, holding a bottle of Triple Sec. "I don't drink except wine with dinner, but you are welcome to this," she said. I compromised my original refusal by agreeing to a quick nightcap. She walked over to the couch with a soft drink and sat down, asking me to do the same.

I did as she requested and Kathy made no effort to come closer, but her eyes alone gave me a better reason to attempt an assault upon her than those in half the cases I heard in court. One gulp emptied my drink. Ten minutes to curfew.

"Let's watch television." Kathy said. "Bobbie will be on in a few minutes with the weather." Bobbie was Kathy's friend who worked as a secretary but did the nightly weather report on the Armed Forces Network. She always wore a miniskirt and finished her bit before the camera with: "Here's wishing you all good things, weatherwise, and, of course, otherwise."

We watched Bobbie, and I was not sure how to interpret the "otherwise" on this particular night. When she finished, though, the late night show began. I took a deep breath.

"This looks pretty good. I'm in the mood for a good movie!" Kathy said.

I did not think that I'd like this particular movie even if I were capable of sitting through it, but the curfew hour had passed. I threw caution to the winds and said: "Well, let's watch."

As the movie progressed, and I do not remember a thing about it, Kathy watched intently, often making comments while sipping from her glass of nonalcoholic whatever. I agreed with all her remarks.

Thirty minutes past curfew. I could wrestle no more with the situation. I'll risk the curfew, I said to myself. When I announced my decision, Kathy did not object but escorted me to the door.

I dashed down the stairs, walked quickly through the maze of shops on the bottom floor, and ran through the rain across the park to the Rex. The armed officer at the door, with clipboard and pencil in hand, stopped me, demanding identification. I complied. He looked at me rather smugly but let me pass without including me in his report of curfew violators.

CHAPTER TWENTY-FIVE

The Bloody Trail

Chu Lai is located forty miles south of Da Nang on a promontory overlooking the South China Sea. In peacetime, it is a virtual paradise. During the Vietnam War, it was headquarters of the Americal Division, and the site where all its general courts-martial were tried. Division personnel were spread out in areas surrounded by the enemy in many villages. They fought in marshy coastal lowlands, in jungles, and on mountain slopes. They fought in the provinces of Quang Tri and Quang Ngai and other areas where the Viet Cong and North Vietnamese army had taken a stronghold. It was difficult to distinguish friend from foe. When they met the enemy in combat, they fought with valor and were victorious. When they doubted who the enemy was, they were perplexed. Many Americal soldiers were killed or injured by unexpected foes.

The desire to liquidate their opponents led members of the division to suspect almost every Vietnamese person in villages of doubtful loyalty. These suspicions led to a hatred (by many soldiers and officers) of every Vietnamese man, woman, and child in areas that were considered to be enemy-infested.

I spent a week trying cases in Chu Lai during the early part of 1969. It was during the Tet season and the enemy was engaged in a second Tet Offensive, although not as serious as the year before. Mortar fire poured into the headquarters compound at unexpected times. Harassment and interdictment of the enemy by division artillery increased the noise level substantially throughout the area.

There were compensations, however, for being in Chu Lai, even though it was the busiest week of my tour of duty in Vietnam. During the noon hour, Lieutenant Colonel Barney Brannen and I jogged on the sandy beach below the headquarters, substituting a bar of candy for the noon meal, before returning to work. When there was an occasional break in the trial schedule, a driver from the legal office took me to the beach for an hour or so of quiet relaxation. In rare evenings when court was not in session, I sat in the general's mess overlooking the China Sea, reading or watching a movie.

The attitude with respect to Vietnamese people in the villages of Quang Nai Province was reflected in the case of Ralph Pilger, a member of a scout dog unit. On two successive days, the dog handlers and their charges had assisted in the sweep of several villages, seeking enemy arms and personnel. But rain on the following morning made it impracticable to use the animals. The handlers were sitting around the command post, chatting with several young Vietnamese boys, when Pilger asked Private Richard Russell to accompany him to a nearby village about five hundred meters away at the end of a trail. Russell refused.

The village Pilger entered was not unusual, consisting of many thatched huts, a small market, and a pagoda. Women of all ages and older men were milling about; children were playing; and three mature younger males, one dressed in the uniform of the Vietnamese Popular Forces and armed with a carbine, were walking among the people.

Thirty minutes after Pilger departed, his fellow dog handlers, who had remained behind, heard two shots from a carbine that they assumed came from the village. A three-minute pause followed, and then many more shots from an M–16, the type of weapon issued to each of the handlers. Before the group could decide what action to take, Pilger came running into the campsite holding a carbine and web belt over his head shouting, "I got a dink up there and there is two more if you want to go get them." A few seconds later, he told Sergeant Pascal Giesler that "I shot a gook, that son of a bitch had shot at me."

With everyone in a state of excitement, Pilger led Lieutenant Samuel Ender, his officer in charge, Sergeant Giesel and Private Russell to the spot on the trail between the command post and the village where the last shots had been fired. A member of the Vietnamese Popular Forces was lying face down, his clothes drenched in a pool of blood. Someone said he thought the person moved. Pilger emptied his automatic weapon into the body, killing him instantly, if he was not already dead. Those facts were undisputed.

Miss Dao Thi Van testified that she observed Pilger in the village near the pagoda. She swore that he approached Than Manh, a member of the Popular Forces, removed his web belt and his carbine, and led Manh out to the trail near the village that led to the command post. Before leading the victim from the village, Pilger fired two shots from Manh's carbine to scare away the children who had gathered around to witness the excitement. A few minutes later, Miss Van heard "a long firing" from the trail. Several villagers corroborated her testimony.

Criminal investigators testified that, on the day following the shooting, Pilger made a statement saying that he went down the trail only to the edge of the village. When walking back to camp, he saw three men behind him, so he started to run. He heard two shots from a carbine, one passing near his eyes and the other near his feet. Then, "I jumped off the trail into some bushes. I waited a minute and the Popular Forces guy ran towards me. I jumped out of the bushes when he was right in front of me and I shot him in self-defense. When I shot him the first time, he spun and I shot him again. He spun more and I must have used a whole clip on him because I just kept shooting. I went to him, took his weapon and gear and ran back to the CP area."

At the trial, Private Russell testified that "Pilger told me that the dink fired at him twice, then he jumped into the brush. He kept on indicating that the dink had fired the two shots first." Russel added that there was no blood on the web belt or carbine that Pilger was carrying when he returned, screaming, to the place where his friends were.

Lieutenant Enders testified Pilger told him that he shot a "dink." He also denied entering the village but was walking toward the village when the "dink" began shooting at him. Later, when Pilger led Enders and two others to the man who had been shot, Pilger began shooting the man again and "the shock of Pilger's weapon firing into the dead or wounded man deafened me. There was a whole lot of mud and dirt flying from the bullets hitting the ground. I saw the dust and dirt going up around the body. The man was definitely dead after that firing."

Investigators from battalion headquarters arrived several hours after the incident to investigate the killing. They searched the area where the man was killed and found nineteen M–16 empty rounds, but could find no carbine or other shells anywhere near the scene where Pilger said the Popular Forces man shot at him. Criminal investigators at the trial, using sketches, testified that they found two carbine casings in the village where Miss Van said she had seen the accused fire a weapon.

Pilger testified in court that he was sorry he could not reconcile all of the statements made during the trial, but the "dink" did shoot at him twice and he jumped into the bushes. When the "gook" passed him, he shot. He could not explain why he shot so many times in the first instance, or why he shot so many times again when he and the others found the man lying in a pool of blood. He swore that he removed the web gear after the man was shot, and not before, inside the village, as Miss Van had testified. He could not explain why the web gear was free from all traces of blood after the shooting.

During Pilger's trial, and especially after supper when darkness had fallen, the noise from mortar fire, both coming into and going out of the area, was deafening. I asked the members of the court whether they would like a recess until the noise abated, or perhaps even until the following morning, but they expressed a desire to continue. One member commented, with a wink towards me, that "We hear this all the time!"

The members of the court deliberated approximately forty-five minutes before returning to announce findings of not guilty. While sitting quietly at the judge's bench after the verdict was announced, not wishing to communicate with anyone, I observed the president of the court walk over to Pilger, put his arm around his shoulder, and say, "Son, you don't let anything like this happen again, because you will never get another chance." Actually, that was another chance for Pilger, because he had been court-martialled twice before. It was not permissible to give this information to the court before findings.

I was totally exhausted after the trial. I departed from the courtroom alone and walked to my quarters thinking of nothing more than a beer and a good night's sleep. Entering my quarters, however, I encountered a delightful surprise. Sitting in the living room of the trailer was a good friend whom I had known in Germany several years before, but had not seen since, and a second person, who looked vaguely familiar, drinking beer together. My friend and I had a hearty reunion, and the stranger introduced himself as Troy Donohue, whom I then recognized. The three of us had a few beers before retiring after midnight.

Early the next morning, we experienced a close encounter with death. An enemy rocket exploded about three meters from our quarters, sending shrapnel through the side of the trailer. My friend and I ran in a couched position to a nearby bunker. I presume Donohue took cover under his bed because he did not follow us, and was still alive when we returned.

CHAPTER TWENTY-SIX

America's Fighting Man

Circumstances of war frequently present occasions in which unsophisticated soldiers are not prepared to cope. Young men who are willing to give their lives for their country, and prove it every day, are placed in situations they are not sufficiently mature to manage. Unplanned crimes occur, therefore, because fighting men are faced with opportunities and temptations to commit offenses.

One of the tragedies of Vietnam was that soldiers who were actually facing the enemy, or were called upon to face the enemy, rather than the eighty-seven percent of troops who supported them, were the ones most often confronted with such opportunities. They succumbed to circumstances that they did not anticipate and now bear the stigma of undesirable discharges that remain part of their lives. Some of the crimes committed took place in the presence of other American soldiers and officers who could have prevented the abuses, but did not. The trial of Corporal Walter Bills, a member of a sister company in the same battalion as the dog handler, Private Ralph Pilger, provided evidence that was typical of this combination of circumstances which led to his court-martial.

At six-thirty on the evening of October 28, 1968, a squad led by Corporal Matt Stahl departed from its company headquarters near Landing Zone Zebra not far from Chu Lai for the purpose of setting up a night ambush close to a nearby village. Nothing of consequence happened before midnight, but early in the morning of the following day, rain began to fall. Stahl took his squad, consisting of himself, Corporal Bills, and five other men to a thatched hut that was empty except for a wooden bunk. The men did not sleep but kept watch, as was their duty.

At dawn, when they were about to return to their company headquarters, the men observed Huynh Thi Chan, an older Vietnamese civilian, about a hundred yards in the distance sitting in a tree looking at them. Stahl, Bills, and Private First Class Ron Darby walked over to Mr. Chan. A group of Vietnamese civilians, including Chan's fourteen-year-old daughter, Huyng Tri Thi, also walked over to Chan, and the two groups converged. Without hesitation or word of explanation, the three soldiers forcibly removed Miss Thi from her father's presence and dragged her into the empty hut where the soldiers had spent the early morning hours. Stahl ordered the other four men of his squad to "keep a watch" on the civilians.

Without much discussion among the three men inside the hut, Stahl undressed the girl who was clothed only in a simple Vietnamese peasant's blouse and pants. Stahl had intercourse with Miss Thi against her will, followed by Bills who committed the same offense. While one was having intercourse, the other held Miss Thi's legs apart. The third soldier, Darby, did not touch her inside the hut. He occasionally looked outside to insure that the civilians, who were being restrained by the other men in the squad, were kept away from the hut.

Stahl, Bills, and Darby were all tried by general court-martial, but I was only involved in the case of Corporal Bills. Although he pleaded guilty to the offense of raping a girl under the age of sixteen, thus admitting all the elements of the offense, the prosecutor chose to present the live testimony of the victim and her father to the court. The papers accompanying the file, including statements from all seven soldiers in Stahl's squad, clearly reflected that members of the squad did nothing to prevent what occurred inside the hut.

Miss Thi testified before the court, as she had previously sworn to investigators, that she was much afraid of the soldiers; that her parents were physically abused when they tried to prevent her removal from their presence; that she was badly bruised by the two soldiers; and that she did not consent to be touched by them at any time.

Mr. Chan testified in substantially the same manner as his daughter with respect to the events outside the thatched hut, and added that when his daughter came out of the hut, she looked exhausted, cried very much, bled profusely, and fell unconscious. Tears came to his eyes when he added that his daughter was only fourteen years old.

During the pretrial investigation, when Stahl was asked, "Why did you rape the girl?" he replied, "Because of hate for the Vietnamese people." When Bills was asked the same question, he replied, "I guess I needed sex." When Kirby was asked, "Why didn't you have sexual relations with the girl?" his response was, "Because these Vietnamese girls don't turn me on."

In extenuation and mitigation, Bills's defense counsel made an effort to explain his client's action to the court members, not as an excuse for the crime, but as a matter to be considered in imposing a lighter sentence. He argued:

> What do they do with these young men over here; eighteen, nineteen, and twenty years old? They have got sex on their minds, they're young. We bring them over here in Vietnam and they make all the villages off limits, so you can't go into them. Gentlemen, these young men get out in the field and do these things because they are no longer what they were in civilian life.

Witnesses who testified in Bills's behalf were unanimous in their praise for him. Officers and noncommissioned officers agreed that he was an outstanding combat soldier who continually volunteered for difficult missions into enemy areas and invariably reserved for himself the position of point man when doing so. His humor helped maintain a high state of morale in his unit even under the most miserable circumstances. He had been assigned combat duties almost from the day of his arrival in the Americal seven months previously and had continued to perform such duties until the day before his trial. He had not even requested the R&R to which he was entitled.

Corporal Bills was sentenced to be dishonorably discharged from the army and to be confined at hard labor for two years.

In an affidavit submitted to the convening authority after the trial, Bills's company commander described him as an example of "America's fighting man." Morale dropped considerably within the company when Bills was taken away to prison after the trial.

I do not have a solution to avoid the tragedy of Corporal Bills and others like him, but I do believe that there is much from his case that should be learned by those responsible for sending young men off to war. More training, better leadership at home and in the field, but most of all, a little more time for the young men to mature. In World War II, the average soldier was twenty-six years old; in Vietnam, nineteen. If there is need for a draft, it should be equally applicable to all men. The burden should not fall upon the disadvantaged and those who are not sophisticated enough to know how to escape being made a part of the military.

CHAPTER TWENTY-SEVEN

It's Prestige, Not Sex

The cases of Private Pilger and Corporal Bills convinced me that it is impossible to predict how a group of soldiers will react to a given situation in a combat zone when there is no combat. The third case in which I was involved at the American Division in February 1969 reinforced that conviction. Lieutenant Donald Pitt and a segment of his platoon were involved in a situation for which there was no prepared script and most of them acted in a manner totally out of character with their true selves.

On the morning of September 16, 1968, Lieutenant Pitt and his men marched into the hamlet of Binh Giang, which consisted of a few thatched huts and a bunker. Seeking a suitable place to establish a temporary command post, Pitt chose one of the huts in which several Vietnamese women, old men, and children, all members of an extended family, were congregated. Accompanied by four of his men, Pitt entered the hut. For a few minutes, only expressions of cordiality were exchanged between the two groups. One American soldier performed an act of mercy by giving medicine to, and playing a children's game with, a sick, retarded child.

One of the men in Pitt's group who did not enter the hut was Private First Class Ted Olsen, a twenty-three-year-old soldier who frequently talked about sex, but had never had sexual intercourse. These personal matters were common knowledge in the platoon and Olsen was frequently ridiculed because of lack of such experience at his age.

While things were still peaceful in the hut, Than Thi Liu, a twelve-year-old, sixty-five-pound, four-and-a-half-foot girl, who had been out gathering grass for her buffalo, returned to the hamlet to find the hut where she lived filled with American soldiers and some of her Vietnamese relatives. When Pitt saw Liu, he called Olsen, telling him to enter the hut. When the latter complied, Pitt pointed to Liu and said: "Look at that girl, look at her long hair, she is beautiful and is probably a virgin. You always wanted a young girl. Take her!"

Corporal Steve Seth, a soldier who had entered the hut with Pitt, approached Liu's mother and said: "Why don't you let babysan make boom boom to this GI?" The mother, although unable to understand English, sensed the threat and threw herself upon Olsen. Other soldiers separated them and forced the woman out of her own home.

The incident with Liu and her mother caused much screaming, pushing, and shoving between the races in the hut. Pitt gave the order to his men to eject all the Vietnamese people, except the little girl, from the dwelling. Olsen picked up Liu in his arms and brought her to the village bunker, where he put her down near the entrance and then shoved her inside. Liu's mother, pleading and crying, watched from a distance with other relatives who had also been forced out of the hut.

Olsen testified at the trial that Pitt followed him and Liu into the bunker, and when he hesitated about touching the child, Pitt told him again: "You always wanted a young girl, take her!" Then, Olsen continued, "Lieutenant Pitt reached over and removed the girl's pants from her body, and then just sat there. I told him to get out. He left the bunker."

Olsen slapped Liu, who was crying, and told her to shut up. "I was thinking only of my prestige, not about sex," Olsen testified. "You might say that I wanted to save face, maybe. I wanted to show them that I could do it. I had been teased for a long time. But, when I had the girl in the bunker, I thought, no. I could not. But, when Lieutenant Pitt pulled the girl's pants down, maybe then I was aroused. Lieutenant Pitt encouraged me to have my first sexual encounter. I was being pressured by the platoon. It was a constant pressure, indescribable."

Liu testified that, inside the bunker, Olsen held her down even though she cried and pleaded that she was too young. She swore he lay on top of her and put something in her body which caused her to bleed. "I had big pain in my stomach. I feel very hurt," she testified.

Five minutes after Olsen and Liu entered the bunker, Pitt stooped down near the entrance to ask, "How are you doing?" "Not so good!" replied Olsen, as he emerged alone from the bunker and proceeded to a water barrel, where he washed his bloody hands. Pitt suddenly felt remorse for his behavior and ordered one of his men to retrieve Liu from the bunker. A soldier went inside and dragged her out by the hands and feet. Liu, crying aloud and bleeding profusely, ran to her mother, who carried her into the family hut.

When one of the soldiers who had seen Liu being physically removed from the bunker was asked whether he did not think it strange to see a little girl being dragged out of the ground, he replied that he did not, because ". . . when we check a bunker, we always send in a kid, so if there is something in the bunker, like a grenade or something, it will blow him up first." I thought this soldier was exhibiting a sense of braggadocio, thinking somehow it would help in the trial of his platoon leader.

The entire group of soldiers left the village shortly after the incident in the bunker. While walking away, Olsen asked a friend if he was angry. "No," replied his companion, "but next time get someone who is bigger and older." Olsen was serious and apparently ashamed of what he had done when he replied, "Yes, I'll never do anything like that again!"

On the morning after the incident, Liu and her mother walked four hours to an American base camp five miles away, seeking medical assistance. Liu was attended by American medical personnel for three days, with her mother at her side. The doctor who took care of her verified that she had been sexually abused but could not determine if she had been raped. When released, Liu could walk without assistance but not climb, even up to a bed or into a jeep.

Lieutenant Pitt was charged with encouraging Private First Class Olsen to sexually abuse a girl under the age of sixteen, thereby being a principal to the crime, and with committing a lewd act on the same girl by removing her pants. He denied both allegations. Two thirds of the court members apparently did not believe beyond a reasonable doubt that Pitt had done the acts alleged, because he was found not guilty. Although Pitt was acquitted, the evidence in the trial revealed a sordid story of American servicemen committing offenses that would never have occurred except for the unfortunate circumstances of being placed in situations in which they had the opportunity to act in a manner inconsistent with their normal behavior. Olsen was later tried and convicted of committing an indecent assault upon a minor. The behavior of Lieutenant Pitt and most of his men reflected adversely upon their honor and the honor of every American fighting man.

CHAPTER TWENTY-EIGHT

Mississippi Lawyer

I was alone in my quarters at the Rex Hotel one evening in February when I received a call from Red Benoit inviting me to his room. He said that he was entertaining a civilian lawyer from Mississippi who had arrived that afternoon and would like me to meet him.

The lawyer was portly, middle-aged, and wore a sharkskin suit with silk tie. He seemed very friendly but loquacious and on the pompous side. Arrangements had been made for him to fly to Dong Tam the following morning, where he was to represent an army client. I got the impression from Red's facial expression that it was about time for me to take a turn at entertaining the gentleman inasmuch as they had already eaten together in the steakhouse and Red wasn't talking very much. In fact, within a few moments of my arrival, Red wasn't talking at all but thumbing through papers on his desk.

"Is it possible to go walking in this city?" the lawyer asked.

I informed him that it was, and offered to escort him. It was not for the honor of the exercise but rather to relieve Red from his obvious boredom in return for the many favors he had done for me and, in a small way, to repay him for causing the firemen to break into his room.

"By golly!" the lawyer said as we left the hotel and walked across the park. "Here I am in the middle of a war and walking around like I was back home in Mississippi. Wait till I get back to tell my friends!"

We were still in the shadow of the Rex, not yet across the park, when the lawyer stopped to light a cigar. He offered one to me from a neat row on the inside pocket of his sharkskin coat, but I declined. As he was lighting up, a Vietnamese man, appearing to be a refugee dressed only in short pants and a ragged shirt, approached us holding a naked baby. There was a fixed half grin on his face, transcending an expression of hopelessness as he stood there, slightly stooping, extending his hand towards us. The lawyer stared at the couple for a moment, neither in a friendly nor unfriendly manner.

"That your baby, boy?" he asked, clouds of cigar smoke engulfing the man, the child, and me. Not having an inkling of what the lawyer said, the Vietnamese man made a gallant effort to broaden the stagnant smile on his face.

"Well, here, I'll help you out!" said the southern gentleman as he put a few coins into the ragged man's hand. The man had no more power within him to broaden his smile but he somehow dipped his body in the form of a crude curtsy as an expression of thanks.

"I like to help poor folk," the lawyer informed me as we resumed our walk towards Le Loi and Tu Do Streets. "In fact, that's why I'm here."

"How is that?" I asked.

"Well, that boy they're trying tomorrow! His case got a lot of publicity back home and I offered to defend him free. That's why I'm here!"

"I'm sure he'll appreciate it."

"Yeah, I know he will. His mama used to work for me. She was a good nigger."

As we walked along Tu Do Street, the lawyer peered into the windows of almost every bar, staring at the hostesses. "There's some right pretty girls in there," he said, "and they're wearing mighty pretty costumes, too!" referring to their au dais.

At each bar and at the sight of more hostesses, the lawyer began to use expressions which indicated to me that he would like to get closer to the action. Finally, he said, "Damn, I wish it was safe to go in there but you can image headlines back home: MISSISSIPPI LAWYER MURDERED IN SAIGON WHORE HOUSE."

"Those aren't whore houses," I explained, "and, if you'd like to stand the expense of buying a couple of drinks for yourself and a hostess, we can visit one."

"Let's do it!" he said excitedly.

I took the lawyer to a little bar situated among the shops and stores within the maze of buildings near the park across from the Rex. It was an out of the way, quiet place off the beaten path, unknown to people who were just walking up and down the more popular Tu Do Street. I had visited the bar on previous occasions when friends came to Saigon from the field for one reason or another and wanted to visit a "notorious" Saigon bar with hostesses. It was the safest and quietest place I could find and was appropriately named the Shangri-La.

One of the hostesses at the Shangri-La was a person who never ceased to fascinate me. She sat on a couch, writing constantly in a ledger when she was not otherwise occupied. As customers entered, she made no effort to approach them unless the other hostesses were busy. She had a soulful face, a perfect complexion, jet black hair reaching below her shoulders, and wore the traditional au dai. She always appeared to be sad. Her eyes stared but never smiled. One night I approached her and asked what she was writing and why she was so preoccupied with the project. She did not seem hesitant to speak as I bought her a couple of Saigon teas, and she told me her story.

The hostess did not expect to live long, although she did not know why and was apparently in good health. She had a daughter born of an American father from whom she had not heard since her baby's birth. She was writing everything she did so that one day her daughter would know about her. Nothing was unimportant. She described her work, her dresses, her customers, her ex-lover, the girl's father, everything. She'd lost count of the number of books she had filled but they were all at her home in a safe place. She worked every night.

As we entered the little bar, the lawyer could not keep his eyes on a single girl but threw furtive glances from one to the other. He was too excited to make a quick choice. When he finally settled on one who appeared to be the youngest and friendliest, the three of us sat around a small table. The hostess who wrote made no effort to stand up when we entered, or make a play for either of us although she did smile ever so slightly as a sign of recognition when she saw me.

"How old are you?" was the first question from the bench.

"Me twenty-two," replied the girl smiling with her eyes, lips, and whole body. The lawyer was enthralled.

Much small talk passed among the three of us, most of which was totally incomprehensible to the hostess, who nevertheless held the lawyer's hand and snuggled up to him, a little closer with each new order of Saigon tea. The lawyer started to perspire and began to jabber nonsense. He didn't know what to do. It was getting late, he had to get up early the following morning, there was a curfew, but most importantly, he was very scared.

"I guess we'd better leave!" he finally exploded after making the momentous decision. He stood up, smiling broadly. The hostess held onto his arm and he slipped her an American greenback that pleased her enough to offer him a kiss on the cheek.

As we left the bar and headed towards the Rex, my new acquaintance was ecstatic. "Did you see that? Did you see that?" he said emotionally. "That girl really liked me! By golly, she even kissed me. Holy hell, what if my wife ever found out?"

And then he leaned over toward me as if to share some deep, dark military secret. "And you know what else?" he said quietly, but animatedly: "I pinched her on the ass and she didn't even mind."

TWENTY-NINE

Travel

I am not afraid to fly in helicopters, although my palms begin to sweat in airplanes at the first sign of turbulence. I have no explanation for this gift of feeling safe in a sometimes unsafe situation except that in Vietnam, disregarding existing facts and evidence of which I was aware, I convinced myself that helicopters could always descend by auto-rotation. It made traveling a lot easier because I was a passenger in helicopters several times a week.

From Saigon, traveling by helicopter was the most practical way to reach Dong Tam, Cu Chi, Lai Khe, Phuoc Vihn, and several other smaller places within the Saigon perimeter. Although I made frequent trips to Long Binh and its environs by helicopter, I also traveled there by staff car, jeep, bus, or an occasional civilian vehicle. On longer trips, airplanes were the only feasible way to travel.

I do not know how many helicopter pads and landing zones there were in Vietnam but surely there were hundreds. Some were equipped with sophisticated paraphernalia; others were mere clearings in forests or swamps. The largest of all heliports was Hotel 3, whose appellation was a mystery to me. Others reflected a more personal touch. In combat areas, they usually bore the names of females or instruments of war, such as Landing

Zone Dottie or Charlotte or Bayonet. Hotel 3 was different. It was a superpad, the busiest in Vietnam, located in a corner of the world's busiest airfield on the outskirts of Saigon. Choppers landed there and took off like dragonflies, usually remaining only a few minutes. I was picked up and returned there dozens of times.

It seemed a miracle of the electronic age that the right chopper usually picked up or deposited the right person or cargo. In the case of departing individuals, we merely gave our names to the radio control operator and waited for our designated carriers. Through the windows and within the VIP lounge of Hotel 3, one was able to witness a microcosm of events taking place throughout Vietnam. There were always high-ranking officers waiting to return to their stations from whatever duty or folly had brought them to Saigon. Media people were usually present, which was not surprising inasmuch as they had easy access to military transportation. I once waited with and shared a helicopter with a young woman reporter going out for stories wearing a sleeveless blouse, miniskirt, and sandals, carrying only camera and writing pad. When I inquired about her luggage, she informed me that it would be no problem returning to Saigon by nightfall. She had always been successful. On other occasions, I saw administration officials from Washington, Pulitzer Prize winners, congressmen, senators, movie stars, professional ball players, and civilian lawyers. None of these people seemed unhappy to me. They were well fed, well paid, had interesting jobs, and the risk for them was not really great. Of course, there were also the grunts who didn't look happy going out to combat zones to replace other grunts.

Flying away from Hotel 3 was never boring. Helicopter pilots were required to remain close to the ground for a few minutes, out of the flight pattern of planes using Ton Son Nhut. That experience, in itself, was harrowing enough, but on one occasion, I was with two young pilots who took pleasure not only in shearing treetops but flying even lower between the trees. They scattered fowl to the wind, forced farmers to dive for cover, virtually touched cattle, and threatened their passenger with a heart attack. I thought perhaps these pilots were exploding with excitement after having landed at a firebase amidst a shower of mortar fire an hour or so before. They also knew that later in the day they might be required to risk their lives evacuating wounded and dying fellow Americans from combat areas. I sympathized with the Vietnamese farmers and repressed the anger within myself because I could not reproach the conduct of these young men.

On two occasions, helicopter pilots gave me opportunities to observe historic places that I would not otherwise have seen. The first was flying away from Camp Evans in August 1968. The pilot made a detour to offer me an aerial view of the ruins of Khe Sanh, where the embattled marines had been making national headlines in the earlier part of the year. Khe Sanh was then silent. The second opportunity occurred when a pilot taking me from Camp Eagle to Da Nang made a detour to allow me to see the great Citadel of Hue, laying in ruins but still beautiful after the extended battle fought there during the Tet Offensive.

Returning to Saigon by helicopter did not usually present a problem. I merely stood at a landing zone and waited for the next chopper to Saigon, or a place closer to Saigon. Occasionally, that closer location was without radio or phone communications. When transportation did not arrive before dark, I reported to the nearest military unit for aid and comfort, and waited there until the following day.

Sometimes I had the good fortune after a trial to discover that a helicopter was already scheduled for a flight to Saigon with room for an additional passenger. Often it was for the convenience of a high-ranking officer. More often than not, the officer gave me a private tour of the area over which we were flying. He pointed out firebases, locations of previous and present engagements, areas decimated by B–52s, and cheerfully bantered all the way to Saigon.

Frequently, a chopper ride was sad and depressing. One or more soldiers, recently killed, had been wrapped in green plastic bags and placed on the floor between the two stationary rows of canvas seats. On these flights, there was little banter among the passengers. Our attention was riveted to the plastic bags. Was one perhaps a young soldier who was away from home for the first time? A man with a wife and children? It was impossible to know, but I never for a moment forgot that my own position was relatively free from danger and before me were bodies of fellow Americans who had left their native land never to return. Had they been killed by the enemy? An avoidable accident, perhaps? Sometimes, I thought it best not to know.

Although I had convinced myself (for psychological reasons) that I would not be involved in an accident, the fact that they did occur was painfully brought home to me when I was peripherally involved in an incident that resulted in the death of an officer. A young psychiatrist who had testified in a case but had not yet been excused came to me during a recess requesting permission to depart before completion of the trial. He was scheduled on a flight from Saigon to Hawaii the following day that would take him to his waiting wife. I granted him permission to depart immediately. He was killed in a crash before reaching Saigon.

The return to Hotel 3 always provided a sense of relief, even though the ever present guns mounted on helicopter doorways and the military installations below were a continual reminder that Saigon was a city at war. For me, it was another mission accomplished and a few days sooner to completing my Vietnam tour. I appreciated, but felt uneasy about, the contrast between my own relatively comfortable lifestyle and that of the people who lived in the myriad little houses covered by tin roofs contiguous to each other on the river banks.

The passengers who exited from helicopters when they touched ground at Hotel 3 reflected different moods of the war. There were those coming in for the last time, having completed a tour of combat, bearing grimaces of persons who could not become detached from memories. Some were deliriously happy on their way to R&R, who quickly departed, afraid to miss connections to Hawaii, Singapore, Bangkok, Hong Kong, Sydney, Kuala Lampur, Manila, or Taiwan. High-ranking officers and others with automobiles awaiting their arrival displayed a suave, sophisticated attitude. There were also the wounded and sick coming in for treatment, prisoners under guard on their way to the Long Binh Stockade, and others, including civilians, traveling for reasons unknown to me. It all became routine, except when the long green plastic bags were removed and loaded on those dreadful trucks destined for the mortuary.

On trips to faraway locations, I usually traveled in the comfort of a U–21 eight-passenger turbojet plane. They were the property of a military airplane company in Long Binh, but controlled by the VIP section at MACV. The planes were dispatched to Ton Son Nhut early each morning to pick up and transport persons on official business to distant places within Vietnam. A simple phone call on the evening before departure was all that was usually required. Planes arrived on schedule with reserved seats. I traveled thousands of miles in these aircraft to Cam Rahn Bay, Pleiku, Nha Trang, Chu Lai, Da Nang, and other points north.

On return flights to Saigon from distant places, there was no easy access to transportation. I accepted anything available. There were usually no waiting rooms or regularly scheduled flights. Some of the better-equipped planes passing through had pressurized cabins and canvas seats; smaller planes, like the Caribou C–7, had no pressurized cabins; some had no seats whatsoever.

In Pleiku, while waiting for a flight, I saw a Caribou scheduled to transport Vietnamese elders, women, and children away from their homes, probably flying for the first time in their lives. All were seated on the floor, holding canvas straps that substituted for safety belts. They appeared to be in panic even before liftoff. Later, I read that, before landing, the wheels of that aircraft were jammed and the pilot prepared for a crash landing. The crewmaster, however, was successful in lowering the wheels manually, but only after chopping away with an ax at an area from which he could work. After a safe landing, the passengers raced for the exit, understandably swearing never to fly again. An experience such as that aggravated the tragedy of the passengers who were being forced to unknown destinations with no information about their future.

The most embarrassing and exasperating experience I had while waiting for air transportation occurred at Cam Rahn Bay after returning from a short trip to Singapore. Although I could have waited five days in Singapore for a regularly scheduled flight to Saigon, I chose to take my chances by accepting an earlier flight to Cam Rahn Bay, thinking that there would be no problem getting from there to Saigon. Most of the passengers on that flight were returning from R&R.

Upon landing at Cam Rahn Bay, I was delighted to learn that a flight to Saigon was about to depart, with space enough for passengers. Not with me on it, however. There were regulations to be followed and I was no exception. All returnees from Singapore were ordered to board buses and be taken to an area distant from the terminal. We were then herded into the largest restroom I have ever seen, with dozens of lavatories.

A sergeant entered the cavernous room and issued to everyone little packets with special soap powder and paper towels. He then proceeded to give a stern lecture on the horrors of venereal disease. He explained what precautions had to be taken, and how to use the contents of the little packets, although, he said, it was probably too late to do any good. Following the lecture, many of those who deplaned began the procedure of using the lavatories and packets, scrubbing their bodies furiously. Many, including myself, made use of neither the packets nor the gratuitous information issued to us. The exercise, however, caused many of us to miss connections to our destinations. I returned to the terminal and waited on the concrete floor until midnight when the next scheduled plane departed for Saigon. It was a joy to be "home" again even during pouring rain in the middle of the night.

CHAPTER THIRTY

Distractions

All courtrooms in Vietnam were different. Although some were simple tents also used for other purposes, improvements were made as time went by. Floors and sturdy supports were usually added. There were also makeshift structures, and buildings already in place in which a room was converted into a place of trial. When a tent was used, it was necessary to raise the side flaps because of the intense heat, day and night. During rainstorms, the flaps were dropped causing an almost unbearable combination of humidity and heat.

Improved courtrooms reflected the ingenuity of personnel in the legal offices. Often during trial, I was distracted by looking at wooden floors constructed of unmatched pieces of wood. Markings on what were crates originally destined for certain people or places were clearly visible. I assumed that smaller parts were the remains of what had been intended for, and should have been used as, pallets for storage of critical materials. In World War II, we obtained such necessities by "moonlight requisition," and I presume the troops were doing the same in Vietnam. Some courtrooms, built without engineer specifications, consisted of whatever materials were available for uprights and siding, with corrugated tin roofs.

The tables and benches never matched. Large boxes, fragile card tables, and steel desks were used as working tables. Folding chairs were the only kind available. The exception, of course, was in Long Binh where the courtroom was perfect. Generally, it was better to avoid an enclosed room with an individual air conditioner. High temperatures were easier to cope with than refrigerated air filtered through machines drowning out the sounds of voices.

The most common distraction during trials was noise. We were almost never free from the sounds of helicopters taking off or landing; of trucks and other war machines passing by; of occasional gunfire and mortar explosions; and most irritating of all, the sound of artillery constantly firing harassment and interdictment rounds into Free Fire Zones.

The problem of noise was partially solved by the ingenuity of Wayne Alley. While on a trip to Okinawa, he discovered the wireless microphone, then a novelty in Vietnam, which could be used with an FM radio to amplify sound. Thereafter, when rainstorms or other outside disturbances made hearing difficult, I positioned my FM radio close to the members of the court, and was able to speak in normal tones into the little microphone without wires. A simple solution to a disturbing problem!

The most irritating minor disturbance was peeping into the courtrooms by off-duty personnel, a totally unnecessary act because chairs were always provided for spectators. I think that peeping through canvas or siding was as irresistible to passers-by as peeping through canvas at a carnival sideshow or fence at a ball game.

In the latter part of January, it was nearly midnight in Dong Tam when the lawyers and I were participating in a lengthy session on legal matters after the members of the court had been dismissed for the evening. We were meeting on the second floor of a structure consisting of two floors and a roof supported by pilings. One crude stairway, more like a ladder on the outside of the structure, provided the only normal access to and from the second floor.

The hearing was being held during a period of almost complete stillness when a mortar shell exploded with a thunderous clap just above our heads. The court reporter removed the mask that formed a part of his recording device, screaming "That's incoming, sir!" and departed the hearing by jumping from the second floor to begin his rush to the nearest bunker. The other participants ran to the exit near the stairway, with me in the rear saying only one word, "Recess!"

We returned to the courtroom a few minutes later to find a part of the roof blasted away. Before anyone else spoke, I entered the word "Recess" for the record, followed by an explanation of what had taken place.

The headquarters of the 101st Airborne Division (Airmobile), known as the "Screaming Eagles," was located at a place called Camp Eagle north of Da Nang and close to the ancient capital of Hue when I was assigned to a case there. Units of that division had served with distinction throughout Vietnam since 1965, and remained until nearly the end of the United States' involvement there.

In the middle of an afternoon, the case at Camp Eagle was progressing slowly with only the usual minor distractions. Suddenly, without warning, loudspeakers sounded off with marches of John Philip Souza, making it impossible to hear anything but the music. I recessed the court. Then, having nothing better to do, I went outside to observe whatever celebration would be taking place.

Remnants of several companies marched by in formation. When the soldiers were in place in front of the division headquarters, members of the staff entered the temporary parade ground. Walking next to the commanding general was a lieutenant colonel who was apparently to be the honoree at the ceremony. When all participants were in proper formation, the music stopped.

Voices from the loudspeakers began to recite the accomplishments of the young lieutenant colonel who had finished his tour of duty in Vietnam and was being recognized with a parade at which he was to be decorated. His achievements were recited in detail and then the medals were presented. First, the Distinguished Service Cross, followed by a Silver Star with oak-leaf cluster, Bronze Star with V for valor and six oak-leaf clusters, two Purple Hearts, three Air Medals, and several other medals that were almost routinely given to personnel who had served honorably in Vietnam. In addition, there was a packet of medals from the Vietnamese government frequently given to officers and enlisted persons who had served with the ARVN forces.

The citations convinced me that this particular officer deserved every medal awarded to him. I feel today, however, that the plethora of medals awarded, especially Air Medals to nonflyers and Purple Hearts to some who were only slightly injured in noncombat situations, diminished the meaning of the awards to those who truly deserved them.

After leaving Camp Eagle, I flew to Lai Khe where a court-martial was again disrupted during a rather routine case. A crowd had gathered about fifty yards away and seemed to be growing as it moved towards the headquarters building. Not only did the commotion disturb the proceedings but curiosity overcame my composure, so I called a recess and joined the crowd.

In the center of the group, standing taller than everyone else, was a regimental commander holding the arm of a wiry little Vietnamese man wearing very little clothing. I was informed that the Vietnamese was a captured Viet Cong being brought to intelligence for interrogation. South Vietnamese and American soldiers armed with M–16 rifles and hand grenades were guarding the little man. I presumed they were his captors.

I have often wondered about the function of that alleged Viet Cong. Perhaps he was responsible for killing American soldiers, or blowing up American helicopters, or perhaps a simple soldier awaiting an opportunity to strike a blow for his cause. Or, just by the slightest coincidence, he may have been a simple rice farmer with no allegiances.

A more severe disturbance occurred at a different place when rapid rifle fire was heard just outside the division compound. I recessed the court and walked a hundred yards or so where I was told that several Viet Cong soldiers had been sighted by guards on the perimeter, and a firefight ensued. Reinforcements from within the compound provided immediate relief and the enemy was quickly subdued. A few minutes later, rifle fire was detected from a house in a nearby village. Division artillery quickly silenced the presumed attack on the installation by destroying the house from which the fire came. Several civilians were killed.

That evening, a Vietnamese woman came to the base camp with heart-wrenching cries complaining that several members of her extended family had been killed in the attack during the afternoon. She received little sympathy.

"Was it necessary to respond with artillery fire into a house within the village?" I asked a division staff officer during cocktail hour at the general's mess.

"Of course it was! People like you are not combat-oriented and do not understand these things," he replied blandly. Then, for emphasis, "We have authority under the Rules of Engagement to use whatever firepower is necessary to silence the enemy."

Colonel George S. Patton III, the Commanding Officer of the 11th Armored Cavalry Regiment, was the senior member appointed to a court at Plantation on which I was the military judge. As such, he was president of the court, whose functions included such duties as announcing findings and sentence, but his vote was no more important than any other member's. As a matter of courtesy, however, he was consulted as to the time for convening the court. For this particular trial, all members and officers of the court were present at the prescribed time. But the accused, who had been confined to the Long Binh Stockade and had no control of his whereabouts, was not present.

Colonel Patton, who had a reputation not unlike his father's, was standing with other court members outside the courtroom about thirty yards from the legal office where I was waiting. Twenty minutes past trial time, Colonel Patton demanded in a loud voice, "What's going on here? Doesn't anyone know there's a war going on?" I sent word that the delay was unavoidable.

When the accused and his guards finally appeared, all participants except the court members entered the courtroom to arrange ourselves properly for the proceedings. When the members were called into the courtroom, Colonel Patton was the first to enter. He gave no impression of being anything but compliant with the rules of military legal procedure. He did not even complain about having to lay aside his pistol.

The defense counsel, when exercising his right to a preemptory challenge, stood up and courteously but firmly announced: "The defense respectfully challenges Colonel Patton!"

A few years later I met General Patton, who since the trial at Plantation had been promoted, in the officers' mess in Nuremberg, Germany. We discussed the case in Vietnam on which we had both been assigned. After thinking a while, he told me: "You know, that defense counsel should never have challenged me. I am the best friend a GI ever had!"

On New Year's Eve, Lieutenant Colonel Hugh Clausen and I were awaiting 1969 in his trailer at Lai Khe, reminiscing about years we spent together in prior assignments. At the stroke of midnight, artillery and rifle fire led us to believe that either Viet Cong or North Vietnamese troops were taking this opportunity to break through the defense perimeter. We took cover in the nearest bunker, but soon realized that what we heard was "friendly" fire being expended by American soldiers on duty ringing in the New Year with the hope, no doubt, that this would be their last in Vietnam.

CHAPTER THIRTY-ONE

Friends

One of the compensations for traveling to combat areas was the opportunity to meet so many lawyers assigned to the legal offices throughout Vietnam. They advised their superiors, gave legal assistance to civilian and military personnel, settled claims, and helped troubled soldiers in and out of combat. It was especially pleasant to work with younger counsel who prosecuted and defended the cases to which I was assigned.

Occasionally, while watching television or reading newspapers, I recognize the names of many Vietnam veteran lawyers whom I knew and who have since become prominent. Some have written books referring to cases in which we both participated; many have become judges; some law professors; several promoted to generals; and a few prosecutors and defense counsel have achieved national attention. Wayne Alley, with whom I spent many delightful hours in Saigon, became, in turn, a general, dean of the University of Oklahoma Law School, and is currently a United States District Court judge in Oklahoma.

There was one captain from the Americal division, however, who made more than a fleeting appearance on the national scene during the Watergate period. I do not remember Captain Donald Segretti from Chu Lai, but he did participate in several of the cases tried while I was there and I am sure that we shared meals and otherwise passed time together when court was not in session. He did not stand out among, above, or below the others. I do, however, remember him quite well from a trip we later took together to Cam Ranh Bay, the largest protected natural harbor in South Vietnam.

Captain Segretti was the appointed defense counsel and I was the appointed military judge on two cases scheduled for trial at Cam Ranh Bay early in 1969. The cases were convened by the commanding general of the Engineer Command in Long Binh, but since the incidents occurred in Cam Ranh Bay and the witnesses lived there, the trials were held at that location. Captain Segretti and I traveled by helicopter from Long Binh and were met at our destination by Captain Juan Figuero, the senior judge advocate there. Acting as a representative of his commanding general, Figuero took great pains to make our stay interesting, instructive, and comfortable. He guided us immediately on a tour of the base, which had previously been used by French and Japanese naval forces but was being developed into an even larger seaport by the Americans. He then brought us to our assigned quarters, a new house trailer that we had to ourselves.

Both of the cases tried at the Cam Rahn Bay were guilty pleas, which meant that each could be disposed of in three or four hours. Furthermore, they were tried on successive mornings, leaving us much free time to ourselves. The prosecutor was a lawyer from Captain Figuero's office who returned to his duties immediately upon completion of each of the cases. Segretti and I visited the Post Exchange, spent an afternoon on the beach, and took a boat tour around the harbor.

On one memorable evening, Figuero took us to the officers' club overlooking the South China Sea. A rock-and-roll group called The Surferers was playing music unfamiliar to me but appropriate to the taste of a younger generation, represented by most of the persons there. (It was only recently, when reading letters written from Vietnam, that I learned the correct name of the musical group. I had, for many years, been under the impression that it was the Beach Boys.) The few women present, special services workers and female members of the armed forces, had little time to themselves, with pressures for dancing partners being made by the men who greatly outnumbered them. The audience was a happy one and most of the patrons gyrated to the music, even those without partners.

During an intermission, someone told members of the band that a judge was in the audience. One of them, feeling happy, joined us, treating me as his best friend. He told me that the group was renting a villa in Saigon, surrounded by a very large wall, and I should visit them when I had an opportunity, it was perfectly safe. For what? I thought. The young man wrote his Saigon address for me on a napkin in a clear, bold hand. When the music resumed, my mood mellowed, perhaps due to the flattering visit by the musician. I began to enjoy the party and, when it ended, I invited The Surferers to join me and Captain Segretti at our quarters. They accepted, and we continued to celebrate there, but in a more subdued atmosphere. (My meeting with The Surferers was nothing compared to Wayne's having dined with Gypsy Rose Lee and Pat O'Brien.)

I probably would have forgotten Segretti's name had it not been for the notoriety that came to him later. Even after I read about him, I did not recall the evening at Cam Ranh Bay as being particularly remarkable. A couple of years ago, however, at a dull gathering, I related the incident as part of a rather mundane conversation. A friend of mine thought it was a remarkable story. "Jack," he said, "you were boozing it up with Donald Segretti and a rock-and-roll band on a moonlit night at Cam Ranh Bay in the midst of a war? It's surreal." When he put it that way, I thought that perhaps it was, but Cam Ranh Bay was a pretty safe place to be. President Johnson himself had visited there two years before.

CHAPTER THIRTY-TWO

Billy Bates

Billy Bates was a patriotic young man, the son of a patriotic father who, himself, had already served a tour of combat duty in Vietnam. Billy volunteered for the army when he was seventeen years old. After training in the United States, he had performed very well in Vietnam during five tortuous months there, until the night before his nineteenth birthday.

Billy was a member of the First Cavalry Division when its headquarters was stationed in Phuoc Vinh. It was there that I went for his trial in March 1969. Upon arrival at the headquarters compound, I introduced myself to the newly assigned staff judge advocate, Lieutenant Colonel Ben Stanley, whom I had never met. He was polite in a strictly formal manner, giving me the impression that he thought he should be able to handle his own disciplinary problems without the assistance of a military judge. Within a few minutes after our introduction, he excused himself, indicating that it was time to meet with other staff officers before dinner at the general's mess.

After my own dinner with two friends from the division, I returned to the legal office to review the file in the case of Corporal William P. Bates. The evidence indicated that on the evening of February 22, 1969, Bates had been ordered by his company commander to participate in a night reconnaissance mission. He refused by saying that he was afraid and would not obey the order. The order was repeated and Bates again refused to comply. The commander warned Billy that he must obey or face charges of cowardly conduct, and repeated the order a third time. Bates began to cry and refused again. On the following day, Bates apologized to his company commander, saying that he could not understand his previous night's behavior and begged to return to combat. "Too late!" was the reply, "I gave you three chances. I can't tolerate your kind of behavior in the presence of other troops." The file included four letters from superior noncommissioned officers who were pleased with Bates's performance of duties as a soldier, especially in combat.

Corporal Bates's case upset me because I knew for a fact that most commanding officers in Vietnam would have gladly accepted his apparently sincere offer to return to combat. Not only would they have a soldier proven in battle and ready to fight again, but they would be relieved of the ordeal of having to prepare for a trial.

After reading the file, I walked over to Colonel Stanley's quarters to discuss the matter with him. I told him that, in my opinion, Bates should be given another chance and that, all things considered, he did not deserve a general court-martial.

"Listen, judge!" Stanley said icily, "This case has already been referred for trial by the commanding general and there is nothing I can do."

"Look!" I replied, "This is certainly your business and I can't interfere or do anything to stop this trial, but you know as well as I do that if you approach the general as his legal adviser, even at this late hour, he'll give you a hearing. Tell him again that Bates wants to go into combat, that he is barely nineteen years old, and that you have reconsidered your original opinion. Tell him that other noncommissioned officers have come forward to say that they want him back in the unit, which happens to be true. In my judgment, he will listen to you."

Stanley became perturbed by my remarks and said that nothing in the world would cause him to approach the general at this hour with such a proposition. Moreover, he would not himself reconsider his original decision. The soldier was a coward and deserved to be severely punished.

At the time prescribed on the following morning, all parties to the trial assumed our proper places. I looked at Bates and he responded with a nervous grin. In my opinion, the defense counsel had given him bad advice by convincing him to plead guilty, a fact that I knew in advance. I called the court to order, and, at the proper time, asked the accused: "How do you plead?"

"Guilty, sir," was the reply.

At that point, it was necessary to excuse the members of the court so that I could question Bates as to his understanding of the plea. Privately, I hoped that he would say something inconsistent so that I would have a basis to reject his plea. Legally, the court members could sentence Bates to life imprisonment, but the commanding general had agreed to disapprove any confinement in excess of four years. I thought the defense counsel could have, and the court would have done better.

"Corporal Bates," I asked, "do you know what it means to plead guilty?"

"Yes, sir."

"Do you know that by pleading guilty you are admitting that you willfully refused to obey your company commander?"

"Yes, sir."

"You don't have to plead guilty, Corporal Bates. You may plead not guilty and then the prosecutor would have to prove that you specifically intended not to go on that reconnaissance mission."

"I understand that, sir."

"On February 26th of this year, did you in fact receive an order from your commanding officer to go on a mission in combat?"

"Yes, sir."

"Did you obey that order?"

"No, sir."

"Why not?"

"Because I was scared."

"Tell me, Corporal Bates, and think about this very carefully. Why were you scared?"

"Well, sir, it's hard to say. I thought I had just about enough of combat at that time, and maybe I got especially scared because I had approval to go to Hong Kong three days later. Something told me I just couldn't make it one more time. It was the night before my nineteenth birthday."

"Did anything in particular make you scared?" I asked, hoping for some response that would have prevented his ability to form a specific intent, which was a required element of the offense of willful disobedience.

"Nothing in particular, sir."

"Do you know that your plea would admit that you specifically intended to disobey your commanding officer? Think about that. Was there something on your mind that may have made you confused?"

"Just what I said."

The defense counsel had him well prepared, I thought. But I would not give up so easily.

"You tell me what intent means. Use your own words."

"Well, that I did not want to go into combat that night. That I would not do what was ordered because I was scared."

"Were you nervous at the time? Were you perhaps not feeling well, or even had a headache or a cold?"

"No, sir, just what I said."

"Now, if I accept your plea, do you realize that, without further ado, you will be found guilty? The members of the court could then sentence you to a dishonorable discharge, forfeitures of all pay and allowances, and confinement at hard labor for life?"

I thought that might scare him, but he knew, pursuant to his agreement to plead guilty, the convening authority would not approve any amount of confinement in excess of four years.

"I understand all of that, sir."

I had no choice but to accept the plea. The court members were recalled to the courtroom (tent) and, after informing the court that I had accepted the accused's guilty plea, the defense had an opportunity to present matters in extenuation and mitigation.

The platoon sergeant who had been with Bates since his arrival in Vietnam testified that they had been out together on a few long-range reconnaissance missions. Bates had been reliable, uncomplaining, and faithful to the missions. He had participated bravely in at least three firefights with the Viet Cong or soldiers from the North Vietnamese Regular Army.

Corporal Bates's first sergeant testified that he knew the accused since his arrival in the company five or six months ago; that he was a good soldier; never a troublemaker; and although he was not a born leader, fitted in well with the members of his unit. There had been no disciplinary problems prior to February 22 when he witnessed the incident between the accused and his company commander. He "felt sorry" for Bates and did not feel that prison would serve any purpose. He would be happy to have Bates back, serving in his company.

Corporal Bates took the witness stand to testify in his own behalf. He merely talked about his childhood, schooling, and military experience. He did not go into details of the case or the nature of the combat he had participated in. I thought that the defense counsel should have prepared the accused for a better presentation.

The defense counsel then made what I considered to be a rather lethargic statement on the accused's behalf. He repeated what Bates and the sergeants had already made known to the court, and added a request for mercy. He made no impassioned plea as I had heard in almost every other case in Vietnam. I had a feeling that the defense counsel thought he had already done as much as he could by obtaining an agreement from the convening authority to approve no more than four years confinement in the case, which was a lot less than life imprisonment.

After advising the court of the maximum authorized sentence and other routine instructions about voting, we adjourned. Everyone except the members left the courtroom and wandered about outside to await the sentence of the court.

As the court deliberated, I saw Bates standing under a tree with one of the sergeants who had testified in his behalf, neither of them speaking. I walked over to him and made a casual introduction and some small talk. The nervous grin remained. He spoke only when I asked about his family.

"My father would kill me if he saw me now," Bates replied. "He was in Korea and a master sergeant here in Vietnam as an adviser in 1963. He has a wall full of medals and citations. He wanted me to volunteer for the army and Vietnam even before I graduated from high school. I did that. I think he wanted me to be a hero like he was."

"Well," I answered, "from your record, I'd say you did very well in Vietnam; probably saw a lot more enemy action here than he did."

"I sure did try to be a good soldier, for my father's sake," he replied. "I killed some gooks one night on a mission and got shot at a lot. I was even helpful in saving the lives of two guys in my platoon who were hit by Charlie. The platoon sergeant put me in for a medal before all this mess happened."

"Where is your father now?" I asked.

"He is still in the army at Fort Bragg."

"Would you like me to write a letter to him?"

"No, sir. I don't know what to do. I don't want him to find out about this court-martial. But I don't know how to keep it from him."

I told Bates that I had asked the staff judge advocate to try to have the case dismissed before it went to trial, but to no avail. I added that, in my opinion, he deserved a break. I could not offer him much consolation except to inform him that his case was subject to automatic appeal and there was a good chance for reduction of the sentence, even below four years confinement, if the convening authority approved that much.

"Thank you, sir," he replied sadly. The nervous grin remained on his face indicating to me that he was not consoled by my attempted words of encouragement. He was convinced he was doomed to be thrown out of the army and serve a long time in prison.

I was upset by the entire proceedings against Bates. I knew that almost any other commander in Vietnam would gladly have accepted his apology and offer to return to combat, if for no other reason than to avoid the paperwork of preparing for a trial. Disobedience of orders under existing pressures was not an unusual occurrence, but intelligent commanders and sergeants, more often than not, diplomatically handled the situation when the offender had a good record, apologized for his conduct, and offered to return to combat.

The prosecutor and defense counsel were sitting under a nearby tree as I was speaking to Bates. When my conversation with him ended, I approached the defense counsel and asked to speak to him alone. He stood up and we moved out of hearing of all others in the vicinity.

"Captain," I asked politely, "how long have you been in Vietnam?"

"Three weeks, sir. This is only my second case here."

"How long were you in the army before coming to Vietnam?"

"Ever since my graduation from law school a little over a year ago."

"What did you do in the army before coming to Vietnam?"

"Well, first I went to the basic course at the Judge Advocate General's School in Charlottesville for three months and then spent about eight months at Fort Carson trying and defending cases, as well as giving legal assistance. I volunteered to come to Vietnam as a career move."

"Captain, may I offer you a suggestion?" I asked.

"Of course."

"First of all," I said, "remember that this is a personal matter and has nothing to do with your performance of duty or career plans. You speak very well, have a good education, and I know that you are a good lawyer."

"Thank you, sir."

"It's about the case we're all involved in now," I said. "Look at Bates over there, standing alone, without even a guard. That's unusual and reflects a certain amount of trust by his superiors, don't you think?"

"Yes, sir."

"I've tried many cases in Vietnam and this is only the second time I've seen an accused at trial without a guard. What I would suggest is that you take a personal interest in the appellate process of this case. I am convinced you can get the sentence of this court, whatever it may be, reduced. You probably won't have much luck at the division here, but write a brief to the Court of Review in Washington, and, if necessary, to the United States Court of Military Appeals. Emphasize everything you already know about the case and talk to Bates to find out more about his life and especially his service in Vietnam. Nothing in the world will be gained by his imprisonment or discharge, as you yourself implied in court. Personally, I feel that he should not be punished at all. Argue that the sentence, whatever it might be, is inappropriate. Would you be willing to do that?"

Looking at the accused still standing under a tree alone, the defense counsel answered: "Sir, I will do all that. I will even ask for a conference with the commanding general here before he takes action on the case."

"Thank you," I replied, "and remember, this is just a suggestion."

The accused was sentenced to be discharged from the army with a bad conduct discharge and to be confined at hard labor for four years, the exact amount stated in the pretrial agreement.

The defense counsel visited the commanding general, requesting that he approve an amount of confinement even less than four years, but without success. He then wrote a brief to the Court of Military Review in Washington where the case would be reviewed from a different perspective, away from combat. The court affirmed the findings of the case but no part of the sentence. Bates was therefore restored to duty without further confinement after the court's action.

I don't know what happened to Bates since the Court of Military Review restored him to duty and I did not have contact with him at all after our conversation under the tree at Phuoc Vinh. I do know, however, that because of my suggestion to his counsel, he was not discharged from the army for refusing to fight one evening in Vietnam. I sincerely believe that whatever service he performed after the Court of Review's decision was pleasing to his father. I also feel that the young defense counsel, who was then about twenty-three, may have learned a lesson that will benefit him throughout the career he was so interested in.

Several years ago, while visiting the Pentagon, I passed the office of Colonel Ben Stanley. He had just returned from lunch at the Pentagon Officer's Athletic Club and was sitting with his feet on the desk, eating popcorn. I recognized only his name and knew that he would not remember me, but I dropped in to chat awhile and introduce myself.

"Do you remember that nineteen-year-old combat veteran who refused to fight one night and was sentenced in Phuoc Vinh to four years confinement?" I asked.

"No," he replied, "but it was tough to teach some of those little bastards how to fight."

CHAPTER THIRTY-THREE

Bearcat

Specialist Fourth Class Mark Saunders loved the area surrounding the village of An Loi and the American installation there, Camp Martin Cox, more commonly referred to as Bearcat. In late 1965, Saunders enlisted in the army, passing all required examinations, physical and mental, although he had only a ninth-grade education. He volunteered for Vietnam and was assigned to a unit in Bearcat during most of 1966. While there, and later during his second tour, he was adept at telling stories, usually casting himself as hero. He told acquaintances that he was a champion boxer with the local YMCA midgets, participated in gang fights, argued with his minister, and accomplished other feats of perceived importance. He was not a bit shy about shading the truth. Those who knew him thought he was a grandstander, and did not want to be his close friend. Most, in fact, considered him a bore. When assigned to Bearcat, he managed to rise to the rank of specialist fourth class, but his request for an extension there was denied.

Saunders did manage to return to Vietnam with help from his congressman (he said) in the early part of 1968 and, as luck would have it, was assigned as a tire repairman to the 169th Engineer Battalion at Long Binh, which was close enough to

Bearcat for him to visit there frequently. After returning from such visits, he told acquaintances that he had been visiting old friends in An Loi and roaming forests that he was familiar with, eating wild fruit, and observing nature.

Almost everyone in Saunders's unit knew that he had a dangerous knife. He told them that it had been discarded by the mess hall before he fashioned it to his own needs. He also owned its leather scabbard, which he had made at the hobby shop. His favorite pastime after duty hours was working on his knife, sharpening it and forming the top six wooden inches to fit the palm of his right hand. The finished knife was fifteen inches long with a broad nine-inch blade. He knew that the possession of knives with blades longer than five inches was forbidden by MACV regulations. When Saunders went off on his journeys around Bearcat, he took both his assigned M–14 rifle and his knife, the latter inside its scabbard, attached to his web belt.

On June 4, 1968, Saunders visited An Loi as was his custom on nonworking days, in possession of both his rifle and knife. He approached a group of elderly gentlemen, including Mr. Nguyen Van Ky, tied the latter's hands behind his back, and forced him at gunpoint into the tall elephant grass outside the village. When they parted, Mr. Ky was still tied and either dead or in the process of dying from three stab wounds, one in the middle of his heart.

The criminal investigation department at Bearcat began an intense search for the person last seen with Ky. Descriptions of the suspect were provided by Ky's friends who were with him at the time of his capture in An Loi. Weeks passed with no success. Then, unexpectedly on July 2, Saunders walked into the Military Police Station at Bearcat to report a Korean civilian who had irritated him by driving erratically. He seemed self-assured and proud when he entered the station to make his report of a vehicle violation.

The military policeman on duty casually took note of the wooden handle protruding from Saunders' scabbard, but was unconcerned until he recognized features of the person described in an all points bulletin, who was wanted on suspicion of murder. The MP called Mr. Alfred Paul, a criminal investigator, who took Saunders into his office for questioning.

After complying with the requirements of military and civilian law with respect to confessions and statements, Saunders agreed to talk. For three hours he denied all knowledge of Ky's death, but after the investigator confiscated Saunders' illegal knife, he began to cry and changed his story. He admitted lying before and said that he was now ready to tell the truth.

Yes, Saunders said, he was in An Loi on the afternoon of June 4, but that was not the first time. He was also there on May 20 looking for a girlfriend from the old days, but could not find her. After failing to find the girl or other old friends, he decided to walk in the woods to watch animals, eat fruit, and observe nature. While in the woods, he stumbled into an area where several friendly Thai soldiers on duty at a guard post "were attacked by five Viet Cong guerrillas." Saunders hid in the tall grass but was seen by one of the Viet Cong, who looked him squarely in the eye and fired at him, too, but missed. He did not return the fire.

On June 4, the date of Mr. Ky's death, Saunders continued in his statement to Mr. Paul, he was again in An Loi looking for old friends. While walking around, he noticed a group of Vietnamese men, casually talking, each in possession of hand tools. He immediately recognized one of them as "the Viet Cong who fired at me" a couple of weeks earlier. He instinctively approached the group, wrote the letters *MP* in the palm of his hand and demanded identification from the man he said he recognized. The man complied. But even with proper identification, Saunders was still convinced that he was the one who had fired at him. Therefore, he felt it was his duty as an American soldier to arrest the Viet Cong and take him to the authorities at Bearcat. He tied the man's hands behind his back with a string from his pocket he always carried when going into woods or forests. Then, using his M–14 as an enforcer, he ordered the man to follow his commands. In order to avoid the stares and contemptuous comments of the villagers, Saunders decided not to go directly to Bearcat but take the man there on a path with which he was familiar, through the woods with tall elephant grass.

While walking through the forest, Saunders continued, they came upon a log used as a bridge to cross a mudhole. The VC crossed without difficulty, but he himself slipped and his rifle fell into the mud. The VC, with hands still tied, ran away. Saunders got up without his rifle, chased his prisoner until he caught him and they both fell to the ground. Ky got up first and jumped on him, so he removed his knife from the scabbard and held it upright. Ky threw himself upon Saunders, again apparently not seeing the knife, and it went to his stomach. Despite the wound, Ky continued to jump, and twice more the weapon entered his body. The VC fell on his back, gurgling and making funny noises. Without knowing whether Ky was alive or dead, Saunders left the scene.

"Why didn't you report this incident when it happened?" Mr. Paul wanted to know.

"What good would it have done?" Saunders answered. "I knew someone would find him eventually."

Mr. Paul arranged for Saunders to be placed in custody until he could be returned to his unit. If there was some doubt about the homicide, there was none about the illegal weapon.

At the pretrial investigation, the Vietnamese men who were with Ky on June 4 identified the accused. Four soldiers who lived in the same tent with Saunders gave accounts of his general behavior and of conversations with him about the events of June 4. Each had seen the knife and witnessed the attention that the accused had given to its care. Two had observed Saunders carving the handle. It was general knowledge in the unit that Saunders repeatedly talked about his visits to Bearcat and An Loi and jaunts into woods and forests in that area. One testified that Saunders had told him that on his days off, he liked going into the woods to eat coconuts and bananas, so he needed a very strong knife.

When the trial date arrived in late September, Saunders pleaded not guilty to the charge of unpremeditated murder but guilty to possession of an illegal weapon.

Mr. Ngau Van Thieu was called as the first witness. He testified that he and Mr. Ky were both laborers who spent most of their time pulling weeds and moving rocks, working at the home of a wealthy Vietnamese. On June 4, after work, he and Ky were standing with two friends in the village square at An Loi talking, when they were approached by the accused. Saunders wrote the letters *MP* on the palm of his hand and demanded to see Ky's identification. He complied. Then, for no stated reason, the American tied Ky's hands behind his back with a thick rope that had been hanging from his web belt, and forced Ky into the nearby forest by holding a rifle to his back. Thieu ran to look for Ky's daughter and when he found her, both went into the woods to look for Ky. They found him about twenty minutes later, bleeding profusely and apparently dead. Thieu's testimony as to Ky's apprehension was corroborated by the second Vietnamese witness, Ngo Van Quan, who was one of those accosted but not forced away by the accused.

Private Louis Smith, a member of the accused's unit, testified that he saw Saunders on the night of June 4 when he returned to the tent they shared. Smith asked about something that appeared to be blood on his clothing, and Saunders told him that, fearing for his life, he killed "one of a group of 'cowboys' who jumped him" in An Loi. Smith did not believe Saunders, he told the court, because it was common knowledge that Saunders was a bullshitter. He did, however, notice Saunders cleaning what appeared to be blood from his knife later that same evening.

Corporal Jack Morris, another tentmate, testified that sometime around June 10, Saunders told him that he had killed a monkey a few days before. Morris didn't care whether or not Saunders had killed a monkey, and didn't bother to question him further; he knew the accused told so many wild stories.

Private First Class Lonnie Vasquez, the person who shared the bunk closest to the accused, testified that he had often seen

Saunders filing his knife in the evenings. As he did so, he talked continuously to whomever would listen. On one occasion, Saunders told him that he used a knife to kill turkeys, bears, and deer in Virginia. On another occasion, in early June, Saunders told him that when he was last in An Loi, he went for the purpose of visiting a short-time house. As Saunders was leaving, a papasan jumped on him and beat him with a stick. He then stabbed the papasan in self-defense and ran away. Vasquez did not know whether to believe the story and did not pursue the matter because the accused was well known for his tall tales.

The trial counsel then read the following stipulation:

> The prosecution and defense, with the consent of the accused, stipulate that the following facts are true: First, Mr. Nguyen Van Ky died on June 4, 1968. Second, the accused had no authority to apprehend any civilian in Vietnam. Third, when Mr. Ky's daughter found her father bleeding in the woods on the day he died, she fainted and had to be carried back into the village. She remained unstable since that time and is not physically able to appear in court today as a witness.

Mr. Paul, the criminal investigator who interrogated Saunders on July 2, testified that he properly explained to the accused his rights under the Fifth Amendment to the United States Constitution and appropriate United States Supreme Court decisions. The statement was introduced into evidence without objection. Mr. Paul then testified that he was quite surprised when he learned that Saunders boldly walked into the MP station, especially since an all-points bulletin had been issued and American and Vietnamese police had been searching for the person who killed Mr. Ky for over three weeks.

The defense counsel began the presentation of his case by stipulating, with the consent of the trial counsel, that Specialist Saunders had been committed to a correctional institute for a year by his parents when he was twelve years old and had received psychiatric treatment during that entire time.

Saunders chose to testify in his own behalf. He began by stating that he was a nature lover and had always liked walking in the woods and forests. On his previous assignment to Bearcat, he had taken dozens of pictures of trees, plants, elephant grass, and animals as well as people and buildings in An Loi. He developed the habit at that time of walking around neighboring villages and forests and was therefore thrilled to be assigned on his second tour in Vietnam to Long Binh. He could easily hitch rides from one place to the other.

Saunders acknowledged that he had previously made several inconsistent and exaggerated statements. He explained that he was always nervous when speaking to superior officers, especially Mr. Paul, who had informed him that he was suspected of murder. He only began to talk about the incident because he could not control his crying. As for statements to his tentmates, he was just "shooting the breeze."

During his testimony, Saunders swore that he was in An Loi on June 4 and had gone there to visit a girlfriend whom he had known during his previous tour of duty at Bearcat. Since she was not home, he walked around the village he loved so much when he saw the man he recognized as a VC who, during a firefight a couple of weeks before, had shot at him. He was positive the man was a Viet Cong guerrilla. This was an opportunity to do something really courageous for his country, since he did not otherwise have such an opportunity, working as he did in the tire shop at Long Binh.

Saunders further testified that he tied the Viet Cong's hands behind his back, but only with string he casually removed from a hammock at the home of his former girlfriend. His intention was to take the prisoner to the proper authorities at Bearcat as an enemy of the people. From past wanderings, he knew a path to the compound through the woods. He treated the VC with great respect by walking twenty paces behind him and holding his rifle on his shoulder as if he was going coon hunting.

The accused continued his testimony by saying that, while walking, he and the VC came across a shallow wet spot in the woods that had to be crossed by walking over a log. The VC crossed without mishap, but he himself felt wobbly on the log and fell into the mud. The prisoner ran away, so he got out of the mud to chase him, leaving his rifle behind. When he caught up with Ky, they both fell to the ground. The VC was quicker than he was, and jumped up and down on his body. He explained graphically:

> He jumped on my face. I couldn't see and then he kicked me in the nuts three or four times. He was like a wild animal on top of me, kicking me in the groin. My temples got to hurting real bad and I couldn't bear the pain. I was getting weak when I remembered I had my knife with me. I pulled it out of the scabbard and lunged forward four or five times knowing that this man had to be stopped or he would have killed me. He fell to the ground. It took about fifteen minutes until I could get my strength back. I could hardly see. I ran away. It was really self-defense, sirs.

On cross-examination, when the trial counsel asked why he liked the area around Bearcat so much, and carried a knife when he went there, the accused responded, "I liked my days off. I liked going down in the woods, eating coconuts and bananas, and I needed a knife, but yet I needed a hatchet for breaking coconuts, so I fashioned me a knife heavy enough to do the job of both ax and knife."

The prosecution and defense made vigorous arguments, the prosecution emphasizing that the accused admitted stabbing the victim and was never consistent in explaining why he did so. There was neither reason nor authority for taking the man into custody. What Saunders did was a deliberate, unauthorized act, even if done in the heat of passion. His action was unwarranted and he was guilty as charged. Moreover, if he indeed thought he was doing a courageous act for his country and was without criminal responsibility, he should have reported the incident immediately to the authorities at Bearcat.

The defense counsel was almost tearful when he spoke of the evidence the accused presented in court. Saunders had fallen to the ground and was being attacked viciously. He was blinded, in pain, and fearful for his life. He was indeed unable to save his life other than acting as he did. The action he took was the only way out of a bad situation.

The court found the accused not guilty of the homicide charge, but guilty of carrying an illegal weapon, as they were required to do because of the plea. He was sentenced to confinement at hard labor for nine months but was not discharged from the army.

I was disappointed with the court's verdict, although I could not express that disappointment. It was my belief that Saunders was not speaking the truth when explaining the events of June 4, and that he was guilty of murder. He testified with a boastful attitude and showed no remorse for Mr. Ky's death. I was convinced that if the victim had been a United States citizen, Saunders would have been found guilty as charged.

The case of Specialist Saunders was reported by a member of the Associated Press, who filed the story shortly after the sentence was announced. My family in Louisiana read about it the very next day. Indeed, the Vietnam War was one in which the American public was living, at least vicariously, close to the action.

CHAPTER THIRTY-FOUR

Lawyers, Clients, and Culture

There were approximately one hundred United States Army lawyers in Vietnam at any one time during 1968–1969. Each of the thirteen headquarters that exercised general court-martial jurisdiction had a staff judge advocate with full compliment of assistants to perform legal duties within the command. These duties included preparation of and participation in trials, supervision of all disciplinary matters, giving legal assistance, adjudicating claims, settling foreign claims by Vietnamese civilians and their government, and other legal matters impossible to anticipate. Smaller organizations such as the Port Command in Saigon also had legal departments with fewer lawyers.

In order to become an army lawyer commissioned as a captain in the Judge Advocate General's Corps, it was necessary to have graduated from an accredited law school in the United States and to have been admitted to practice before the highest court of a state within the United States. Acceptance in the corps was not a routine matter, inasmuch as there were more applicants than available positions. Most army lawyers in Vietnam were of a rank higher than captain and had served in the army for as much as twenty years, many of them in Korea and World War II. Some had extensive practice in civilian life.

Military judges were selected on the basis of merit and past service. In Vietnam, Lieutenant Colonel Alley, with twelve years service, including time as an instructor at the Judge Advocate General's School in Charlottesville, Virginia, had served the least amount of time. Colonel Tobin, the oldest and most experienced, had served in almost every position available to a judge advocate officer during the previous twenty-one years. I had been a civilian and army lawyer for eighteen years.

A military lawyer was assigned to represent a soldier or officer as soon as he became a suspect, but the accused could request any other military counsel who was reasonably available to represent him free of charge, as well as hire civilian counsel if he so desired. It was unfortunate that some servicemen and their families distrusted military lawyers in Vietnam as counsel. The United States Court of Military Appeals carefully monitored the trial of cases and had pioneered the rules that led to the United States Supreme Court decision in *Miranda v. Arizona*.

Civilian lawyers from the United States frequently came to Vietnam for the purpose of defending servicemen. My experience was that those lawyers offered no more, and sometimes less, to the defendant than military lawyers who were already in Vietnam, and had expended much time in the preparation of the cases. They often traveled great distances to interview clients confined in the Long Binh Stockade and other witnesses scattered about the country. Moreover, the army lawyers in Vietnam, having no family or other home to return to, often spent evenings working for their clients. Preliminary work on an accused's behalf had usually been accomplished before civilian counsel arrived.

Every amenity available to a military lawyer was offered to a civilian lawyer who came from the United States to defend a client. He was met in Saigon by military personnel, furnished necessary transportation and quarters, and escorted in military aircraft to the place of trial.

In December, a civilian lawyer named Roger Rogers, who had come to Vietnam to act as defense counsel in a particular case, was quartered in the Rex Hotel, where I was living. I had not met him, but others had made arrangements for us to share ground and air transportation to Dong Tam on the date of trial.

I met Mr. Rogers by chance at breakfast on the roof of the hotel, shortly before departure. He mentioned to me that he was taking the case at great expense to himself only because he was a friend of the accused's father, with whom he played golf regularly. He was gregarious and obviously enjoying the experience of being in Vietnam. On the way to the helicopter pad at Ton Son Nhut, he spoke without pause, commenting about the people, the horrendous traffic, and whatever else he observed, especially the presidential palace and the sight near the Notre Dame Cathedral where a Buddhist monk had immolated himself in 1963.

Most aircraft used to transport passengers to places not far from the Saigon area were UH–1 Huey helicopters that carried as many as eight passengers. The chopper waiting for us, however, was a much smaller Cayuse, an egg-shaped aircraft capable of carrying only four persons, including the pilot. The pilot and front passenger were relatively comfortable, but the rear space, resembling the shape of the smaller portion of an egg, was a tight squeeze for two people. Since helicopters in Vietnam were not equipped with doors, one or both passengers in the rear of a Cayuse usually found it more comfortable to keep one leg on the outside of the aircraft.

When Mr. Rogers saw the little chopper, surrounded by dozens of large warships, he blanched, assuming that I would be sitting next to the pilot. He made no objection but became absolutely silent, losing his composure and enthusiasm for the adventure. Seeing his distress, I said to him, "Mr. Rogers, I am about to do a great favor for you."

"How's that?" he remarked without a smile.

"You may ride in the large seat beside the pilot," I said, whereupon his ebullient mood returned. I mention this small and seemingly inconsequential incident only to reflect our concern for the safety and comfort of visiting civilian lawyers.

Mr. Rogers met his client for the first time shortly after our arrival in Dong Tam, two hours before the trial was scheduled to begin. He was offered, but did not accept, the opportunity to have additional time to talk to his client and further prepare the case. He had, as was customary, been previously furnished with all the allied papers in the case.

The accused in Mr. Rogers's case was charged with premeditated murder and there were many important issues of law and fact that had to be decided during trial. The accused and a fellow soldier, both on guard duty, had become involved in a heated dispute over an insignificant matter. Each threatened the other, but the accused fired his weapon at and killed his companion, who had drawn a switch-blade knife from his pocket. There were issues of premeditation, intoxication, self-defense, and lesser included offenses to be decided during the period of trial. Both the prosecutor and military defense counsel were thoroughly prepared.

Except for introducing himself, Mr. Rogers did not address either the court members or me during the trial, although he frequently whispered comments to his cocounsel. The accused was acquitted. In my opinion, it was the convincing closing argument of military defense counsel that tipped the balance in favor of the accused.

After his return to the United States, Mr. Rogers wrote gracious letters to me and others connected with the case, thanking us for the assistance we had given him. In his letter to me, he mentioned that he was scheduled to address students from the state university law school on the subject of military justice, with particular emphasis on his experience in Vietnam.

General courts-martial, even when tried under adverse conditions in Vietnam, were conducted according to standards equal, if not superior to, trials in civilian courts in the United States. Common law rules of evidence and strict rules of procedure required by the *Manual for Courts-Martial* were applied. Witnesses requested by the defense were called from wherever they might be, including combat; some were held over in Vietnam beyond their scheduled dates to rotate home; others were returned from the United States.

The trial of a general court-martial was recorded verbatim and the accused furnished a copy of the transcript. The record was reviewed by the commander who convened the court and later by the Court of Military Review in Washington, where counsel was also provided for the accused. Finally, appeal was available to the United States Court of Military Appeals, which consisted of three civilian judges appointed by the president, and comparable to a United States Circuit Court of Appeals.

The conditions under which the United States entered and fought the war in Vietnam were factors in the behavior of the American forces. Young soldiers could hardly be expected to understand a culture that the architects of the war did not understand. Those men with keen and analytical minds did not believe that our armed forces, possessing such great planes, tanks, and other implements of war, could possibly lose to a group of people who used pieces of old rubber tires as shoes to fight in the jungle. Neither Washington officials nor good soldiers could understand that the Vietnamese people fought foreign invaders and even civil wars to preserve their culture for over two thousand years.

In 1954, the last of the foreign invaders, the French, learned that they could not destroy the will of the Vietnamese people and departed in disgrace. The United States then attempted to do what the French could not do. The ordinary soldier did not understand that he was participating in a futile effort to preserve what was euphemistically known as the doctrine of containment.

Soldiers in Vietnam referred to the United States as the real world. To them, it was a world where things were as they should be. Vietnam was indeed a different world. In 1964, the entire Congress of the United States, with the exception of two senators, gave its approval, in the Gulf of Tonkin Resolution, for the president to act freely in determining who the enemy was and how the enemy could be destroyed. The president was exercising that prerogative.

In the months between November 1963 and July 1965, the political and military leadership in Saigon was in shambles, but we took it upon ourselves to solve their problems. The number of

American fighting men rose exponentially until it exceeded one-half million in 1968, when over two hundred young men were being killed every week. The people in the United States were becoming agitated, but Congress continued to furnish the president with the funding required to continue the killing. The administration depended upon the fighting men to do that.

Although there were crimes committed in Vietnam by American servicemen, they were few in number compared to crimes committed in cities the size of Denver or Seattle where the number of citizens was similar to the number of servicemen in Vietnam. Moreover, most of the crimes committed in Vietnam were of a military nature.

About twelve percent of the servicemen sent to Vietnam actually participated in combat. Those who did matured quickly and fought bravely, even beyond expectations. Wherever the enemy was encountered face to face, the Americans prevailed. During the eight years of severe fighting, young soldiers fought through cities, villages, jungles, mountains, and deltas, never certain what enemy forces might be lurking in the vicinity. It is remarkable that they accomplished so much at such tender ages. About 58,000 made the supreme sacrifice while fighting, mostly without complaint. It should be a source of great pride to loved ones to know that the soldiers in combat consistently risked their lives without question to care for their wounded or endangered comrades. Helicopter pilots did not hesitate to fly to the rescue of the wounded or stranded, regardless of the danger that accompanied their missions.

United States servicemen have traditionally been among the most likable and generous of soldiers anywhere. They played with children on the streets of the cities and in the villages. They gave out candy and chewing gum and taught kids how to throw a baseball. In Vietnam, the American servicemen visited orphanages, donated to charities, and showed other kindnesses to people less fortunate than themselves. They liked and joked with the people who worked in their offices and hooches. Boysan and mamasan were the friendliest of people. Sad to say, however, too many friendships were not based upon equality of status but rather upon a superior-inferior relationship.

It was not uncommon, even by witnesses testifying in court, to refer to Vietnamese people as gooks, dinks, slopes or other obnoxious names. The word "gook" was so common that it was used to refer even to those who worked happily and playfully for and with Americans. When the word "gook" was used, even the most sensitive of Americans in the vicinity did not blink at the use of the pejorative term.

In addition to a feeling of superiority, there was a feeling of privilege, not only by Americans stationed in Vietnam but many who came to visit, under whatever pretext that might be. Kathy told me that an aide to a United States senator, after taking her to dinner, sexually assaulted her in the hallway of the building in which she lived and then attempted to forcibly enter her apartment. When she saw him the next day in the officer's mess, he showed no remorse and casually joined her, uninvited, for breakfast.

Perhaps a reason for failure to communicate more sympathetically with Vietnamese people was the sometimes difficult task of distinguishing friend from foe. They looked alike, spoke the same language, ate the same food, and were of the same cultural background. Unfortunately, the word "enemy" has a connotation of evil and fear, and sometimes innocent Vietnamese civilians were treated as enemies with unnecessary and overzealous caution.

United States servicemen in Vietnam were well clothed, regularly paid, provided with transportation to and from exotic locations for R&R, given the best medical attention any soldiers ever had, and often furnished with more ammunition than needed. Usually, those not in combat were entertained by movies, swam in beaches and canvas swimming pools, worked regular hours, visited cities, and were armed wherever they went. Because of the status attributed to him, the feeling of authority perhaps accompanied the serviceman in uniform, and contributed to a prevailing feeling of superiority.

I have read references to use of the term "mere gook" in pub-lished works as well as having heard it myself on several occa-sions. The phrase was understood to mean that the mistreatment or even the negligent killing of a Vietnamese citizen was regarded with less concern than if the victim had been American. In the case where a sergeant shot his carbine into a group of Vietnamese civilians merely to clear the way for quick passage of his truck, a civilian was killed but the sergeant was acquitted. In Cam Rahn Bay, after the acquittal of a soldier who negligently killed three Vietnamese civilians while driving his jeep around a corner at high speed, the defense counsel casually mentioned to me later that the result of trial was application of the "mere gook" rule.

In the chapters "I Want a Body Count" and "Bearcat," included in this memoir, I have suggested that I felt at the time of trial, as I do now, that the acquittals resulted only because the victims were Vietnamese. Light sentences or acquittals for this reason alone, however, did not always result. In the case described in "Tragedy in White," the court was obviously dis-tressed by the behavior of the accused and had no sympathy for him whatsoever.

United States personnel in Vietnam, both military and civil-ian, contributed much to illegal activities that were apparent in most of the large cities. Prostitution flourished, encouraged by the American dollar. Black-market goods intended for the Post and Base Exchanges could only have been obtained with the cooperation of Americans. Wayne Alley tried a case in which an American civilian assigned to the Exchange System attempted to divert $25,000 worth of batteries in his custody to an agent of the underground. MPCs were issued as payment to United States Armed Forces personnel and those accompanying the armed forces, because the use of United States currency was prohibited by regulation in an attempt to keep dollars off the black market. MPCs were freely accepted on the black market, however, and exchanged for Vietnamese money. On the day the color of MPCs was changed, in an effort to prevent misuse of the scrip, an Amer-ican civilian lawyer in Saigon, not a part of the United States

Armed Forces, came to MACV in an attempt to exchange over $3,000 in MPCs that he had acquired illegally.

The Vietnamese people recognized the fact that sometimes justice did not prevail when they were the victims. In a village near Pleiku, a soldier shot and killed a farmer whom he "suspected of being a VC." The soldier was charged with but acquitted of manslaughter. When a colonel tried to go into the village on the following day to offer a "sympathetic" payment to the family of the deceased, the angry villagers banded together to prevent the colonel's helicopter from landing.

On my last day in Vietnam, a vehicle dispatched by the motor pool, and driven by an armed soldier, came for me at the Rex shortly after lunch. While driving down Cong Ly Boulevard on the way to the processing center at Ton Son Nhut, we came upon an empty pedicab, but there appeared to be a body beneath a sheet at its base. There was no activity at the scene other than the presence of a few onlookers. Our first concern was that an American had been assaulted by a "zapper," which occasionally happened. We stopped, and the driver rushed to the scene, raised the sheet, replaced it hurriedly and returned to the jeep. "Thank God it's a gook!" he exclaimed, as we prepared to continue our journey.

CHAPTER THIRTY-FIVE

A Week in Dong Tam

My predecessor, Dick Snyder, had advised me that I would not like Dong Tam. The place was frequently attacked by rockets; there was not much to do, no place to relax, and the heat was unbelievable. "Avoid the place if you can," he cautioned, "it's the pits."

Dick was wrong. My first visit to Dong Tam for six days was like a vacation. I arrived there on a Sunday evening, having come directly from Cu Chi, where I had been in court until noon. I had more freedom in Dong Tam than I dared hope for, and enjoyed it all except the first few minutes. The helicopter in which I was being transported experienced difficulties before landing and we descended by auto-rotation. That was certainly better than crashing, but a frightening experience nonetheless.

Dong Tam was one dusty square mile of tents and other temporary structures, surrounded by green rice paddies. American ingenuity had created the compound by dredging dirt from the Mekong Delta and using it to build a compound for the Ninth Infantry Division Headquarters, three feet higher than the surrounding marshy areas. Vietnamese peasants watched in awe as the work progressed and said that only Americans could turn a rice paddy into a desert.

Lieutenant Colonel John Webb met me at the helicopter pad. He allowed a few moments for me to recuperate from the experience of landing without a working engine. Then, apologetically, he advised me that the case scheduled for the following day was canceled, although others for the remainder of the week remained on target. It would be impracticable to make a round trip to Saigon in the time available, so I would just have to entertain myself on the following free day. Then he took me to my assigned quarters, an air-conditioned trailer mounted on the bed of a truck with no working parts. Inside was a steel cot, a lavatory, and a card table with lamp.

Colonel Webb should never have apologized. I was delighted to be alone for a change, with this wonderful gift: a day of splendid air-conditioned solitude, no phones to answer, no cases to authenticate, and no office traffic.

After refreshing myself and putting away my luggage, I went with John to the general's mess. I was told that the Vietnamese cook's daily round to local markets was responsible for making this the best eating place in Vietnam. Lobster, other delicacies from the sea, and fresh vegetables cooked to perfection were the norm rather than the exception. After dinner, I retired early to enjoy some of the reading material I always carried for just such an emergency. There was no incoming mortar fire that night.

Monday was my first completely free day since arriving in Vietnam. After breakfast, I picked up a well-thumbed copy of John Updike's *Couples* from the office and returned to my quarters, an experience so luxurious that I skipped lunch. That evening I went again to the general's mess. Unexpectedly, after dinner, excitement was provided that I could never have anticipated.

A troupe of USO entertainers was visiting Dong Tam and invited to the general's mess for dinner before their scheduled performance. Young female troupers from the group sat on each side of the commanding general as a special treat because it was his birthday. At the request of the officers, one of them presented him with a surprise gift, a small wooden elephant with the division crest embedded on its side. The general wanted to express his appreciation by kissing the young lady on her cheek but she bolted like a spooked horse. I wrote home what a shame that was, but the boss took it with gracious humor and was not offended.

The unplanned entertainment of the evening, however, came a little later. One of the other members of the troop, Ellen Brugger, had been sitting next to the Protestant chaplain, Captain Charles Gross, who was, by inclination and training, also a herpetologist. Ellen was fascinated with his stories about the care and feeding of his reticulated python, Henrietta, which Chaplain Gross kept in a footlocker at the far end of his room. Acquired in Vietnam, Henrietta was nurtured until she grew from six feet and twenty pounds to eight feet and forty pounds under the chaplain's care.

Each week, Chaplain Gross purchased a small live duck from the local village market as food for Henrietta. He tied the fowl's legs together and placed it in the python's path. A sad ending for the victim, but the duckling was already doomed at the market by whomever purchased it for food. Feeding Henrietta in this manner was the only way to satisfy her nutritional needs because, from her enclosure, she was not able to otherwise forage for food. Before the feeding, a group of curious officers and enlisted men usually gathered to witness the event. Henrietta coiled and crushed her quarry, opened her mouth, and took the offering whole.

Miss Brugger, who was dressed in a miniskirt in preparation for her performance later in the evening, became so engrossed with the chaplain's stories that she begged for and received permission from the general to allow Henrietta to be brought into the mess. When the chaplain arrived a few minutes later with the python around his shoulders and torso, Ellen was enthralled. "Could the snake be wrapped around my body?" she asked. The chaplain was dubious but consented.

Gently, very gently, Chaplain Gross wrapped Henrietta around Ellen's body. This done, he stood back to admire his accomplishment with a wide grin. The officers applauded. One who had a camera could not resist commemorating the event for posterity. Without warning, the photographer set off a flash with the snap of his shutter. Henrietta panicked and excreted on poor Miss Brugger. Worse, she began to constrict her grip on the lady. Now it was the chaplain who panicked and, I'm sure, prayed harder there in the mess than he did in the chapel on Sunday. Carefully, he cajoled and, thankfully, was successful in coaxing Henrietta to loosen her grip. He was able to transfer the snake to his own body and promptly removed her from the mess, presumably to her restraining area.

Whether the footlocker in Chaplain Gross's room was really effective enough to restrain Henrietta was a subject of much debate. There were, among the officers, both pro- and anti-Henrietta factions. On one occasion, she escaped from her confinement and writhed under a partition into a room occupied by the Catholic chaplain, who promptly fainted dead away when he saw Henrietta.

When I appeared at the legal office after breakfast on Tuesday morning, I was informed that the accused and his counsel had proposed a plea of guilty, which had been accepted only a few minutes before by the commanding general. The case was over before lunch. I could hardly believe that I would have another afternoon with no scheduled work. After lunch, once again I retreated to my trailer to finish the Updike epic. Later, I joined the officers again for dinner, and retired early.

That evening before midnight, I was awakened by the sound of incoming mortar fire and ran to my assigned bunker. Inside, I recognized an acquaintance from my last duty station in El Paso. He was seated on a wooden bench with only a towel around his waist, his head lowered in his hands. He did not look up when I entered, even after calling his name. He was repeatedly mumbling "Damned communists! Damned communists!" and a few other choice epithets about those who were responsible for his misery. When he departed a few minutes later, he did not take notice of me or the deaf division psychiatrist who entered after I did. My former acquaintance apparently did not appreciate being awakened from a deep sleep by the damned communists.

On the day following the mortar attack, to my surprise, there was a repetition of the previous day's event when the accused decided to enter a plea of guilty. A few hours in court and it was all over. But I still could not return to Saigon because cases were scheduled Thursday and Friday. Subconsciously, I was happy but a sense of guilt tugged at my conscience. I did not feel that I deserved another free afternoon in an air-conditioned trailer. I selected another novel to occupy my time.

After returning to the trailer in the early afternoon, I fell asleep before beginning to read, but was awakened by a rapping at the door. It was an officer from the judge advocate section who wanted to ask a favor. Would I be willing to speak to a sergeant who had appeared at the office, seemingly desperate, asking to discuss a serious matter with a lawyer? Since I had no duties on three consecutive afternoons, he thought that I would not mind taking on this task. I was happy to oblige. A few minutes later, the sergeant appeared at my quarters and we introduced ourselves.

Sergeant First Class Robert Graves was clean-cut, polite, and looked more like a stockbroker than a soldier. We seated ourselves across from one another. It was obvious that he was deeply troubled.

"Sir," he began, "I have a problem and it does not concern military matters."

"I'll be happy to help you in any way that I can," I responded. He told me the following story:

"Well, sir, I've only been in Vietnam a short time and really would like to complete my obligation here, but I received news from the Red Cross that makes it very difficult, if not impossible. I can't sleep or concentrate and must talk to someone who can help me."

"Tell me whatever you like, Sergeant. I'm here to listen and we'll see what, if anything, can be done."

"Colonel, I met my wife last January in Tacoma when I was stationed at Fort Lewis. She was a teller in a bank and we met through mutual friends. We began dating immediately and I had never experienced the feeling of love with anyone like I did with her. I knew right away that the feeling was mutual and I began to see or call her every day.

"One evening about four weeks after we met, I went to her apartment and saw immediately that she had been crying. She continued to sob when I asked what was bothering her. She suggested that we have something to drink and did not speak again until we sat down for coffee.

" 'I have something to tell you,' she said.

"I told her that she need not be concerned about anything she had to tell me. 'I'm pregnant!' she said.

"Of course I was taken by surprise, but my feelings for her were unchanged. I only wanted to know how she felt about me under the circumstances; I asked whether there was another man who was important to her.

" 'No, no, really,' she replied, 'I can't excuse myself for doing what I did. There's no use trying. The man who is the father means nothing to me now and never did. He hasn't even called in five weeks, and I haven't thought of him until today.'

"We talked a long while and decided that we should spend a few days thinking about our lives. We would continue to see each other. As for myself, I did not doubt that I loved her.

"I thought seriously about marriage for the first time in my life. I knew I could be happy with Susan. I was twenty-nine and far enough along in my career to know that I could, and would, be happy to support a small family. I made up my mind that I would ask her to marry me. It was not out of pity, or any altruistic motive. I was willing to claim someone else's child as my own.

"When I proposed to her later, she was not altogether surprised. I think she suspected I would. By that time, we could anticipate each other's thoughts. She didn't give me an answer immediately, but promised to think about it. When I saw her again two days later, she was prepared to respond to my proposal.

" 'I want to marry you, Bob, but I can't ask that you mortgage your future for my sake. I think I will accept your proposal, but only after the baby is born and we have had more time to think about our futures.'

"Her reply did not satisfy me. I wanted to marry her, especially before the baby was born. We took a long walk along the Puget Sound near Fort Lewis, then returned to her apartment for a talk late into the night.

"We reached a compromise that did not satisfy me but was absolutely the only way she would consent to an immediate marriage. I would have to go away until after the baby was born. Meanwhile, she would arrange for its adoption. She wanted only my children, but she cared enough for the one she was carrying to insure that it would be adopted by someone she knew welcomed the responsibility. She could not be persuaded to consent to my wishes.

"I volunteered to come to Vietnam and we were married a few days later in a chapel at Fort Lewis. The happiest weeks of my life were spent while waiting to be shipped here. During the past three months we have corresponded daily. I couldn't bear it in Dong Tam without her letters. She never complained and wrote mostly about plans for our future.

"Susan arranged for the adoption through a Catholic organization in Seattle. She accepted the character reports on the family who would be responsible for her child. She was satisfied and looked forward to our life together, as I did. Even being in Vietnam did not detract from my happiness.

"Until last night!"

"What happened last night?" I asked.

"I received a communication from the Red Cross. The baby was born. Susan was well but the child has a defective heart and the prospective parents backed out of the agreement to take the baby. My wife is on the verge of a nervous breakdown. She had to leave the hospital but the little girl is still there."

"What are your feelings about all this?" I asked.

"I have not changed my mind. I want Susan and I want the baby. I sent a message to her via the MARS station here today. What I want now is for you or someone to arrange an emergency leave so that I can explain my feelings to her in person. I want both her and the baby."

I was not in a position to grant the leave, but Colonel Webb took on that responsibility, willingly and successfully. Sergeant Graves was out of Dong Tam on his way to the United States the following day. This soldier, I thought, deserved a medal for something that had nothing to do with combat.

When I arrived at the judge advocate office on the morning following Sergeant Graves's visit, the prosecutor told me that, for the third consecutive day, an accused decided to plead guilty. Another free afternoon loomed in Dong Tam. I could not depart for Saigon until completion of the case set for the following day, which I was assured would be a long one.

That Thursday afternoon, free from legal work, I had an opportunity to visit a section of the Ninth Division's area of operations, and a little more of the Mekong Delta. The area had long been infiltrated by enemies of the established government, first the Vietminh and then the Viet Cong. Additionally, the area was home to the Hoa Hao religious sect, which had its own army and was very protective of their enclave.

Colonel Webb had previously scheduled visits to some of the division's subordinate units and offered to take me with him. I accepted. We visited the artificial harbor at Dong Tam where a part of the Riverine Assault Force was operating. An entire brigade of the Ninth Division was occupying navy barges and ships, substituting for marines who had earlier been called north to defend the fortress of Khe Sanh. The river barges had 105-mm guns mounted fore and aft, with ammunition stored under the hulls. Navy ships were a little farther away in the Mekong River. We visited two firebases on small islands, using Air Cushion Vehicles, an experimental-type boat, for transportation.

When the official visits were completed, I asked John to take me to the city of My Tho, which had been in the war news frequently, harassed alternately by one or the other of the occupying forces. It was also historically significant as the capital city of Dinh Tung Province. At first he declined, but later said, "Keep your helmet on, your head low, and I'll see how fast this jeep can go." We took the trip and returned without incident, not much worse for a bone-jarring and dust-flying ride.

The entire day on Friday was spent in court, excluding time-out during the noon hour. As in the three previous days at Dong Tam, I had lunch with a dermatologist from Walter Reed Hospital who was doing research on the effect of Mekong Delta terrain on the feet of American soldiers. We had become friendly, having in common the fact that we were both visitors to the division. During a lull in our conversation, I thought it would be an opportune time to ease my mind about a personal matter. For years, I had had a small red spot on my face that did not really bother me except sometimes when shaving.

"Colonel," I asked, "no big deal, but what is this spot on my face?"

He looked carefully and replied: "Nothing to worry about. Just a little cancer."

"Cancer?" I said, horrified.

"Well, if it makes you fell better, don't call it cancer. Just know that it's a basal cell carcinoma. And if that still sounds serious to you, drop by the first-aid station after your case this afternoon and I'll remove it."

I was presented with a dilemma. If it was nothing to worry about, should I not wait until I returned to the United States where I could have the carcinoma removed in a fully equipped military hospital; or should I relieve all concern about cancer, or carcinoma, or whatever, by having it removed in the aid station down the street?

"I'll be there," I said, "probably."

A few hours later, after completion of the case being tried, I walked to the medical aid station where the colonel was sitting in a steel chair looking at slides and files.

"So you decided to come?" he asked. "Just lie down on that gurney behind the sheets there and I'll be with you in a minute."

There was dust on most of the papers and furniture in the station, but the small enclosure where I lay on the gurney looked clean and contained sterilizing equipment. Besides, I trusted the doctor. I trusted all the doctors I met in Vietnam, having seen their remarkable work in a dozen different locations.

I was not asked to remove my shirt, or boots, or anything other than my steel helmet. The colonel cleaned my face with alcohol and a newly opened piece of gauze. There was no assistant. He administered a local anesthetic before removing the carcinoma. The doctor and I then chatted about twenty minutes before he decided that I could get up, and we would go to dinner together. I looked in a mirror and was surprised to see a hole in my face much larger than I expected. There was no bandage and the only instruction I received was to keep my face clean, which I thought was superfluous advice. I bear a scar to this day as a memento of that small operation after work and before dinner on my last evening that week in Dong Tam.

On Saturday, after a case that lasted only through the morning, I returned to Saigon. Everyone in the MACV legal office stared at me in surprise and wanted to know what in the world happened to my face in Dong Tam.

"Nothing much," I replied. "Only a little cancer operation."

CHAPTER THIRTY-SIX

Hi Si

I was not assigned to any case in Vietnam involving the use or sale of hard drugs prohibited by army regulations, but other judges presided over ten such cases during my tour. I was, of course, aware that such drugs were readily available, some legally purchased in Vietnamese drugstores. Serious problems with these substances were more common in the years after President Nixon was elected on the assumption that he had a plan to end the war. The diminishing number of troops in Vietnam was obvious to those who remained. Soldiers saw their comrades leave, knowing that an end to the American presence was approaching. Morale was weakening. No one wanted to be the last to die in Vietnam.

In my opinion, company commanders did a creditable job of adjusting to the changing mores of the time concerning the use and sale of less-powerful drugs. Good soldiers who were first-time users were rarely punished. Small sales to friends for private use were handled by company punishment or special courts-martial that had no jurisdiction to impose a discharge from the army.

Personnel charged with possession, use, or sale of small amounts of marijuana did appear in general courts-martial frequently, but only in conjunction with more serious offenses.

I was the military judge in two cases involving possession of marijuana only. The first occurred near Di An when Corporal Steven Phares attempted to return to his base, apparently stoned, after a night in a nearby village. Without attempting to conceal evidence, he carried a large clear plastic bag containing a green leafy substance, clearly visible to anyone who saw him. The guard at the entrance to the firebase confiscated the bag and its contents. Phares protested that he came from a free country that was fighting the communists and had a right to possess whatever was legally his. The substance in the bag was later confirmed to be thirty-three ounces of marijuana, a fact readily admitted by Phares the following day. After a short trial, Phares was sentenced to serve four months confinement in the Long Binh Stockade. That case was much simpler and less interesting than that of Private First Class Simon Bordes.

Simon Bordes was not a particularly good soldier. He was a supply clerk in the 576th Ordinance Company in Long Binh, but never ambitious enough to advance above the rank of Private First Class. He was a bit lazy and smoked pot occasionally, but clever enough to keep out of serious mischief. His intelligence was limited. Singapore was not in his vocabulary until a buddy advised him to go there on R&R. When his tour of duty in Vietnam was completed, he was leaving without any evidence of misbehavior, but no evidence of particularly good service, either.

On the date of his scheduled departure, Bordes was given probably the only favor any officer had offered to him in Vietnam. The company commander allowed his personal jeep to be used for Bordes's transportation to the processing center at Ton Son Nhut. Everything seemed to be in order at the end of that supposedly last journey when he thanked the driver and told him goodbye.

Before processing began, all departees were required to pass through a large unattended room in the center of which were two large barrels painted yellow. At the door was a sign informing those leaving the country that the barrels could be used for voluntary disposal of any unwanted materials. The conspicuous absence of guards inferentially informed those departing that this was a convenient place to dispose of unauthorized weapons, drugs, pornography or any other material forbidden by regulations. Bordes walked through the room with a duffel bag and two large plastic dolls, one under each arm, without making a deposit.

After passing the yellow barrels, Bordes stopped in the next room for the first step of his processing, which consisted of a routine observation and possible questioning by two military policemen. Their eyes focused on the cheap dolls and Bordes was immediately under scrutiny. The MPs had seen hundreds of persons pass before them and were quite knowledgeable about sizing up persons suspected of misconduct. Without talking, they looked at Bordes and the dolls for half a minute before one of them observed a green leafy substance fall gently to the ground from a fractured part of one of the plastic dolls. He was not so naive as not to suspect that the substance he observed was prohibited by regulation.

"Look, buddy, why don't you go back into the room you just came through?" he asked nonchalantly, being neither polite nor impolite.

"Why should I?" answered Bordes.

"Please make my day easier and return to the room," the MP pleaded.

"I didn't do anything illegal. I don't have anything to hide. I don't want to go back there," Bordes replied.

The MP took a little field kit for testing drugs, used it on the fallen substance, and became convinced that Bordes was carrying a lot of marijuana.

"Look, friend, there are over two hundred people waiting to come through this line, and I'd like to see every one of them get on a Freedom Bird tonight. I'm not accusing you of anything, but please go back right now. I will not ask you again," the MP pleaded, now a bit irritated.

"I went through that room once and I'm not going through it again!" was the final reply.

"Okay, let's have the dolls. I saw enough and have enough evidence to prevent you from proceeding to the rest of the processing routine."

Bordes gave up the dolls without argument and was ordered to sit down to await the officer of the day. After reading the provisional test results, the officer confiscated the dolls and ordered Bordes to be placed in temporary custody where he remained until the following morning when he was returned unceremoniously to his unit. Charges of illegal possession of forty-six ounces of a controlled substance were preferred and investigated. Four weeks later, after all pretrial formalities were properly completed, Bordes appeared for his trial by general court-martial in the courtroom at Long Binh. I was the appointed military judge.

The trial counsel called the two MPs who had first become suspicious of Bordes and the plastic dolls, and a crime laboratory technician who testified that the substance removed from the dolls was indeed marijuana. The defense counsel did not contest any of the evidence. I surmised that Bordes would deny knowledge of the forbidden substance, and indeed that was the case, as reflected in the following testimony:

Defense Counsel (DC): Now, Private Bordes, you heard all of the evidence. What do you have to say?

Accused (A): Yes, sir, I heard the evidence, but I did not know anything was inside those dolls.

DC: What were you going to do with those dolls?

A: Bring them to my little sister.

DC: Are you a good soldier?

A: Yes, sir. I've never been in any kind of a court in my life before and as long as I've been in the army, I never even had company punishment.

DC: I have no further questions.

The trail counsel (TC) cross-examined:

TC: Now, Private Bordes, you say that you have been a good soldier, is that right?

A: Yes, sir.

TC: Have you been given any decorations since you've been here in Vietnam?

A: Everybody gets ribbons, sir.

TC: I mean something special, like the Bronze Star, or the Soldier's Medal, or even the Good Conduct Medal?

A: No, sir.

TC: Were you given a letter of commendation from your commanding officer or anyone else before you were scheduled to depart?

A: No, sir.

TC: Okay. Well now, let's talk about the case. Where did you get those dolls?

A: From a man in a Vietnamese bar, sir.

TC: Did you know this man?

A: Not really, sir. I just met him when I spent the night in the house there.

TC: Why did he give you those dolls?

A: He asked me if I had any little sisters, and I said yes, so he gave them to me.

TC: Where is this Vietnamese bar located?

A: In some little village not far from Long Binh.

TC: Can you be more specific? What is the name of this little village?

A: I don't know, sir. I couldn't even find it if I went looking.

TC: Well then, this man. Did you spend some time with him?

A: Yes, sir, we had a couple of beers and smoked a little pot.

TC: Did you learn what his name is?

Bordes thought a while, then answered.

A: Yes, sir. It was Hi.

TC: Was that his first or last name?

A: His first name, I think.

TC: Well, what was his last name?

Bordes thought again for a moment, then answered hesitatingly.

A: Si.

TC: So your testimony is that you were with this man named Hi Si drinking beer and smoking pot in a house of good times, and, out of the goodness of his heart, he gave you two large plastic dolls?

A: That's exactly what happened, sir.

TC: Is there any way in the world you could tell us where we could find Hi Si, or anyone who might know him, so that we might make an effort to get him into this court to testify?

A: No, sir.

TC: Was Hi Si a Vietnamese?

A: I don't know, sir.

TC: Was he an American?

A: I don't think so, he couldn't speak English very well. He looked like he could be a Vietnamese, or Cambodian, or something.

TC: Did you put anything into those dolls after the man gave them to you?

A: No, sir.

TC: Did they seem to be a bit heavy for two plastic dolls?

A: I don't think so.

TC: I have no further questions.

The defense counsel had no redirect examination. He did, however, make a motion that Hi Si be subpoenaed as a witness.

"Well, defense counsel," I asked, "can you give us any indication where this man might be found, or even the spelling of his name?"

"I have no idea, sir. I think the burden is on the government to produce Mr. Hi Si."

I denied the motion, adding, "I do not think the evidence warrants me to order United States Army authorities to conduct a search for Mr. Hi Si, who might be a Vietnamese and probably lives somewhere in Vietnam or maybe Cambodia."

The defense rested. The prosecution had nothing further. I instructed the court, and Bordes was found guilty about fifteen minutes later. I was not surprised about the conviction, but was surprised at the speed in which the verdict was reached.

After a passionate plea by the defense counsel, emphasizing the accused's lack of prior convictions or punishment, the court sentenced Bordes to be discharged from the army with a bad conduct discharge and to serve six months confinement at hard labor.

Upon completion of the case which, like many others, was being reported by the *Overseas Weekly*, the prosecutor held the two dolls high above his head smiling broadly for the camera. He loved the publicity.

It was my impression that during all of the proceedings, the trial counsel was more amused than serious. I did not hold him in high regard. He continually joked during the recesses of this and other cases. My view of him was apparently shared by his superiors because they approved a three-week drop from his scheduled rotation date to the United States, which was an action almost unheard-of. His request was based upon an invitation he received to become a duke in New Orleans at a supposedly important Mardi Gras function.

Four months later, I received the decision of the Court of Military Review in Bordes's case. The only issue raised on appeal by the appellate defense counsel was that I made an error prejudicial to the accused by refusing to issue a subpoena "for Mr. Hi Si, located somewhere in Vietnam or Cambodia." The issue was not favorably acted upon, but the court disapproved the bad conduct discharge, and approved only so much of the confinement as had already been served. Bordes, by that time, was probably home again ready to start life anew as a seasoned Vietnam veteran with an honorable discharge.

CHAPTER THIRTY-SEVEN

Plantation

Plantation was the name of a compound twenty-three miles north of Saigon located within the Long Binh area. It was headquarters of II (pronounced "two") Field Force, airlifted to Vietnam in March 1966 to provide combat assistance to the South Vietnamese army. Its mission was also to control United States military operations on the approaches to Saigon. II Field Force was a corps-level headquarters and exercised general court-martial jurisdiction over several large military units.

On the occasion of an assignment to a case at Plantation, Colonel Bob Jones emphasized that it was imperative for me to be there on the evening of January 27, 1969. The case to be tried was scheduled for 7:00 A.M. the following morning, an unusual hour to begin a case, but necessary because witnesses were scheduled to depart Vietnam on the evening of that day.

On January 27, I returned to Hotel 3 from Cu Chi about seven in the evening, which normally would be too late to board a helicopter as a passenger. Without returning to my room or office, I contacted Colonel Jones and advised him of my predicament. I heard him order Warrant Officer Bill Heaton to get me to Plantation without delay, even if he had to come for me by jeep with armed guards. Warrant officers in the army are the people to depend upon when an assignment requires extraordinary effort. Mr. Heaton was no exception. He had friends within the headquarters.

Twenty minutes after my call to Colonel Jones, while I was still at Hotel 3, a helicopter appeared. Prominently displayed in the rear seat closest to the right-hand exit were three large stars. Mr. Heaton was sitting next to the pilot, giddy as a child and proud of his accomplishment. He took a picture of me with the seat of stars before returning to Plantation. There were neither door gunners nor copilot, because the urgent demand for transportation did not allow time to secure the personnel. Mr. Heaton was not so happy, however, when we landed at Plantation to find the commanding general's aide and two senior officers waiting, demanding an explanation of how in hell a warrant officer managed to acquire use of a three-star general's chopper. I walked away, and did not find out how Mr. Heaton managed to extricate himself from the crisis, but he was in the office the next morning, although not on the night of my delivery to Plantation.

The case to be tried was one in which two soldiers, Privates William Sellers and Sandy Pollock, were charged with unpremeditated murder. These two young men, each nineteen years old, had been dispatched on November 28 from Headquarters Battery, 5th Battalion, 42nd Artillery, to obtain parachutes at Bien Hoi. On the road there, they had the misfortune of running over a particularly sharp stone, puncturing one of the tires. Sellers and Pollock were not born to fix flat tires. They pulled up to one of those ubiquitous little buildings on the roadsides of Vietnam where one could have trucks or tanks washed, tires changed, buy beer, chat with hostesses, and probably get private entertainment upon request.

When a Vietnamese worker began to change the tire, Sellers and Pollock each bought two bottles of beer and strolled over to a small stream behind the store. They sat down to relax and drink peacefully when Pollock decided to test his rifle by shooting several rounds into the stream. Caught up in the excitement of the firing, Pollock placed a new magazine into his weapon. Sellers did the same with his. They were going to do some shooting, they told each other.

"Are there any VC in the area?" Sellers asked a young girl passing by. She replied in the negative.

Across the stream about eighty yards from where the soldiers were standing, six Vietnamese men were cutting wood in an old rubber plantation that belonged to the village. Together, the soldiers, ignoring the men cutting wood, fired about seventy rounds into the trees, expending all of their ammunition. A bullet struck Nguyen Van Hang. He fell to the ground, and was picked up by his son, who was also cutting wood. When they arrived at a little bridge crossing the stream, a village doctor pronounced Mr. Hang dead.

After the firing, but before learning about the stricken man, Sellers and Pollock returned to the nondescript building to order another beer. A few minutes later, a man who witnessed the shooting ran into the building, hysterically shouting that a person had been shot and killed. Sellers nonchalantly answered that only VC were in the woods, and he could not see them, anyway.

"No VC," said the hysterical man, "and he lay down." A summons went out to the village police. They, in turn, called the Military Police, who took the soldiers into custody.

A perfunctory investigation revealed that Mr. Hang had been shot in the stomach and killed by a single bullet fired by either Sellers or Pollock. Although apparently dead, Hang was placed solemnly on a wooden cart and brought to the local hospital. There was much wailing and cursing of Americans as the little hand-drawn wagon rolled down the street to its destination.

The trial that resulted was ready to proceed as scheduled in the early morning of January 27, when all parties were present. The court members were assembled in the deliberation room, and I was in the legal office across the street when the prosecutor, Major Herbert Green, came to inform me that everyone was ready to proceed. As I entered the courtroom, I accidentally kicked over one of two M–16 rifles that were propped against the side of the inside wall. I said nothing until I reached the judge's bench.

"Major Green!" I intoned seriously. "What are those weapons doing in the courtroom?"

"They belong to the accused, sir. The company commander sent the men over this morning with their weapons, which they apparently always carry."

I paused a moment. The courtroom was silent except for the noise of the air conditioner. "Major Green!" I said with all the composure I could muster. "Get those weapons out of here!"

"Yes, sir!" Green replied as he hurried to the rear of the courtroom and disappeared with the weapons. Upon his return, I asked: "Major Green, how is it possible, first of all, that two soldiers charged with murder are allowed to be carrying weapons and, secondly, to bring them into a courtroom?"

"I don't know, sir. Well, they're not charged with premeditated murder. I don't think their company commander considered them dangerous."

There was no way for me to respond to that kind of logic. I shook my head, and told Green to call the members of the court from the deliberation room.

The case proceeded as expected, the Vietnamese witnesses testifying to the actions of the accused and the untimely death of the victim. Mr. Hang's son brought a stunned silence to the trial when, after his testimony, he solemnly pleaded:

"I make here the request to the United States government to pay for my father's funeral."

When the prosecution rested, both accused admitted firing their weapons but denied seeing anyone near the trees into which they were shooting. They were found not guilty of unpremeditated murder but guilty of negligent homicide, which required only a finding of simple negligence. Each was sentenced to nine months confinement at hard labor and limited forfeitures of pay but no discharge.

After the review was completed by the staff judge advocate, he recommended to the commanding general that since there was no discharge imposed upon either of the accused and two months had passed since their imprisonment, the remainder of the sentence be remitted. The general agreed and the two accused were returned to their unit.

Two years after the trial, I was military judge on a case in Nuremberg, Germany, in which an accused was charged with maiming. He had thrown a live hand grenade out of a window toward his first sergeant, who was walking alone outside the building, causing permanent damage to the intended victim. "Fragging" is the term for throwing a fragmentation grenade at a person, usually a superior, to dispose of that person without leaving evidence of the person who committed the crime. Such offenses were rather common in Vietnam in late 1969 and thereafter, but I had no prior experience with such a case.

William Sellers was the name of the accused in the Nuremberg case. I did not recognize the name, nor the accused himself, during the first part of his trial. After he was found guilty, the prosecutor introduced a record of previous convictions that included an earlier one for negligent homicide in Vietnam.

When Sellers took the witness stand to present matters in extenuation and mitigation, he talked about his life back home, which was more or less normal, although he had never finished high school. His father had been gainfully employed by the City of New York, and he got along with his siblings. He lived in one of a group of homes that had common walls but separate closed-in back yards. When he finished testifying, nothing was brought out, in my opinion, that might evoke sympathy from the court. The trial counsel did not examine him. Out of curiosity because we were in Vietnam at the same time and also hoping to bring out something appropriate that might bear upon his apparently unsympathetic attitude toward human beings, I decided to ask a few questions.

"I note that you were tried by court-martial in Vietnam, is that correct?"

"Yes, sir, for unpremeditated murder, and you were the judge."

I gasped — and then remembered the Sellers and Pollock case.

"Are you sure you were convicted of unpremeditated murder? Your record of prior convictions says negligent homicide, and there is quite a difference."

"Well, sir, I was charged with murder, but you or somebody else in that courtroom knocked it down."

"OK. Now tell the court whether there was anything at all in your childhood that caused you to become bitter about anyone?"

"No, sir. People didn't like me a lot but I didn't like them either, except some special friends."

"Did you have any hobbies?"

"Well, yes, sir, I had one. Three turtles appeared in our back yard one day and I took care of them all the time I was in high school."

I had no further questions. In his argument for leniency, the defense counsel commented upon routine matters, such as youth, service in Vietnam, lack of a good education, but nothing really that seemed to gain sympathy from the members of the court. In frustration, feeling that he was getting nowhere, the defense counsel concluded: "After all, anyone who cares for three turtles during his high school years can't be all bad!"

I wanted to cite the defense counsel for contempt!

The court sentenced Sellers to be dishonorably discharged from the army and to be confined at hard labor for fifteen years. There was little chance he would ever see the day when he would be convicted again by court-martial.

CHAPTER THIRTY-EIGHT

Ears and a Finger, Too

There is a postcard of a beautiful beach in my office. Children are pictured selling balloons and playing in the water. Along the nearby boulevard, colorful hotels and palm trees are visible. Visitors ask whether the scene is from Hawaii or the Caribbean. "No," I tell them, "that is a postcard from Nha Trang, in Vietnam, on the coast of the South China Sea."

Nha Trang was the site of Headquarters, I Field Force, which controlled American operations in the central highlands of Vietnam and along a large part of the China Sea coast. It was a pleasure to go there because I was regularly assigned to a room in one of the hotels near the beach, which was within walking distance to the staff judge advocate office, the courtroom, and the mess hall.

Lieutenant Colonel Ralph Hammack, the staff judge advocate, was a gracious host. Sometimes, when there was a break during a trial, we sat on the beach to escape the heat and catch the gentle sea breezes, whiling away time without thoughts of war or work. Sometimes we ate at a run-down French restaurant where the cook prepared fresh fish and lobster with taste, loving care, and superior skill. Colonel Hammack made his jeep available to me in order to visit nearby installations where I had friends.

Late in April 1969, I was at I Field Force to participate in a case, which involved mutilation of a corpse and two serious assaults. Stories of soldiers desecrating enemy bodies were not uncommon, but except for the incident in which a cameraman for a national news network paid a soldier to cut the ear off a dead Vietnamese, I was not personally aware of any such incident. I heard stories, of course, but thought then, as I do now, that they were exaggerated.

The case to which I was assigned in Nha Trang was my first experience with that type of conduct. After killing a Vietnamese man, Private First Class Herbert Stoss cut off his ears and a finger, and grievously assaulted a second Vietnamese man.

On the afternoon of January 9, 1969, members of a platoon assigned to C Company, 1st Battalion of the 173rd Airborne Brigade, were on a minesweeping mission four kilometers from their company's Forward Operating Base (FOB). One of the tracks (armored personnel carriers) overheated and they could not proceed. It was a break for those who did not have to work on the broken vehicle.

Second Lieutenant John Jones, the platoon leader, was a recent graduate of Officer Candidate School and had been in Vietnam about four months. Neither he nor Private Stoss had yet reached his twenty-second birthday. Jones was considered to be an immature officer by his superiors, and even more so by the sergeants under his command. Although Jones was intellectually superior, having graduated from college, Stoss was by far more aggressive and charismatic.

The ubiquitous Vietnamese "Coke girls" who seemed to be wherever a group of American soldiers gathered for whatever purpose, were also present near the breakdown, selling Cokes, beer, souvenirs, and themselves. All of the men bought beer. Lieutenant Jones went to a nearby "boom boom" shack with one of the girls, told the men to make themselves happy, and disappeared into the tiny building, which consisted of one small room. A soldier took one of the girls down into his track, while two friends watched from above. The others took the beer they had purchased, sat down in the shade of a tree, and began to speak without paying much attention to one another. The beer and the heat contributed to making this an idle conversation.

Sergeant Alfred Mano, the platoon sergeant, was the center of the group in the shade. Private Stoss and four of Mano's subordinates were the other participants in the conversation. Stoss began to speak of the bravery of his best friend, who had departed that morning for Manila on R&R.

"You're not a man like your friend! You cannot kill or hurt anybody! You're just a baby," Sergeant Mano said to Stoss.

"Hell, I've only been here a couple of months! What can I do to prove that I'm a man?"

Although Stoss was inexperienced, he was not afraid of work, always pulled his share of duties without complaint, and had many friends. Lacking in formal education, he nevertheless freely asserted himself, but he was seldom offensive. He was especially respectful to his superiors, even Lieutenant Jones.

"Well," said Mano, "you could bring back some gook ears next time you shoot one! That would be proof of your courage and ability to stand up under fire."

Private Stoss had been in the army less than a year. He was drafted in December 1967; went through basic and advanced infantry training with no problem in six months; and, after a short leave home, was sent to Vietnam in July. He was several years younger than his platoon sergeant.

There was no doubt that Mano spoke to Stoss about "brining back gook ears." One of the witnesses to the conversation said that the sergeant did not sound serious. Others, including Stoss, said that Mano did not appear to be joking. Mano said he was just teasing.

After tending to the overheated track, the platoon returned to the company's FOB. Their only duty before supper was to chase away other "Coke girls" who had somehow managed to infiltrate the company's perimeter. During supper, each soldier was furnished one can of beer. Several, including Stoss, had already drank several that had been purchased from the girls.

Shortly before sunset, the battalion intelligence officer directed the C Company commander by radio to set up a listening post near a small creek just south of the hamlet of Dien Tieu, about four kilometers south of the FOB. It was known that Viet Cong soldiers came down from the mountains into the surrounding villages and hamlets at night.

Dien Tieu hamlet, however, was considered secure. It was surrounded by barbed wire, and a few of its inhabitants were members of the Vietnamese Popular Forces, who presumably were able to protect everyone within the compound, including a few refugees. The battalion intelligence officer was specific in stating that there was no reason to enter the hamlet.

Lieutenant Jones was chosen to lead the small patrol scheduled to begin an hour and a half before midnight. Stoss volunteered for the mission. A medic, Corporal Bill Rhodes, a radio operator, and three other soldiers were chosen to complete the detail. Instructions were repeated to bypass the hamlet, as quietly as possible.

At 2230 hours, the patrol set out, following a ditch line that passed close to, but did not enter, Dien Tieu. When the soldiers approached the hamlet, the members heard laughter and dogs barking from within.

Private Stoss was ready to prove he was a man. He told Lieutenant Jones that suspicious noises were heard in the hamlet and requested permission to enter. Jones told the radio operator to check with the command track back in the FOB. He received a negative reply. When the patrol arrived closer to the entrance of the hamlet, Stoss once again tried to persuade Lieutenant Jones that there were suspicious noises inside and it was his duty to investigate, overriding the prior refusal for permission. While Jones was pondering an answer, Stoss decided on his own to enter the hamlet.

Inside the village, a group of Vietnamese men were seated, talking and laughing on the outside of a hooch. When they saw Stoss approaching with a weapon pointed in their direction, most retreated inside, but one of them, Do Phat, began to run.

Stoss shouted "Dung lai!" which he understood to mean "stop." The man did not stop. Stoss fired a burst of automatic fire at the man's feet, but Phat continued to run. Another burst above the man's head did not have the desired result. Then, four bullets of a third burst of fire entered Do Phat's body, causing him to fall to the ground. Stoss bent down, heard the victim breathing heavily, grabbed Phat by the collar and dragged him to the village entrance, where other members of the patrol had gathered after hearing the three bursts of fire. The medic, Corporal Rhodes, took Phat's pulse and announced that he was breathing and still alive. According to all of the witnesses, Stoss struck Phat on the head with the butt of his rifle, causing breathing to stop. Rhodes checked his pulse again, and pronounced Phat dead.

Two of the inhabitants of the hamlet tried to go to Phat's assistance, but Stoss forced them to lie face down on the ground. He was acting as if he were leading the mission. He demanded identification from Dan Dinh Xuan, one of the men who had come to assist Phat. The man moved upward and handed Stoss a piece of paper. Not satisfied, Stoss said that he was not interested in laundry lists, and struck Xuan with the barrel of his rifle, rendering him unconscious. Rhodes checked Xuan and found that he was "fairly well cut, pretty good, pretty deep."

While Rhodes was administering first aid to the injured man, Stoss became angry and shouted that he should not help a gook because "the gook would not help you if the tables were turned." Another soldier standing by ridiculed Rhodes for helping Xuan. Lieutenant Jones looked on awkwardly and walked away, lacking the courage to intervene. He told the radio operator to report that his platoon had just killed a Viet Cong. A report was made by radio that "one VC was killed."

Stoss asked Rhodes, who was administering first aid to Xuan, for a knife. He denied having one, suspecting that Stoss was preparing to make good on a threat he made earlier to "get some gook ears." Stoss angrily ran to the nearest hooch and returned with a curved knife similar to those used by Vietnamese who work in the fields, making a boast that he "was going to cut off the gook's ears."

The medic turned his head and the other soldiers walked away. Rhodes heard noises "like a dull knife cutting flesh." When he turned to protest, he saw that Mr. Phat's ears had been cut off.

"Are you satisfied?" the medic asked Stoss, who was now acting "like a wild man." "No," was the reply, "I still want a finger."

Corporal Rhodes swore that he "heard the same cutting sound, and then a bone snapped."

When Rhodes once again reprimanded Stoss, the latter said "Here, you want a finger?" and threw it and the knife at him. Lieutenant Jones returned to the scene as the knife was thrown, observed what happened, and gathered together the men of the patrol. He ordered everyone to head back to the company area, saying nothing about the killing or the brutality, except that there would be hell to pay if the company commander found out about the ears and finger. The mission to secure a listening post was abandoned.

When the patrol returned to the company, Stoss went directly to Sergeant Mano and handed him a green handkerchief with something wrapped inside. Mano unfolded the handkerchief and two bloody ears fell to the ground. The sergeant was benumbed and told Stoss to get rid of the ears, but did not reprimand him. Stoss asked Mano if he was now a man and the sergeant, shaken, meekly replied, "Yes, I guess so."

"All right then, you can't call me a baby anymore, you have to call me a man!" Stoss admonished.

Stoss was not charged with killing Do Phat, but assaulting him by striking him on the head, and mutilating his corpse by cutting off both ears and one finger. He was also charged with assaulting Xuan with intent to commit grievous bodily harm. The convening authority apparently believed that Stoss was justified as a soldier in shooting Phat, who was running away from a lawful apprehension.

At the trial, Stoss admitted the three firings and killing Do Phat. He denied every other piece of inculpatory evidence that was presented against him. He specifically denied cutting off Do

Phat's ears and finger, hitting him with his rifle butt, and assaulting Xuan with his rifle barrel. He said he did not throw a finger or knife at Corporal Rhodes, but possibly he did "throw a rock because I always kept a bunch of rocks in my pocket."

I had a rather unique problem in formatting instructions for the members of the court. There was the matter of close timing with respect to the assault and death of Do Phat. If he was dead at the time Stoss allegedly hit him on the head, there could be no assault. If Phat were alive when the ears and finger were severed, there could be no mutilation of a corpse.

The trial counsel argued quite graphically that "by the time the ears and finger were removed, Do Phat, yes, was dead. But at the time that the blow was struck, although dying, Do Phat was alive gasping, wheezing, gurgling, or whatever." Rhodes had indeed testified that Phat was alive when Stoss struck him, but dead when the mutilation took place. All this within a period of minutes, and Rhodes was by no means an expert.

The defense counsel asked the court to believe the accused's testimony. He introduced evidence by stipulation that former employers in the United States praised Stoss highly and would believe him under oath, and that his mother said he was always a good boy, working four years at the same factory to help support the family and was polite to everyone. Sergeants in the accused's company testified they would like to have him back in the unit because of his willingness to work hard.

The court members, according to their verdict, did not believe that Phat was alive when Stoss struck him, or perhaps that Stoss did not strike Phat at all, because they found him guilty only of mutilating the corpse. They also convicted him of committing an assault upon Xuan. I personally believe that it was a compromise verdict, the jury unable to decide the time factor. The court members sentenced the accused to be dishonorably discharged from the army and to be confined at hard labor for one year.

I did not understand then, and I do not understand now, why Private First Class Stoss was not charged with homicide. In my opinion, the evidence I heard was sufficient to prefer a charge of murder against him, and the court members should have been allowed to determine whether the killing was justified.

CHAPTER THIRTY-NINE

DEROS

DEROS. Date Eligible to Return from Overseas. Mine arrived on July 9, 1969. I was up at five in the morning to allow time for a hundred little details that remained before reporting to the processing center in the early afternoon. At the open mess for breakfast, I was pleasantly surprised to find Kathy ahead of me because we had not visited in several weeks. A good way to start the day that ended my tour. We sat together for my last meal at the Rex.

"I've been looking for you these last few days," she said. "I wanted to invite you to a barge party on the river today."

"Sorry, I can't make it, but my day has arrived," I replied.

"It's a pity you can't come!" she said, "It'll be great fun. It's being given by the civilian we visited that evening we were looking for a place for Dianne. All kinds of people will be there. From the embassy, from USAID, two congressmen, and lots of important civilians who have villas."

"Where did your friend get the barge?" I asked.

"I don't know, but I'm sure it's legal. He's very careful about things like that. I'm really sorry you can't come. There will be lots of good food and you would enjoy meeting new people!"

"By the way," I asked, "what ever happened at the picnic you invited me to attend on Con Son Island a few weeks ago?"

"It was great!" she replied. "My pilot friend managed to get hold of a cute little plane, a U–21, I think, and we had a great time. A couple of us bought all the goodies from the commissary and we cooked outside. We spent the whole day at a beautiful beach. And, I want you to know that we did not see those horrible Tiger Cages you told me about."

"Well, I didn't think you would. Beautiful beaches are not the sight for anyone in cages. Besides, they're in a prison which is pretty well secluded."

"Anyway, it was gorgeous, and there was no hint of anyone being tortured there."

Sometimes it's not so difficult to separate appearance from reality, I thought.

Kathy had been afraid of nothing (except, perhaps, being alone) and she enjoyed the excitement of living in Saigon. She was there during the 1968 Tet Offensive and was excited by every minute of it. From her apartment, she could hear the shootings, the mortar shells, and all the uproar. She went outside to get a better view of the action. She walked to the United States Embassy where she watched General William Westmoreland and Ambassador Ellsworth Bunker peering over bodies of Viet Cong soldiers who had been killed while attempting to occupy the building. She never refused a trip that promised excitement. She had been to dozens of places outside Vietnam, including the R&R destinations of Kuala Lampur, Hong Kong, and Manila. She always had friends, especially civilian reporters and pilots who were willing to take her along on noncombat missions.

After reminiscing for an hour or so about her eighteen months and my twelve months in Vietnam, we shook hands and said goodbye. She was off to the barge party before I reached the stairs to return to my room.

After processing in the afternoon, I had dinner with others whose DEROS had arrived. We were then bussed to the waiting room at Ton Son Nhut, where our flight was scheduled to depart in a couple of hours. I sat on a long, hard bench experiencing for the last time the smell of combat uniforms and the sight of young new arrivals who could not know their destinations. I thought about the thousands of United States servicemen and women who had entered Vietnam since my arrival there, but had not lived to experience this, the ecstasy of having reached the day on which they would be returning home.

The dispirited Vietnamese beggars milling around the airport were no different than those who were there a year before. It saddened me to think that, insofar as they were concerned, nothing had improved. I fell into a slight depression trying to make sense of the war, especially since my arrival in Saigon.

My experiences in Vietnam did not change my perspective of the war. How could I, or any one, determine whether we were winning, losing, or making progress? Vietnam was not a war about which the nation could become excited. There was no capture of great cities like Paris or Berlin or stories of General Patton racing to Trier in World War II, or General MacArthur landing at Inchon during the Korean War.

It was nonetheless necessary for those responsible for the continuation of the war to justify to the American people that our efforts were not in vain. This was unfortunately done by announcing that we were killing more of the enemy than the number of losses we were suffering. The particular phrases used were "body count" and "kill ratio." To aggravate the situation, everyone seemed to know that the body count was exaggerated to our advantage. I sat several times in briefings where battalion and higher commanders were reporting the day's results of casualties within their commands. I had never experienced a situation where the kill ratio did not favor the United States.

The terms "body count" and "kill ratio" were bandied about uncritically in combat and in the media. If it were necessary to announce the somber news that one hundred American servicemen had been killed in a particular action, could we take comfort because the announcement also included the fact that nine hundred of the enemy had been killed on the same day?

After the sweep across a village, or destruction of Viet Cong and North Vietnamese soldiers by bombs, bullets, and napalm from the air, we counted the enemy dead. The count sometimes included old men, women, and probably children. We assumed victory in terms of body count. Geography was not the method of determining success, mortality rates were.

Victories that gained territory usually proved ephemeral. In 1967, the United States deployed thirty-two thousand troops using intensive bombing and chemical warfare, including napalm, to clear a 125-square-mile area known as the "Iron Triangle," destroying the village of Ben Suc in the process. The enemy retreated into Cambodia, but returned to use the same land as a staging area for the 1968 Tet Offensive.

A few weeks before my departure from Vietnam, the United States Army and Air Force spent ten days capturing Ap Bia Mountain, better known as Hamburger Hill because of the carnage in that small space. Heavy artillery, napalm, B–52 strikes, and fierce hand-to-hand combat bought that victory at a cost of sixty American lives and over three hundred other casualties. Two weeks later, the enemy returned to the mountain without opposition.

Vietnam made heroes and offered opportunities to turn theories into experience. The majority of regular combat arms officers in Vietnam volunteered for combat duty. Many had to wait their turn for six months in a noncombat position, after which they were given a command of their own. The idea was to gain experience and prepare for the next war.

Many who had proved themselves in combat spoke of their experience with bravado. "I was shot down from helicopters three times and survived," a colonel said to me. Another boasted of sweeping through four villages in two weeks with only three fatalities. Ninety-seven "enemy" killed.

When not in combat, or scheduled for combat, the officers and enlisted persons were not having an unpleasant experience, except for incoming mortar fire. Every division and higher headquarters had a general's mess where the food was excellent.

Often, there were hors d'oeuvres, steaks, fine desserts, and stereophonic music. At some locations, officers enjoyed volleyball or other sports before retiring for showers, cocktails, and dinner. Post exchanges, swimming pools, guaranteed R&Rs, USO shows, and showers were generally available to everyone not in combat. Payroll deadlines were seldom missed and, for those who survived, a guaranteed return to the United States in one year.

When President Nixon was inaugurated, and immediately thereafter, the situation did not improve; protests increased, women marched on Washington, clerics accused the United States of war crimes, students participated in sit-ins, professors advised young men how to avoid military service. Combat operations in Vietnam continued; there was no progress at the Paris Peace negotiations; Vietnamese Vice President Nguyen Cao Ky hinted that perhaps he would talk peace with the National Liberation Front; refugees were still flooding into the cities as their homes and villages were destroyed.

During March, in a supposedly secret operation, President Nixon authorized the bombing of Cambodia, thus extending the war into a neutral country. Two months later, the *New York Times* revealed "the secret bombings." Personnel of the administration, including National Security Adviser Henry Kissinger, became obsessed with trying to prevent leaking secret information. It was interesting to consider that anyone could think the bombing of a neutral country by B–52 stratafortress jet bombers, dropping tons of bombs with each sortie, would be kept secret. There were almost eight hundred media reporters in Vietnam. Once, while the "secret bombings" were taking place, I stood with friends outside the courtroom in Cu Chi listening to bombs falling into the Cambodian countryside. In May, over three thousand tons of bombs were dropped by B–52s alone on areas near the Cambodian-Vietnam border.

In April, Secretary of State William Rogers told the Senate Foreign Relations Committee that "We are not seeking a military victory, nor do we want an escalation." This statement was difficult to comprehend. Few favored an escalation, but it seemed incongruous to say we were not seeking a military victory when, at the same time, the number of United States forces reached its peak at 543,000 and the war had been extended into a neutral country.

A few weeks before my departure, *Life* magazine published individual pictures of 242 American soldiers who had been killed during one week in Vietnam early in May. I think that those pictures of young men happily posing in new military uniforms, sports coats, high school graduation caps and gowns, brought home to me, more than anything I had observed, graphic evidence of what had been occurring in Vietnam and the war in which I was participating. If my views on the war had not been clear when I arrived in Vietnam, they had been defined before the date of my departure.

So many people had advised our past presidents of the futility of our presence in Vietnam. In addition to senators, members of Congress, and ordinary Americans doubting our stated cause, President Charles de Gaulle of France, whose country had experienced the agony of defeat in Indochina, and General Douglas MacArthur, who had almost a lifetime of experience in the Far East, had warned President Kennedy that our goal in Vietnam was unattainable. The greatest tragedy to me, however, was that I could conceive of no solution for victory without giving up on the South Vietnamese people whom we had recruited to our cause.

While occupied with these depressing thoughts and staring at nothing in particular, I saw a smiling face. Kathy had entered the terminal, escorted by a young marine officer. I gave up my space on the hard bench and walked over to them.

"I came to tell you goodbye again," Kathy said. "And to tell you that the party you missed today was not worth going to. The barge leaked, there was no protection from the sun, and the people were mostly stuck up."

"Did you go to the party, too?" I asked the young marine.

"No," he answered, "I'm just one of Kathy's pals she can always depend upon, and she needed a ride here to tell you good-bye."

Kathy's smile faded, and she looked sad. Her feelings were not for me in particular, I thought, but rather a reflection of bidding one more farewell to one of her many friends who merited perhaps a short note in her diary. Impulsively, she embraced me briefly and whispered "God bless you" before turning around and departing without another glance. Thus ended my tour of duty in Vietnam.